Negotiation Analysis

Negotiation Analysis

H. Peyton Young, *editor*

Ann Arbor
THE UNIVERSITY OF MICHIGAN PRESS

Library of Congress Cataloging-in-Publication Data

Negotiation analysis / H. Peyton Young, editor.
    p.   cm.
   Includes bibliographical references and index.
   ISBN 0-472-10251-6 (alk. paper). — ISBN 0-472-08157-8 (pbk. :
alk. paper)
   1. Negotiation in business.   2. Game theory.   3. Decision-making.
I. Young, H. Peyton, 1945–   .
HD58.6.N438   1991
658.4—dc20   91-28044
                                                              CIP

British Library Cataloguing in Publication Data

Negotiation analysis.
   I. Young, H. Peyton
   158.5

   ISBN 0472102516
   ISBN 0472081578 pbk

Foreword

This volume originated in a suggestion that Howard Raiffa put to me several years ago. As a teacher of negotiation analysis, he said he felt frustrated because there are many results in game theory, economics, and psychology that have a bearing on negotiation analysis, but that are inaccessible to most students and practitioners because they are presented in such a technical way. Although he had incorporated some of these subjects in his superb textbook, *The Art and Science of Negotiation,* much had been omitted. Furthermore, research in these topics has been developing so rapidly that many results had not been available when he wrote his book at the beginning of the decade. The question was how to remedy this situation. Could a group of people be found who were familiar with the technical literature and attuned to the needs of students in negotiations courses, and could they be persuaded to present some of these results for a nontechnical audience? I rose to the bait, and with Howard's encouragement and advice, organized a group of theoretically inclined teachers of negotiation to see if we could agree on a list of topics that would be suitable for presentation in this manner. This negotiation proved to be surprisingly painless, and the result is the set of articles contained in this volume.

Our aim is to show how recent work in game theory, decision theory, and experimental psychology lends insight into the negotiation process. The major topics are: the design of incentives for communicating information, the uses of third parties, the role of fairness arguments in bargaining, the analysis of trade-offs, the effects of cognitive biases, the dangers of escalation, and the dynamics of coalition formation. Some of these topics also appear in Raiffa's text, but are treated there in less detail. Others, such as the design of incentives, escalatory traps, and cognitive biases, were scarcely discussed there at all. The book should therefore be seen as a supplement to Raiffa's text, and is intended for a similar class of readers. The articles are aimed at students and practitioners who do not have much training in mathematics, but who are sufficiently motivated to follow detailed arguments. Basic ideas are illustrated by examples rather than formal definitions. We have taken pains to point out the limitations of these concepts, not only to paint a balanced picture, but also to challenge ourselves and our colleagues to extend the theory in ways that will be even more applicable.

Throughout the book, the frequent references to Raiffa's work show how much we owe to him as colleague, mentor, and friend. He, more than anyone else, put negotiation analysis on the map.

Contents

CHAPTER 1

Negotiation Analysis

H. Peyton Young

Negotiation is the process of joint decision making. It is communication, direct or tacit, between individuals who are trying to forge an agreement for mutual benefit. The original meaning of the word is simply to carry on business,[1] but negotiation is also a central activity in diplomacy, politics, religion, the law, and the family. It encompasses arms control talks, legislative logrolling, the interpretation of religious texts, child custody disputes, the allocation of household chores, and the decision about where to go with one's spouse for dinner. Everyone negotiates. Until recently, however, the subject has not been studied very systematically. Of course, the art of negotiation has long been a staple of diplomatic training, and the classical treatises on diplomatic strategy (Nicolson 1939; Machiavelli 1950; de Caillières 1963) still make profitable reading for students of negotiation. But these accounts tend to be anecdotal rather than systematic, and they view the field through the lens of international relations rather than in its entirety.

During the last decade, however, negotiation has emerged as a topic of study in its own right, and courses on the subject have become standard fare in schools of law, business, and public policy. Whereas research on negotiation used to be conducted in isolation in a variety of fields—experimental psychology, game theory, economics, and international relations—the subject is increasingly being seen as a whole. Why this sudden interest in a subject that seems so natural to study? The answer appears to be the growing recognition by professional schools that their graduates—lawyers, businessmen, bureaucrats, and politicians—spend much of their time negotiating. Hence, teaching the art and science of negotiation has become an integral part of professional education in these disciplines.

The subject can be—and is—taught in a variety of ways, depending on students' analytical dispositions and their professional goals. Some approaches emphasize the interpersonal relations aspect of negotiations and the need to be cooperative and candid (Fisher and Ury 1981); others stress the

---

1. *Webster's New Collegiate Dictionary,* 1974.

competitive aspect of bargaining and the difficulty of achieving full cooperation or complete candor when individuals act strategically (Schelling 1960;
Myerson 1979); others, such as Raiffa (1982), attempt to strike a compromise
between these points of view. In spite of these differences in emphasis, however, there is much common ground between the various approaches.

I became interested in negotiation when presented with the challenge of
teaching the subject to master's students in business and public policy. Students come to a course on negotiation for diverse reasons. Some are thinking
of careers in politics, others want to become lawyers, some are planning to
run a company, some simply want to improve their ability to relate to others.
Meeting all of their expectations is not easy. Moreover, the analysis of negotiations requires various technical concepts—choice under uncertainty, information, rational behavior, strategic equilibrium—that presume some mathematical background. The instructor's problem is to illustrate the relevance of
these theoretical concepts through real-world examples. In trying to discover
such examples, delving into case materials in business, politics, and the law,
it soon becomes apparent that present theory is often inadequate for explaining the complexities of real negotiating situations. Creativity, experience, and
sound intuition are at least as important to successful negotiation as any
amount of analysis. Nevertheless, intuition and creativity are not enough.
Some analysis is necessary to correct our intuition and to force us to reex-
amine our assumptions. The aim of this book is to show how analytical
reasoning, backed up by empirical evidence, can deepen our understanding of
real-world negotiating situations. Here I shall briefly sketch the major themes
in the chapters to follow.

Game-Theoretic Models of Negotiation

The principal theoretical tool for analyzing negotiations is the theory of
games. Game theory is a misnomer in some ways, since the theory covers
much more than parlor games. It applies to any situation in which the outcome
of one person's actions or decisions depends, in a definite way, on the actions
or decisions of others. In this sense, every negotiation is a game. But the bulk
of game theory deals with situations in which the moves available to the
protagonists—the rules of play—are clearly spelled out. Negotiations are
different because the rules of interaction—the permissible moves and counter-
moves, who can communicate to whom and when (about what)—are defined
ambiguously, if at all. They are *incompletely determined* games. Indeed,
shrewd negotiators often exploit this fact by trying to change the game, or by
changing others' perceptions of what the game is, as Lax and Sebenius demonstrate in chapter 8.

A negotiating situation may be described in broad outline as follows.
There is a set of interested parties called "players" who can make various

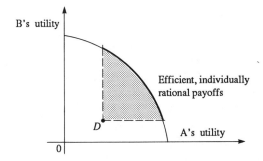

Fig. 1. The bargaining set for a two-person negotiation

agreements called "outcomes." Each player is assumed to be able to evaluate, on a numerical scale, the attractiveness of every conceivable outcome, including the possibility of no agreement. The value that a negotiator assigns to an outcome is called his subjective *payoff* or *utility* for the outcome. (A method for making such value assessments is outlined in chap. 7 by Keeney and Raiffa.) The set of all payoff combinations from the various possible agreements is called the *bargaining set*. Under standard assumptions about the players' utility functions, the bargaining set is bowed outward (convex) as shown in figure 1.

Each party is presumed to have a *b*est *a*lternative *t*o a *n*egotiated *a*greement (BATNA; see Fisher and Ury 1981). It seems reasonable to suppose that no party will accept an agreement that leaves him worse off than his BATNA. This condition is known as *individual rationality*. The utility of each party's BATNA, therefore, places a lower bound on the utility that the party must realize from a negotiated settlement. These minimum payoffs define the *disagreement point* (point *D* in fig. 1). The shaded region to the northeast of *D* delineates the agreements that are individually rational for both parties.

A second reasonable criterion of a negotiated agreement is that all potential gains should be realized. In other words, it should not be possible to make some parties better off while making no party worse off. An agreement that satisfies this criterion is said to be *efficient*. The efficient agreements correspond to points that lie on the northeastern boundary of the bargaining set. The agreements that are both individually rational and efficient correspond to the section of the boundary in bold outline in figure 1.

The bargaining set is, of course, only an idealization of an actual bargaining situation. Typically, the parties do not know each other's utility functions with any degree of accuracy. Sometimes they are not too sure of their own. Usually they do not know each other's BATNAs; at the same time they may be hard at work trying to improve their own. In other words, the location of the disagreement point and the shape of the utility frontier are not fixed in the players' imaginations, as is often assumed in formal bargaining theory.

They are fluid and to some extent under the control of the players themselves. Part of the strategy of negotiation is to change the bargaining set, or at least to change the way in which the other players perceive it.

Even if the bargaining set is completely known, however, the outcome is often far from clear. Any solution that is both individually rational and efficient can be called reasonable, but there are typically many such solutions. Which of them is *most* reasonable? The more reasonable bargains there are, the more difficulty reasonable bargainers may have in reaching agreement, simply because they are faced with too many choices. Somehow they must coordinate their expectations and converge on one outcome. But how do they do it?

Fair Bargains

In chapter 2, I argue that this coordination problem is closely connected with the issue of *fairness* in bargaining. People customarily discuss the outcome of labor negotiations, arms negotiations, divorce suits, and even business deals in terms of its fairness or unfairness to the parties concerned. Yet there has been relatively little agreement in the literature about what this term means, or what role (if any) it plays in negotiated agreements. In fact, some would maintain that fairness considerations are largely irrelevant to bargaining. The outcome of a bargain depends on the opportunities of the bargainers, their attitudes toward risk, and their strategic skills. It depends, in short, on the *power relation* among them, not on considerations of fairness. According to this view, appeals to fairness are mere window dressing. If this is so, however, then it remains to be explained why experienced negotiators often frame their arguments in terms of precedent and principle—on notions of fair share, customary procedure, objective value, and so forth. If these terms are so transparently a fraud—a mere fig leaf to disguise what is essentially a naked contest of wills—then why does anyone bother with them?

The answer, I submit, is that fairness arguments help the parties to reach an agreement by coordinating their expectations. The power relation—the alternatives of the various parties, their utility functions, and their strategic skills—does not typically determine a unique outcome; it merely delimits the range of reasonable outcomes. The greater the degree of indeterminacy, the greater the risk that the negotiations will break down because the negotiators are unable to settle on any one of them. The problem for the bargainers, then, is to find some device for reducing the number of credible outcomes.

It is at this point that fairness arguments come in. The negotiators search for some generally accepted principle or standard—customary shares, splitting the difference, reciprocity—that allows them to come to closure while avoiding a contest of wills that may cause the negotiations to break down. By appealing to standards of fairness, the negotiators increase the likelihood of an agreement by narrowing the range of possible disagreement. A further benefit of relying on standards of fairness is that it relieves the bargainers of responsibility for having "given in." It converts what might otherwise degenerate into an arbitrary contest of wills into a "principled" or "objective" solution that can be justified—both to the bargainers themselves and to their constituents (Fisher and Ury 1981).

Of course, if there are as many plausible standards as there are possible outcomes, then this approach has little to offer. It is the uniqueness, or near uniqueness, of the salient standard that makes the appeal to standards valuable as a negotiating tool. This is not to say that there is exactly one standard that would be considered appropriate in every situation; typically, each side will find some standard that favors its cause. But relatively few such choices are credible, and this serves to narrow the scope of disagreement. Moreover, a contest between two standards can sometimes be resolved by applying some metastandard, such as splitting the difference between the outcomes suggested by the two standards.

The specific fairness standards that are salient in a given situation vary widely from one class of negotiations to another. In wage negotiations, for example, it would be normal to tie the wage increase to an industry norm, adjusted for specific circumstances such as the firm's level of profitability. In sharing the profits from a joint enterprise, it would be natural to allocate in proportion to some measure of contribution. In negotiating the dues owed by various member countries to an international organization (e.g., the IMF), it is customary to look for some visible criterion of ability to pay—such as the country's gross domestic product. These formulas define the parties' fair shares.

An alternative to using a *formula* is to rely on a *procedure* to determine a fair outcome. When two children must share a piece of cake, for example, it is customary for one to divide it into two pieces and for the other to get first choice. Custom also has it that the older child plays the role of divider, though the privilege may also be decided by the toss of a coin (which is, itself, a fair procedure). This method is more than mere child's play; for example, it is an integral part of the Law of the Sea Treaty (Sebenius 1984). A particularly thorny issue addressed by the treaty is how to allocate the rights to mine the deep ocean bed between the industrialized countries and the less developed countries (LDCs), who lack the technology and resources to compete with the former. The solution was to create an international mining entity known as the Enterprise to mine the seabed on behalf of the LDCs. To protect against the possibility that commercial mining interests in the industrialized countries will steal a march on the Enterprise and lock up most of the desirable sites, the treaty provides for allocating the sites according to the divide and choose procedure. Every time that a mining company applies to the Seabed Authority for permission to mine at a given location, it is required to develop two parallel sites, from which the Enterprise chooses one. This site is then banked for future development by the LDCs.

The justification for the divide and choose procedure is that each party can assure himself of a portion that he values at least as highly as the other's portion. The divider can guarantee this by creating two pieces of equal value to himself; the chooser can do so by taking the piece that she prefers. This outcome is "fair" in that neither party envies the other's portion. Divide and choose is a "fair game" in the sense that, if played rationally, it leads to a fair outcome. The negotiators may prefer to play such a game rather than risk the hazards of free-for-all bargaining.

The Offer-Counteroffer Model of Negotiation

There are a variety of procedures for transforming an unstructured bargaining situation into a game that has an arguably fair outcome. A particularly interesting and natural example is the *offer-counteroffer procedure* (Stahl 1972; Rubinstein 1982) that I shall now briefly describe. (A more complete account is given in chapter 2.) Imagine that two protagonists, A and B, are bargaining over how to divide a perfectly divisible good, say a sum of money m. First, A proposes a division of the m dollars, which B either accepts or rejects. If B accepts, then the game is over. Otherwise, B proposes a division, which A either accepts or rejects. Offers and counteroffers alternate between the two parties until one of them accepts and the game ends. This procedure captures, in a stylized way, the give-and-take of many real negotiating situations.

What prevents the offer-counteroffer procedure from degenerating into a permanent standoff in which each bargainer persists in making an extreme proposal that the other rejects? The longer it takes to reach a settlement, the less valuable the settlement is to both bargainers, because people are impatient. Define an individual's *degree of impatience* to be the percentage increase in utility that he demands as compensation for deferring the payoff until a future date. For example, if a person's impatience is 5 percent per day, then he would just as soon have a utility of 1 today as a utility of 1.05 tomorrow. Impatience—aversion to delay—is the force that drives the parties toward compromise.

Assume that the degree of impatience of each party is common knowledge. Then the offer-counteroffer game has the following solution (Rubinstein 1982). On the first day, A demands a certain amount of money x, leaving $m - x$ for B. The following day, B plans to offer $y < x$ to A, keeping $m - y$ for himself. In equilibrium, these offers have the property that B would just as soon accept A's proposal now as wait one more day in the expectation that A will accept B's proposal tomorrow. Similarly, B's counteroffer is calculated so that *tomorrow* A would just as soon accept it as delay for yet another day. Assuming that each player's impatience for waiting one more day is small, and that the utilities are proportional to the amounts of money received, then the more impatient player ends up with less than half the money.[2]

The assertion that the players will actually arrive at this solution depends on several important assumptions. First, each agent must know the other's rate of impatience; moreover, each must know that the other knows it, that the other knows that he knows it, and so forth. In other words, the time preferences of the players must be *common knowledge* (Lewis 1967; Aumann 1976). Second, it is assumed that each agent is *rational* in the sense that he maximizes his expected payoff given his beliefs about what the others are going to do. Third, these expected payoffs are assumed to obey certain consistency conditions known as the von Neumann-Morgenstern utility axioms (von Neumann and Morgenstern 1944). Finally, each player must believe that the others are going to act rationally, and that they believe that *he* will act rationally, and so forth. Rational behavior must be a common belief.

Virtually all of game theory is predicated on common knowledge and common beliefs, for otherwise the players cannot reason their way toward a solution. Aumann puts it as follows: "The common knowledge assumption underlies all of game theory and much of economic theory. Whatever be the model under discussion, whether complete or incomplete information, consistent or inconsistent, repeated or one-shot, cooperative or noncooperative, the model itself must be assumed common knowledge; otherwise the model is insufficiently specified, and the analysis incoherent" (Aumann 1987, 31). This assumption is obviously very demanding and, in many cases, quite unrealistic. Nevertheless, game-theoretic models such as the offer-counteroffer procedure can capture important aspects of a negotiating situation. In particular, it predicts that the more impatient a negotiator is, the less he or she is willing to settle for. This prediction accords with common sense, but it goes further by showing the magnitude of the effect.

---

2. Let the total amount of money be one unit. Let r be A's degree of impatience and let s be B's degree of impatience, where the unit of reference is the length of time between offers, say one day. We assume that r and s are small. On the first day, A demands x and offers $1 - x$ to B. On the second day, B plans to offer y to A, where $y < x$, and to keep $1 - y$ for himself. In equilibrium, B is indifferent between $1 - x$ and $(1 - y)/(1 + s)$, so $1 - x = (1 - y)/(1 + s)$. Similarly, A is indifferent between y and $x/(1 + r)$, so $y = x/(1 + r)$. The solution to these equations is $x = (s + rs)/(r + s + rs)$ and $y = s/(r + s + rs)$. If A is less impatient than B ($r < s$), then A gets more than half the money. If B is less impatient than A ($s < r$), *and* if rs is sufficiently small, then B gets more than half of the money (Rubinstein 1982).

Arbitration Procedures

The offer-counteroffer model can be thought of as an idealization of the bargaining process. Alternatively, it can be construed as a procedure that the parties might agree to follow instead of engaging in unstructured negotiations. In this sense, it is a form of arbitration. More generally, an *arbitration procedure* may be defined as a formal process that the parties submit to as an alternative to negotiating in an unstructured way. Brams, Kilgour, and Merrill examine the properties of various arbitration procedures in chapter 3.

Arbitration has been used since ancient times, when the local priest or magistrate traditionally served as arbitrator. In modern societies, arbitration is frequently imposed in negotiations where society has an interest in a speedy resolution of the case. Labor negotiations involving public employees, for example, are often referred to arbitration if the parties cannot reach an agreement within a specified time. The objective is to avoid strikes that might jeopardize public safety. Arbitration is also standard in contract disputes between players and owners in various team sports, and in disputes between customers and firms in certain industries (e.g., the brokerage business).

In conventional arbitration, an arbitrator is selected who is believed to be impartial and is familiar with the substantive issues raised in the dispute. The parties present their arguments, and the arbitrator renders a binding judgment. This process certainly assures an outcome, but it does not necessarily encourage the parties to work out an agreement on their own. The problem is that the process creates no incentive for the parties to compromise. The onus is placed on the arbitrator to find the middle ground; hence, to the extent that the arbitrator's decision is influenced by the parties' arguments, it encourages them to exaggerate their demands. The prospect of arbitration may therefore drive the parties further apart instead of helping them to settle on their own.

In an attempt to mitigate this problem, new forms of arbitration have been proposed that give the disputants more control over the process. One method that is now extensively used in public and private sector bargaining is *final-offer arbitration*. Under this method, each party submits its "final offer" to the arbitrator, who must then choose one of them. The only discretion given to the arbitrator is to make one of the negotiators' final-offers binding. This gives the parties more incentive to compromise, because an extreme offer is almost certain not to be chosen. Each side tries to make an offer that is a little more reasonable than the other offers in the hope that it will be the one selected.

But does this procedure actually cause the parties' offers to converge? Brams, Kilgour, and Merrill show that, while final-offer arbitration may promote some convergence, it can still leave the parties far apart. Consider the following example. Labor and management are negotiating a new wage contract. If they fail to reach an agreement in thirty days, the case will be referred to final-offer arbitration. Labor's initial demand is a wage increase of $3 per hour, whereas management insists that it cannot afford any increase. Recent wage settlements in this industry have generally yielded increases between $1 and $2 per hour, and the outcomes are more or less uniformly distributed between these two values. Both labor and management are aware of these precedents, so they know that their offers are relatively extreme. Do they have an incentive to compromise?

To answer this question we need to make some assumption about how the arbitrator will decide the case. It seems reasonable to suppose that the arbitrator will refer to the other wage settlements in trying to determine a fair outcome, and that she will then choose the final offer that comes closest to her idea of a fair outcome. Two possibilities suggest themselves: (1) the arbitrator's idea of a fair outcome is the mean of the other wage settlements ($1.50), or (2) it is some value between $1.00 and $2.00 but the specific value is uncertain. In the first case, there is a definite incentive for the parties to compromise in their "final offers." Each side wants to come closer to the arbitrator's position than the other does (in the hope of having its offer chosen), and the end result is that both offer $1.50. Notice that this outcome could even occur in anticipation of final-offer arbitration, in which case it would not be necessary to go to arbitration at all.

Now consider the second case, in which there is uncertainty about the wage increase that the arbitrator considers to be fairest. Suppose that both labor and management believe that all values between $1.00 and $2.00 are equally likely to be the arbitrator's preferred outcome. Here again there is an incentive to compromise, but not as much as before. If management and labor continue to make extreme demands of $0.00 and $3.00 respectively, then their offers will be accepted with equal probability (depending on whether the arbitrator's judgment happens to fall below or above $1.50). Thus the *expected* settlement will be $1.50. But if labor offers $2.00, then it is certain that this offer will be less extreme than management's, and the expected settlement will be $2.00 for sure. Therefore, labor is motivated to lower its offer to $2.00. Similarly, management is motivated to raise its offer to $1.00.

Beyond this, however, there is no incentive to compromise. To see this, consider the expected value of the settlement when the offers are $1.00 and $2.00 respectively. There is an even chance that the arbitrator will accept either offer, so the expected outcome is $1.50. Suppose now that labor were to compromise slightly and offer $1.90 instead of $2.00. Labor's new offer will be accepted if the arbitrator's position is closer to $1.90 than to $1.00, i.e., if it is above $1.45. This will be the case 55 percent of the time. Thus, the probability of labor's offer being accepted has increased by 5 percent. But labor gets $0.10 less if its offer is accepted. Thus, labor gets $1.90 with probability 55 percent, and $1.00 with probability 45 percent, so the expected outcome is $1.49, which is $0.01 less than before. So it makes no sense for labor to compromise. A similar argument shows that management has no incentive to compromise either. So the equilibrium outcome is that management offers $1.00, labor insists on $2.00, and the case must go to arbitration.

This example shows that, contrary to our initial intuition, final-offer arbitration does not necessarily cause the parties to converge. In fact, it may leave them quite far apart unless all parties are fairly sure that the arbitrator's preferred settlement is some specific number, and they also believe that the arbitrator's judgment will not be swayed by their final-offers. The example also illustrates the value of game-theoretic reasoning: by being explicit about how the negotiators interact with each other and examining the equilibrium outcomes, we can sharpen, and in some cases correct, our intuition.

Game theory can also be used to design new forms of arbitration. For example, one might wish to design an arbitration procedure that creates more of an incentive for the parties to compromise, i.e., that brings their final offers closer together. This is desirable because it removes the onus from the arbitrator of imposing a decision. Brams and Merrill (1986) propose a variation of final-offer arbitration that has this property. Suppose that there are two bargainers, labor and management, who are negotiating an issue that can be measured along a single dimension, for example, a salary increase. The arbitrator writes down his or her preferred settlement A; simultaneously labor and management write down their final offers L and M. It is reasonable to assume that L is greater than or equal to M. If the two offers agree (L = M) then this is the outcome. If A falls between L and M, then the offer closest to A is selected (as in final-offer arbitration). If A is not between L and M (and L ≠ M), then A itself is chosen (as in conventional arbitration). This ingenious scheme is called *combined arbitration*, since it is a mixture of final-offer arbitration (if A is between the two offers) and conventional arbitration (if A lies outside the two offers).

Combined arbitration creates more of an inducement for the parties to compromise than final-offer arbitration does. To see why, consider the labor-management negotiation discussed above, and suppose that the arbitrator's preferred position is equally likely to be any value between $1.00 and $2.00. Under final-offer arbitration, management will remain entrenched at $1.00, labor will insist on $2.00, and there is no incentive to compromise. Now consider the situation under combined arbitration. Suppose that labor were to compromise slightly and offer $1.90 instead of $2.00. Labor's new offer will be accepted if the arbitrator's position is closer to $1.90 than to $1.00 and it lies between the two offers, that is, if it is between $1.45 and $1.90. This event has a probability of 45 percent. Management's offer will be accepted if the arbitrator's position lies between $1.00 and $1.45, which also has a probability of 45 percent. Finally, the arbitrator's position will be binding if it falls between $1.90 and $2.00, which has a probability of 10 percent. Hence, labor's expected payoff is .45 × $1.90 + .45 × $1.00 + .10 × $1.95 = $1.50, which is exactly the same as before. In other words, there is no harm in compromising. A similar conclusion holds for management. Moreover, if the parties believe that the arbitrator is more likely to choose the median value of $1.50 (for example, if the arbitrator's position is normally distributed around $1.50), then the parties' final offers will actually converge to the median value.

In practice, of course, other factors enter into the parties' thinking that may alter these conclusions. On the one hand, there may be an intangible bonus to having one's offer chosen, which lends it legitimacy. This effect induces *more* convergence than if the parties only tried to maximize their expected monetary gains. On the other hand, each party may be overly optimistic that the arbitrator is predisposed to favor its side. This effect induces *less* convergence than if the parties shared the same beliefs about the arbitrator's position. Thus we cannot say that combined arbitration necessarily induces convergence in the parties' offers. We can say that, under certain circumstances, it is more likely to induce convergence than final-offer arbitration.

Mediation of Disputes

In the above example, it was implicitly assumed that the parties have a fairly accurate idea of each other's payoff function. Management knows that labor wants a higher wage, while labor is sure that management wants the reverse. What neither can be sure of is the other's "bottom line"—the minimum that the other side must obtain in order to settle. For example, the union leaders may feel that they cannot settle for less than a $2.00 raise and win the approval of the rank and file. Management may feel that the firm cannot remain in business if they allow an increase of more than $1.00. If both of their claims are true, then there is no room for agreement. On the other hand, one or both of them may be bluffing. Perhaps labor would actually accept no increase as the alternative to a plant shutdown; perhaps management would really be able to grant an increase of $3.00 without going into the red. Each side suspects the other of bluffing but cannot be sure of it.

This dilemma is common to many negotiating situations. Each negotiator attempts to learn about the opportunities and preferences of the other parties; simultaneously each tries to influence what the others believe about him. In this process, everyone has reason to be wary, since they recognize that the information conveyed may not be correct. There is a temptation to bluff, to try to fool the other party into thinking that your threshold for acceptance is higher than it really is. Myerson analyzes this problem in chapter 4 using the theory of games with incomplete information.

In Myerson's terminology, a negotiator is *strong* if he really must have a high payoff in order to accept an agreement; otherwise he is *weak*. Note that these definitions refer to the bargaining strength of the parties, not to their ability to control their destinies. (Paradoxically, a lack of options often translates into strength at the bargaining table [Schelling 1960]). We shall say that management is strong if it cannot accept more than $1.00; in other words, it is in a strong bargaining position if it is a weak company. It is weak if it is willing to accept up to $3.00. The labor negotiator is in a strong position if his hands are tied by the rank and file to accept no less than $2.00, that is, if he lacks flexibility. He is weak if he is willing to accept no increase at all.

If both parties are strong (or merely say they are), then there will be no agreement because management will not meet labor's minimum demand. If one or both admit to being weak, then there is scope for agreement. Let us suppose that in the latter case they split the difference. Thus, if labor admits to being weak and management maintains that it is strong, then the outcome will be $0.50—the average of $0.00 and $1.00. If labor says it is strong and management says it is weak, then the outcome will be $2.50. If they both admit to being weak, then the outcome is $1.50.

When does it pay to bluff? The answer depends on how likely it is that the other side is bluffing (or is strong, in fact). Let p be the probability that management *says* it is strong (i.e., cannot pay more than $1.00), either because it really is strong or just says so. Suppose that labor is actually weak, that is, it could accept as little as $0.00. If the labor negotiator admits it, then the payoff will be $0.50 with probability p and $1.50 with probability $1 - p$. If the labor negotiator bluffs and says he needs at least $2.00, then the payoff will be $2.50—assuming that management does not insist on $1.00 or less. In the latter case there will be a strike because their demands are incompatible. Assume that a strike is so costly that it is equivalent (to labor) of getting a wage increase of $0.00. Then labor's expected increase from bluffing is $0p + $2.50(1 - p)$, whereas the expected increase from not bluffing is $0.50p + $1.50(1 - p)$. The latter is larger if and only if p is greater than two-thirds. In other words, it pays for the labor negotiator to bluff unless it is quite likely that management is also bluffing (or strong).

Myerson shows that, in situations like this, each side will be tempted to bluff some of the time. But when both of them bluff, they miss an opportunity for agreement and are both worse off than if they had revealed themselves to be weak. Bluffing is inherently wasteful because potential gains are sometimes left on the table.

Is there any way the two sides can be persuaded to level with each other? One approach would be to bring in a mediator who is trusted by both sides. We can imagine that such a person approaches each party privately and asks whether he or she is "really" strong or weak. The understanding is that the information reported will be kept in confidence. Based on these reports, the mediator suggests a specific agreement. Of course, the two sides may demand to know exactly what process the mediator plans to follow before they agree to such a scheme. A naive plan would be for the mediator to announce an agreement that reflects what the bargainers have revealed. Thus, if one says he is strong and the other says he is weak, then the mediator would announce an agreement that is consistent with these reports. This procedure is ineffective, however, because if the parties know in advance that the mediator plans to do this, then they will have an incentive to misrepresent their true positions, just as in the unmediated case.

A better strategy would be for the mediator to plant some uncertainty in the bargainers' minds about whether she believes them. Consider this plan. First, the mediator asks the parties confidentially whether they are weak or strong. Then she suggests an agreement that is consistent with these reports being true. For example, if they both say they are weak, then she suggests a wage increase of $1.50. If they both say they are strong, then she walks away and there is no agreement (i.e., a strike). If one says strong and the other says weak, then she chooses an agreement that is consistent with these reports, which (of course) gives a bonus to the person who claims to be strong but really is not. In addition, however, she stipulates that, if one party says strong and the other says weak, then she will *reject* their reports and recommend no agreement with some positive probability. In effect, she says that she does not necessarily believe the statements made by the participants. If the probability of rejection is sufficiently large, then, Myerson shows, the parties will be motivated to report honestly. Ideally, of course, one wants to find the lowest rate of rejection that is still high enough to get them to report the correct information.

In general, a mediation plan is said to be *incentive compatible* if: (1) it induces the bargainers to admit their true situations to the mediator, and (2) it offers them expected payoffs at least as high as their BATNAs. The mediation plan described above is incentive compatible. Note, however, that it does not remove the possibility of wasted opportunities. It could happen that one of the bargainers really is strong and the other really is weak—so that an agreement is possible—but with a positive probability the mediator rejects it. Nevertheless, if the probability of rejection is appropriately chosen, then the expected loss may be less than if the bargainers had negotiated directly without the intervention of the mediator. Mediation can reduce the potential losses that arise from posturing by the negotiators, even though it may not eliminate such losses.

The central message of Myerson's chapter is that, when negotiators have different information, it may be *impossible* for them to communicate it credibly to the other side. As a result, they may be unable to reach an agreement, even when it is in their mutual interest to do so. Because there is a natural incentive for the negotiators to misrepresent and exaggerate their bottom lines, and they all know this, they may be unable to overcome their well-founded suspicions and reach an agreement that really is there—if only they could discover it.

While some types of mediation can motivate the parties to report honestly to the mediator, these procedures necessarily leave some gains on the table some of the time. This is actually a provable result—a kind of "uncertainty principle" of bargaining (Myerson 1979). It has an important implication, namely, that even the most intelligent negotiators will not always be able to extract fully the potential gains from a negotiating situation. This result contradicts many popular treatises on negotiation, which imply that if only the parties were sufficiently cooperative (and followed the recipe for success advanced in that book), then mutually advantageous agreements would never go begging.

The concluding part of Myerson's chapter addresses a second problem that bedevils many negotiations, namely, the tendency to stall. When is it desirable to drag one's feet, to seek delay? Delay is costly because of the impatience factor—a benefit now is generally preferred to a similar benefit in the future. Pushing off an agreement, therefore, causes it to lose value for everyone concerned. Nevertheless, it may pay some party to delay if he or she thinks that this tactic will wring a concession from the other side that outweighs the loss associated with delay. In fact, it is possible that all sides are motivated to delay in the hope that someone else will blink first. While these delaying tactics may be rational, the result can be very costly overall. Even though each side conjectures (correctly) that it would be better to stall for a little while longer because the other might give in first, the resulting standoff equilibrium may go on for so long that the potential gains from the bargain are almost completely squandered. It would be better, Myerson argues, for the parties to accept a mediated settlement now—even though this may sometimes lead to missed opportunities—than to risk a lengthy stalemate.

Escalation and Coercive Bargaining

Delay is a relatively innocuous example of coercive bargaining, a tactic in which one imposes, or threatens to impose, costs on the other side unless it yields to some demand. In chapter 5, O'Neill examines more overt types of coercion—threats, escalations, and ultimatums—and asks how well they work as bargaining tools.

O'Neill defines escalation as "a new and stronger action, an intensification or widening of the conflict, aimed at promoting the escalator's gain from an agreement at the expense of the other's." Calculated escalation has two purposes. One is to convey information, to tell the other side who you are, and (most important) to demonstrate resolve. The second purpose is to change the objective situation to your advantage (or to the other side's disadvantage) and thus make the other side more eager to compromise. The theory of controlled or strategic escalation has permeated U.S. military thinking during much of the postwar period, and it has been tried with greater or lesser success in several conflicts, notably the Cuban missile crisis and the Vietnam War. The central question that O'Neill examines is whether escalation can, in fact, be controlled, or whether in certain cases it takes on a life of its own, impelling both sides to higher and higher levels of damage that were not initially part of the game plan. O'Neill argues that certain types of games tend to "entrap" participants. A classic example is the "dollar auction" game devised by Martin Shubik (1971). Two individuals bid for a sum of money (say one dollar) that is held by the auctioneer. The bidding occurs in successive rounds, the bids being in nickels. In the first round, each player must bid at least one nickel to be in the game. (If only one of them bids, then he gets the dollar.) In each successive round, each bidder must raise the previous bid by at least one nickel or fold. The game ends when some player fails to raise. The winning bidder gets the dollar, but *both* of them must pay their last bids.

This game can be seen as a metaphor for the arms race: Each side invests in more powerful weapons in an attempt to stay ahead of the other. The "winner" is the one who invests the most, but in the end, both pay. Experimental tests of this game demonstrate that it tends to entrap participants in the sense that both bidders lose money. In other words, the bidding typically goes to more than one dollar.

O'Neill suggests several explanations for this entrapment phenomenon that apply more generally to escalatory situations. First, while each player could, in theory, calculate his optimal strategy—which depends, among other things, on his estimate of the others' staying power, and also on his estimate of what they believe his staying power to be, etc.—in practice it is very difficult to carry out the necessary computations. Furthermore, people have cognitive biases that interfere with making such calculations correctly. Second, there is a sense in which the situation itself takes control and changes the players' payoff functions. Once the parties are engaged and have incurred sunk costs, the goal becomes one of winning instead of minimizing expected losses.

While in theory the players should be able to anticipate this shift in perceptions, in practice they usually do not. For example, if a player makes a credible threat—one that he either wants to or has committed to carry out— then a rational opponent ought to yield, assuming that he has no credible counterthreat. Yet, in fact, the threat may simply enrage the other side and stiffen resistance rather than compel submission. While this response might be irrational, the would-be threatener needs to take the possibility into account. One solution, O'Neill suggests, is for the threatener to veil the threat or be deliberately ambiguous about his intentions. This softens the impact on the opponent, and leaves room to maneuver as events unfold. According to this theory, it may be desirable *not to commit*—or, at least, to give the appearance of not having committed completely—rather than to follow a commitment strategy that attempts to corner the other side.

Relaxing the Assumption of Rationality

This discussion highlights one of the problems with traditional game theory, namely, the assumption that each player acts rationally and bases calculations on the belief that the others will act rationally. This model of human behavior has the advantage of generating interesting and nontrivial results. Yet, in practice, it is not necessarily a good assumption. Indeed, if one takes seriously the idea that one should optimize against an opponent, then it is self-evident that one should optimize using one's best estimate of what the opponent is likely to do, not using some theory about what *he ought* to do. To assume that the opponent's behavior is rational is clearly irrational if there is good evidence to the contrary.

The need to make realistic estimates of the other side's motives and responses has been argued for most persuasively by Raiffa (1982). In his view, the principal function of the negotiation analyst is to give good advice to negotiators. Since the analyst will (typically) only be advising one side, he is faced with an asymmetric problem: he needs to give the best *prescription* to his client based on his best *description* of the other side's likely response. To carry out this function, therefore, the analyst must be acquainted with the prescriptions offered by game theory as well as the descriptions offered by behavioral psychology and everyday observation. Of course, if the other side is being similarly advised, one must also take this into account. But even in this case it is not necessarily correct to suppose that both sides will play a rational game. Many negotiators continue to make (predictable) mistakes even after they have received good advice. It appears that people suffer from specific cognitive biases that must be overcome to play the game well, but one cannot assume that these biases will be overcome simply because they have been pointed out.

Chapter 6, by Bazerman and Neale, surveys some of the more prominent cognitive biases that have been revealed in experimental situations. One pervasive problem is overconfidence. Given the same information about an uncertain situation, subjects assigned to different roles tend to bias their probability assessments toward the outcomes that are favorable to themselves. This has implications for choosing a strategy in situations where the probability of an event is not given explicitly, but is judged from the circumstances of the case. Consider, for example, the arbitration procedures discussed in connection with chapter 3. The assumption there was that both sides have the same probability distribution over the arbitrator's choice of settlement. If negotiators tend to be overconfident, however, then, in practice, one would expect labor's distribution to be biased toward a higher settlement and management's toward a lower settlement. The result is that combined arbitration might not cause the parties' final offers to converge (though combined arbitration may still be superior to final-offer arbitration in promoting convergence).

A second problem is that people do not necessarily maximize expected payoffs as standard utility theory would predict. Systematic departures from the expected utility hypothesis have been documented in a variety of experimental situations. One of these is the certainty effect, in which subjects overweight certain outcomes relative to outcomes that are merely probable, even if they are highly probable (see Kahneman and Tversky 1979; Kahneman, Slovic, and Tversky 1982). Another empirical phenomenon is the reflection, or framing, effect. As a rule, subjects tend to be risk averse in their attitudes toward expected gains, and risk seeking in their attitudes toward expected losses. For example, a subject will typically prefer $5 for certain than taking an even chance at winning $10 or nothing. But if this same subject has just lost $10, he will typically prefer an even chance at winning it back to a certain payment of $5 (i.e., a certain loss of $5). Though the money payments are the same in both cases, the typical subject reacts differently to the choice, depending on whether he perceives it as maximizing gain or minimizing loss.

These effects have important implications for negotiators, since the outcome of a negotiation can depend on whether it is framed positively or negatively. For example, Bazerman, Magliozzi, and Neale (1985) presented subjects with a business negotiation that was constructed so that risk-averse negotiators had a larger zone of agreement than risk-seeking ones. One group of subjects was instructed to maximize net profits; the other group was instructed to minimize expenses. The result was that the positively framed negotiators reached agreements with greater frequency than negatively framed negotiators did; furthermore, their agreements had a higher average profitability than those reached by the negatively framed negotiators. Framing and overconfidence effects do not contradict game theory, but they must be built into the assumptions about how players evaluate outcomes in order for the game-theoretic analysis to be a useful predictor.

Assessing Trade-offs in Multiple-Issue Negotiations

The examples discussed so far deal primarily with two agents negotiating over a single issue. While they are useful pedagogical tools, and elucidate important issues related to the formulation of strategic choice, they are oversimplified compared to most real-world negotiations, which typically involve multiple agents dealing with multiple issues. In this case, matters become considerably more complex. For example, one of the most apparently innocuous assumptions of game theory is that each agent has a well-defined utility function that represents the choice he would make when faced with multiple options and uncertain outcomes. The fact is, however, that negotiators often have great difficulty in articulating their preferences.

In chapter 7, Keeney and Raiffa discuss various ways in which bargainers can sort out their preferences when there are several issues on the table. The basic theme of the chapter may be described as "preparation for negotiation through systematic introspection." How does a negotiator or a negotiating team determine the relative value that they would place on various possible outcomes? The brief answer is that they would compare all possible outcomes pairwise, and, for each pair, determine which of the two options is preferred. From this they could, in theory, deduce their utility function, that is, a numerical representation of their preferences. Keeney and Raiffa go beyond this general prescription—which is usually impractical to carry out anyway because it involves too many comparisons—to discuss various shortcuts that are available for estimating trade-offs. They then go on to argue that a systematic analysis of trade-offs can be helpful even for qualitatively minded negotiators who will not use the output literally, but who may discover, in the process, important qualitative features of their preferences that they had not been conscious of before.

The Keeney-Raiffa approach begins with the assumption that the set of issues is specified in some preliminary way, that the range of possible outcomes on each issue is known, and that the negotiator has determined his best alternative to a negotiated agreement. The object for the negotiator is to determine how much of each issue he or she would be willing to give up in return for a specific concession on some other issue. Under certain conditions that Keeney and Raiffa spell out, it is possible to score each issue separately, and then to score a proposed agreement by adding up the scores achieved on the various issues. This is the *additive preference model*. It is analogous to scoring an exam by adding up the scores that a student receives on each of the individual questions.

It often happens, however, that preferences are not additive in this sense. Consider, for example, a wage agreement involving two classes of workers employed by a company. The union representative might determine a "utility" or point value for various levels of increase for the class 1 workers, and similarly for the class 2 workers. But it might not be the case that the utility (to the union) of a total wage package equals the sum of the utilities of the wage increases for each group. They might be concerned about the equity of the agreement, that is, the *difference* between the percentage increases achieved by the two groups. Keeney and Raiffa argue that, even in such cases, it may be helpful to adopt the additive model as a starting point in order to reveal nonadditivities. Once they are discovered, it is often possible to re-define the issues in such a way that the preference structure becomes additive. In this case, for instance, the appropriate issues may be (1) the average wage increase for the two groups together, and (2) the difference between the two groups. Preferences over these two issues may be more or less separable.

Another qualitative benefit of preference evaluation is that it helps the negotiator to distinguish between basic interests and derivative interests. Examples of basic interests include economic well-being, security, and liberty. The issues in a negotiation represent specific ways of realizing these (and other) underlying interests. In the Camp David negotiations between Egypt and Israel, for instance, one issue was the extent to which Israel would withdraw from the Sinai. The immediate issue was the degree of withdrawal. The underlying interests, however, were Israel's need for secure borders and Egypt's need for self-respect, which in this case meant reassertion of sovereignty over its traditional territory. As Fisher and Ury (1981) have so forcefully argued, it is the fundamental interests that matter in a negotiation, not the specific way in which these interests are realized. Negotiators need to bear in mind that the utility of the "issues" derives from these fundamental interests. Value analysis can help make this dependency explicit by constantly asking *why* an issue is important, thereby revealing previously unarticulated goals and interests.

In sum, the systematic analysis of trade-offs between issues has several potential benefits. First, it forces the negotiators to be explicit about the issues under discussion and the range of outcomes that might result. Second, it helps them to articulate their underlying interests and devise ways of meeting these interests that they may not have previously recognized. Third, it provides a benchmark for measuring the degree to which a proposed agreement improves upon the negotiator's best alternative to a negotiated agreement. Finally, it helps to carry out a similar analysis of the other side's preferences, since this may reveal where joint gains are possible.

Coalitional Dynamics in Multiparty Negotiations

The final chapter, by Lax and Sebenius, examines the problem of coalition formation in multiparty negotiations. In the game theory literature, this problem tends to be treated in the following way. First one delineates all of the potential coalitions that could form; then one specifies the gains that each coalition could realize by its own actions. The analysis focuses on how the gains from cooperation would be distributed in some final agreement. The key question here is: What agreements are stable? One of the most general concepts of stability is the *core* (Shapley 1952; Gillies 1953). A core agreement is one that no coalition has both the power and the motivation to overturn. There is no coalition that could, *by its own action,* make each of its members better off under some alternative agreement. Unfortunately there is no guarantee that such an agreement exists.

A somewhat more flexible notion of coalitional stability is based on the notion of objections and counterobjections. Imagine that a coalition has formed and that the members are debating how to distribute the potential gains among themselves. We assume that no member of the coalition is worse off than he would be on his own, that is, the agreement is individually rational. Suppose that two members, A and B, are comparing their shares. A might object that B is getting too much. To bolster his claim, A would point out that he can form an alternative alliance with certain other individuals, C, C' . . . such that all of them will be better off than under the proposed agreement. On the other hand, B has a credible *counterobjection* if B can form an alliance with some of A's proposed partners, and perhaps others, that leaves the former as well off as under A's proposal and leaves the latter as well off as under the *original* proposal. If to every objection there is a valid counterobjection, then the agreement is said to be *stable.* Stable bargains typically exist, and the set of all of them is called the *bargaining set* (Aumann and Maschler 1964; Davis and Maschler 1967).

These classical prescriptions generally assume that the payoffs can be precisely specified and are known to the participants, that is, there is full information. Lax and Sebenius, by contrast, adopt a more process-oriented look at coalition formation and examine its qualitative aspects in the absence of such information. A common tactic is to pressure one's partners in a coalition by threatening to form an alternative alliance. This is the underlying idea in the definition of the bargaining set, but Lax and Sebenius demonstrate its practical application through a variety of real examples. In 1971, for example, Malta and Britain had to renegotiate the terms under which Britain would continue to use Malta as a base for naval operations. To enhance its bargaining position, Malta made overtures to the Soviet Union about possible base rights. Simultaneously, Malta approached Libya and other Arab states about the possibility of receiving assistance payments in return for declaring neutrality. On the one hand, this tactic created an attractive alternative for Malta should the negotiations with Britain break down. On the other hand, it worsened Britain's alternative to a negotiated agreement, since Britain and its

NATO partners viewed a Soviet presence on Malta with alarm. The tactic, then, was to bring in a third party with whom one could strike a potentially favorable deal that also worsened the situation of the other side. What had been a two-party negotiation became a three-party negotiation. Malta had changed the game.

A second useful tactic identified by Lax and Sebenius is to build a coalition by creating a "bandwagon" effect. First, the coalition builder wins over A, whose opinion is known to carry weight with B. Once A and B are on board, C may want to go along because C owes a favor to B. Next, D decides to join in because he believes that the coalition is unstoppable, and so forth. Lax and Sebenius illustrate the bandwagon effect in a number of recent international negotiations. For example, in the 1985 accord to manage the value of the dollar downward, Secretary of the Treasury James Baker began by quietly forging an alliance between the United States and Japan. These two then worked together to gain the cooperation of the Germans. Once this coalition was in place, they could apply pressure on France and Britain. The strategy worked, but there is no reason to believe that this particular coalition was the only stable one. Indeed, had Britain and France formed a coalition with Germany first, they might well have been able to block Baker's move. But they did not move first, and found themselves outmaneuvered.

The general tactic being applied here is to commit first. Once several partners have committed to a position, even tentatively, there are costs to undoing it. Hence, the remaining negotiators will find it more difficult to break this tentative alliance than they would have had they made the initial overtures. This is so for several reasons. First, there is a cost in credibility to reversing an earlier position. Second, if a position already has many adherents, then it becomes more credible. Third, patterns of deference exist that can be exploited by first building up coalitions of leaders, who then pull the followers in. Coalitions do not form and dissolve costlessly and spontaneously, as is often postulated in the classical formulations of the problem. Rather, the dynamics of coalition formation are path dependent, and the payoffs from subsequent actions may depend on previous actions. An astute negotiator may be able to lock a group into a favorable decision by exploiting this phenomenon.

The larger point of chapter 8, however, is that negotiating situations are often highly fluid, unstructured affairs that basically defy mathematical analysis. The formal results in game theory cannot be applied in any direct way because "the game" is indeterminate. It is precisely this fact, however, that opens up all sorts of new opportunities for entrepreneurial negotiators to change the game. Lax and Sebenius vividly document this with a selection of fascinating accounts of behind-the-scenes maneuvering in the worlds of diplomacy and high finance, including a bureaucratic negotiation in the U.S.

State Department, the 1975 U.S.-USSR grain agreement, the Maltese Base negotiations, the 1985 Plaza Accord on stabilizing the dollar, and the Law of the Sea negotiations.

It is this type of example—with its personalities, intrigues, and unexpected complications—that makes negotiation analysis such an interesting subject to teach. It is also this type of example that poses a healthy challenge to theory, by forcing it to stretch its boundaries, and draw still more of the complexities found in real-world negotiations within its compass.

REFERENCES

Aumann, R. J. 1976. "Agreeing to Disagree." *Annals of Statistics* 4:1236–39.
Aumann, R. J. 1987. "Game Theory." In *The New Palgrave: A Dictionary of Economics,* ed. J. Eatwell, M. Milgate, and P. Newman. New York: Schocken.
Aumann, R. J., and M. Maschler. 1964. "The Bargaining Set for Cooperative Games." In *Advances in Game Theory,* ed. M. Dresher, L. S. Shapley, and A. W. Tucker. Princeton: Princeton University Press.
Bazerman, M. H., T. Magliozzi, and M. A. Neale. 1985. "Integrative Bargaining in a Competitive Market." *Organizational Behavior and Human Performance* 34:294–313.
Brams, S. J., and S. Merrill III. 1986. "Binding versus Final-Offer Arbitration: A Combination Is Best." *Management Science* 32:1346–55.
Davis, M., and M. Maschler. 1967. "Existence of Stable Payoff Configurations for Cooperative Games." In *Essays in Mathematical Economics in Honor of Oskar Morgenstern,* ed. M. Shubik. Princeton: Princeton University Press.
de Caillières, F. 1963. *De la Maniere de Negocier avec les Soverains.* Notre Dame, Ind.: University of Notre Dame Press.
Fisher, R., and W. Ury. 1981. *Getting to Yes: Negotiating Agreement without Giving In.* Boston: Little, Brown.
Gillies, D. B. 1953. "Some Theorems on N-Person Games." Ph.D. diss., Department of Mathematics, Princeton University.
Kahneman, D., and A. Tversky. 1979. "Prospect Theory: An Analysis of Decisions under Risk." *Econometrica* 47:263–91.
Kahneman, D., P. Slovic, and A. Tversky. 1982. *Judgment under Uncertainty: Heuristics and Biases.* Cambridge: Cambridge University Press.
Keeney, R., and H. Raiffa. 1976. *Decisions with Multiple Objectives: Preferences and Value Tradeoffs.* New York: Wiley.
Lax, D., and J. K. Sebenius. 1986. *The Manager as Negotiator: Bargaining for Cooperation and Competitive Gain.* New York: Free Press.
Lewis, D. 1967. *Convention: A Philosophical Study.* Cambridge, Mass.: Harvard University Press.
Machiavelli, N. 1950. *The Prince.* Trans. Luigi Ricci. New York: Modern Library.
Myerson, R. 1979. "Incentive Compatibility and the Bargaining Problem." *Econometrica* 47:61–74.

Nash, J. 1950. "The Bargaining Problem." *Econometrica* 18:155–62.

Nicolson, H. 1939. *Diplomacy.* 3d ed. London: T. Butterworth.

Raiffa, H. 1982. *The Art and Science of Negotiation.* Cambridge, Mass.: Harvard University Press.

Rubinstein, A. 1982. "Perfect Equilibrium in a Bargaining Model." *Econometrica* 50:97–110.

Schelling, T. C. 1960. *The Strategy of Conflict.* Cambridge, Mass.: Harvard University Press.

Schelling, T. C. 1966. *Arms and Influence.* New Haven: Yale University Press.

Sebenius, J. K. 1984. *Negotiating the Law of the Sea: Lessons in the Art and Science of Reaching Agreement.* Cambridge, Mass.: Harvard University Press.

Sebenius, J. K. 1990. "Negotiation Analysis: An Emerging Approach." J. F. Kennedy School of Government, Cambridge, Mass. Photocopy.

Shapley, L. S. 1952. "Open Questions." In *Report of an Informal Conference on the Theory of N-Person Games.* Department of Mathematics, Princeton University.

Shubik, M. 1971. "The Dollar Auction Game: A Paradox in Noncooperative Behavior and Escalation." *Journal of Conflict Resolution* 15:109–11.

Stahl, I. 1972. *Bargaining Theory.* Stockholm: Economics Research Institute.

von Neumann, J., and O. Morgenstern. 1944. *The Theory of Games and Economic Behavior.* Princeton: Princeton University Press.

Zartman, I. W., and M. Berman. 1982. *The Practical Negotiator.* New Haven: Yale University Press.

CHAPTER 2

Fair Division

H. Peyton Young

Every society has rules for settling disputes over property. If a person dies without leaving a will, the family members are allotted specific shares of the estate depending on their relationship to the deceased. When a business firm fails, the unsecured creditors are paid in proportion to the amount of their claims, that is, so many cents on the dollar. If two parties are haggling over the price of a second-hand car and they are reasonably close in their offers, it would not be surprising for them to settle by "splitting the difference." In parts of the midwestern United States, it is customary for tenant farmers and landlords to split the proceeds of the harvest 50-50, a custom that is known as "farming on the halves." Even children have customs for dividing property. A standard method of sharing a piece of cake, for example, is for one child to divide it into two parts and for the other to choose. Custom usually has it that the older child plays the role of divider, though the privilege may also be decided by the toss of a coin, or by letting the one who was chooser last time be divider this time.

Such customs help negotiators conclude their business more efficiently. They serve as signposts without which a negotiation can degenerate into a contest of wills. They create common expectations in the minds of the negotiators; to deviate from them requires special arguments and extenuating circumstances. They are focal points that guide the negotiators toward a cooperative solution (Schelling 1960).

This is not to suggest, however, that rules of division are fair merely because they are customary, or that, once established, they are immutable. Customs change to reflect the changing norms and values of society. In earlier times, men and women were not considered to be equals. The Old Testament suggests, for example, that a woman should be valued at three-fifths the rate of a man: "the male from twenty years old even unto sixty years old, even thy estimation shall be fifty shekels of silver, after the shekel of the sanctuary. And if it be a female, then thy estimation shall be thirty shekels."[1] While this

---

1. Lev. 27:3–4.

ratio may have been considered an appropriate standard in ancient times, today we would consider it inappropriate and unfair. In our society, fairness entails equality. But equality of what? Equality can be given many different formulations, and the most appropriate one depends on the situation. If two people contribute different amounts to a joint fund and the fund loses money, should the loss be divided equally among the claimants? Surely this would be unfair. The customary solution is to divide the loss in proportion to their contributions. It is not the persons, but the dollars of contribution, that are treated equally. Suppose, on the other hand, that two persons pile dirt against a wall and the wall falls down. If one pile of dirt is twice as large as the other, should the damages be apportioned in a 2:1 ratio? The common-law view is that, if each pile separately could have caused the wall to fall down, then both parties are equally liable (Hart and Honore 1959). Both are guilty of a tort, and the extent of the tort is not measured by the size of the pile.

Sometimes there are several plausible interpretations of equality in a given situation, and the bargaining is over which notion of equality shall prevail. Consider the division of representation among the states in the U.S. Congress. This was one of the most hotly debated issues in the Constitutional Convention of 1787 (Farrand 1911). Some delegates argued that, since the primary function of government is to protect property, representation should be divided among the states in proportion to their wealth or economic product. Others held that the purpose of government is to promote the welfare of persons rather than property, in which case representation should be divided among the states in proportion to their populations. Still others maintained that the states themselves are equal partners in the federation, and should therefore be represented equally.

Each of these theories entails some notion of equality, and the argument was over *what* should be treated equally: persons, states, or property. The Great Compromise was to create two chambers, one with equal representation per capita, the other with equal representation per state. The advocates for representation based on wealth lost out, though a vestige of the wealth criterion was retained in the old "three-fifths rule" whereby slaves (who in those days were regarded as chattels) were counted at the rate of three-fifths of all other persons for purposes of apportionment.[2]

In this chapter I will examine various conceptions of fairness in two negotiating situations: the sharing of joint costs, and the division of inheritances. In both of these cases there exist several plausible interpretations of fair and equal treatment. The role of analysis is to lay bare the assumptions implicit in these various formulations of equality, and to explore their logical consequences.

---

2. U.S. Constitution, art. I, sec. 2.

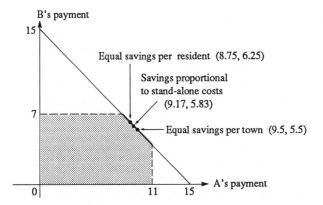

Fig. 1.   Cost allocations of $15 million between towns A and B. The shaded region is the set of allocations that do not exceed the stand-alone costs.

Cost Sharing

The Case of Two Parties

Consider two nearby towns who are considering whether to build a joint water distribution system. Suppose that town A could build its own facility for $11 million without any cooperation from B. Similarly, B could build a separate facility for $7 million without any help from A. The estimated cost of a facility that serves both communities is $15 million. By cooperating, the towns can save $3 million, but to realize these gains they must agree on how to split the costs.

Imagine that each town sends a representative to negotiate a solution. What strategies and arguments should they adopt? To begin with, neither is likely to agree to a division of costs that leaves his or her town worse off than if there were no agreement. The representative from town A will not agree to a division of costs that saddles it with more than $11 million, while B's representative will not agree to pay more than $7 million. These *stand-alone costs* delimit the range of plausible agreements, as shown in figure 1. The shaded segment represents the set of all divisions of $15 million such that A pays at most $11 million and B pays at most $7 million. In a two-party bargaining situation, the divisions that do not exceed the stand-alone cost of either party constitute the *core* of the cost-sharing game.

The core excludes several solutions that one might otherwise find quite reasonable. One possibility, for example, would be to divide the costs equally between the two towns. The argument for this solution on fairness grounds is that the towns have equal power to enter into an agreement, so they should shoulder an equal burden. Alternatively, they might have equal property rights to the source of the water. Whatever the arguments might be for equal division on fairness grounds, however, B has no incentive to be party to such an agreement. It would be saddled with costs of $7.5 million, when it can build its own system for only $7 million.

Of course, an equal division of costs might be considered inappropriate if the towns have different numbers of residents. Suppose, for instance, that A's population is 36,000 and B's is 12,000. An equal division between the towns would imply that each resident of A pays only one-third as much as each resident of B, even though they are served by the same system. A fairer solution in this case might be to treat the persons, rather than the towns, equally. The total costs of $15 million would be equally divided among the 48,000 persons served by the system, and each individual would be assessed $312.50. Once again this poses a problem, however, because the total assessment to town A would be $312.50 $\times$ 36,000 = $11.25 million, which exceeds its stand-alone cost.

Costs versus Cost Savings

Some of these difficulties can be sorted out once we recognize that it is not the cost that is the main object of interest to the negotiators. The reason for entering into a joint agreement is to reduce costs. It is the expectation of *cost savings*, rather than the costs themselves, that motivates the discussions. Hence the fairness issue needs to be examined in the light of how the savings will be distributed. Let s_A denote the cost savings for town A, and s_B the cost savings for town B, where $s_A + s_B$ = $3 million, and both s_A and s_B are nonnegative. How should these savings be distributed? Three possibilities suggest themselves: (1) split the savings equally among the towns; (2) split the savings equally among the residents; or (3) split the savings in proportion to the stand-alone costs. These three solutions are shown in table 1, and their location in the core is illustrated in figure 1.

TABLE 1. Three Methods for Sharing Costs among Two Towns

Town	Stand-alone Cost	Equal Savings	Equal Savings per Capita	Savings Proportional to Costs
A	11	9.5	8.75	9.17
B	7	5.5	6.25	5.83
Total	18	15.0	15.00	15.00

Three or More Parties

Now consider how these ideas can be extended to the case of three or more parties. Suppose that a third town C would like to join the consortium. Say that it would cost C $8 million to build its own system, whereas to include it in the joint system would cost an additional $5 million. Thus, it makes economic sense to include C in the project. The total cost if none of the parties cooperate is $11 + $7 + $8 = $26 million, whereas the cost is $20 million if they do cooperate. So the potential savings total $6 million. Assume that A and C can build their own system for $14 million (a savings of $5 million over their stand-alone costs), whereas B and C can build their own system for $13 million (a savings of $2 million over their stand-alone costs). (See table 2.) To simplify the discussion, assume that the towns are to be treated equally. Then the most natural solution is simply to divide the cost savings equally. Thus A would pay $11 − $2 = $9 million, B would pay $7 − $2 = $5 million, and C would pay $8 − $2 = $6 million. Unfortunately, this solution is not likely to be accepted by A and C, because together they are charged $15 million, whereas they could build their own joint system for $14 million. In other words, the equal savings rule does not respect the stand-alone costs of *groups* of claimants.

In general, the stand-alone cost of a subgroup of claimants is the cost that they would incur if they formed a consortium by themselves. An allocation of costs is in the core of the cost-sharing game if: (1) the costs are fully distributed, and (2) no subset of claimants is charged more than their stand-alone cost. The core is the set of cost allocations that gives all of the parties an incentive to cooperate. Thus, if a, b, c are the charges to A, B, C respectively, then the charges are in the core if and only if

$$a \leq 11, b \leq 7, c \leq 8$$
$$a + b \leq 15, a + c \leq 14, b + c \leq 13$$
$$a + b + c = 20$$

TABLE 2. Potential Costs and Cost Savings for Each Group of Towns

Group	Cost of Group	Sum of Stand-alone Costs of Individuals in Group	Cost-Saving for the Group
A	11	11	0
B	7	7	0
C	8	8	0
A&B	15	18	3
A&C	14	19	5
B&C	13	15	2
A&B&C	20	26	6

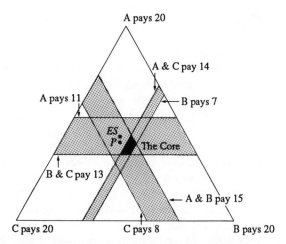

Fig. 2. The core of the cost-sharing game for three parties, A, B, C

The core is the shaded set illustrated in figure 2. Each corner of the large triangle represents an extreme solution in which one town is assessed all of the costs ($20 million). Each interior point of the triangle represents an intermediate solution in which the towns split the $20 million among themselves in some manner. For example, point *ES* represents equal division of savings. The perpendicular distance from *ES* to the base of the triangle is 9 units (A's payment), the perpendicular distance from *ES* to the left-hand side of the triangle is 5 units (B's payment), and the perpendicular distance from *ES* to the right-hand side of the triangle is 6 units (C's payment). The sum of the three perpendicular distances is 20 for every point in the triangle, so every point represents a different way of dividing 20 among the three parties.

In general, the core of a cost-sharing game may be large; it may be small; it may even be empty. Suppose, for example, that B and C could build their own joint system for $9 million, and that all other costs are as in table 2. Then there is no allocation of the $20 million that satisfies the stand-alone cost test for all subgroups, as the reader may verify.

Assuming that the core is nonempty, which of its solutions is *fairest?* Note that the solutions that worked well in the two-person case are not satisfactory here. For example, the equal savings solution may not even be in the core, although for two-person games it is at the center of the core (see fig. 1). Allocating savings in proportion to stand-alone costs is always in the core when there are two parties, but not necessarily when there are three or more parties, as in this case (see point *P* in fig. 2).

A natural approach to choosing a point in the core is to choose one that is centrally located. Consider point *N* in figure 3. This represents the cost allocation: $7.75 million for A, $6.50 million for B, $5.75 million for C. If we fix

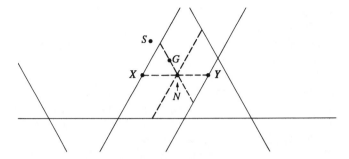

Fig. 3. Cost allocations for three towns

A's payment at $7.75 million, then there is a range of values that B and C could be charged while staying within the boundaries defining the core. This range is represented by the horizontal dotted line segment passing through N. It will be seen that N is the midpoint of this line segment. This means that B and C are situated in the middle of their bargaining range. Moreover, this is true for A and C, and also for A and B. If the core is nonempty, then there always exists at least one allocation in the core such that *every* pair of players is situated in the middle of its bargaining range.

> An allocation is in the intersection of the kernel and the core if it situates every two parties in the middle of the bargaining range defined by the core constraints.[3]

A second notion of fair division is to award equal savings to all subgroups of the parties. In other words, we would like to find an allocation such that the difference between each subgroup's stand-alone costs and the amount that it pays is the *same* for all subgroups. Unfortunately, this condition is too demanding, for typically no such allocation exists. A less demanding criterion in the same spirit is to make the least well off group as well off as possible, the next least well off group as well off as possible, and so forth, where the measure of "well off" is the difference between each group's stand-alone cost and the amount that it pays.

The *nucleolus* is the unique allocation that satisfies this criterion and does not exceed the stand-alone cost of any individual claimant.[4] This criterion is similar to a general principle of distributive justice known as Rawls's "difference principle," which holds that the position of the worst-off group in society

---

3. The kernel is also defined for all games, even those with empty cores (Maschler and Davis 1965).

4. More precisely, for each proper subset of players S, define the *savings* of S to be the difference between its stand-alone cost and the amount that it is charged under the proposed

should be maximized (Rawls 1971). A refinement of this idea due to Sen (1970) states that, subject to the worst-off group being as well off as possible, the next worst-off group should also be made as well off as possible, and so forth. The nucleolus is the analogous criterion applied to subgroups of claimants in a cost-sharing game.

Remarkably, the nucleolus is always in the kernel of the cost-sharing game, that is, the nucleolus situates every two parties in the middle of their bargaining range, as defined by the core constraints (assuming that the core is nonempty). In the present case, then, the nucleolus is the point N.

A third solution to the fairness question is to allocate the savings in proportion to each claimant's contribution to savings. According to this theory, the claimants are treated equally only to the extent that they contribute equally. Define the *marginal contribution* of a claimant to be the difference between the maximum savings that can be achieved with the claimant and the maximum savings that can be achieved without the claimant. In this example, the total cost savings are $6 million. If town C is excluded, then the total savings are only $3 million, so the marginal contribution of C is $3 million. Similarly we find that A's marginal contribution is $4 million and B's is $1 million. If the savings are allocated among A, B, and C in the ratio 4 :1 :3, then the associated cost allocation is: A, $8 million; B, $6.25 million; C, $5.75 million (point G in fig. 3). This method is known in the civil engineering literature as the *alternate cost avoided method*, a variation of which is the standard procedure for allocating the costs of multiple-purpose reservoir projects (James and Lee 1971). When there are just three parties and the core is nonempty, then the alternate cost avoided solution is typically in the core, but this is not the case when there are four or more parties (Straffin and Heaney 1981).

The extent of the claimants' marginal contributions can be measured in yet another way. Suppose that the claimants commit themselves to the project in some definite order. For example, suppose that A commits first, B second, and C third. By itself, A does not contribute anything to joint savings, so its marginal contribution is zero. The addition of B saves $3 million compared to A's and B's stand-alone costs, and these savings are attributed to B. The addition of C saves a further $3 million, which is attributed to C. Thus the incremental savings implied by the order of commitment A, B, C are: $0 for A, $3 million for B, and $3 million for C. But this ordering is purely hypothetical: any other ordering seems equally credible a priori. Thus it would seem fairest to compute, for each of the six possible orderings, the incremental savings attributable to each claimant and take their average over all order-

---

allocation. The nucleolus is the unique allocation such that the minimum savings among all proper subsets S of N is as large as possible and is achieved on as few sets as possible, the next-lowest savings is as large as possible and is achieved on as few sets as possible, and so forth, subject to the condition that no individual party is charged more than its stand-alone cost (Schmeidler 1969).

ings. The resulting allocation is called the *Shapley value* (Shapley 1953). In this example, the Shapley value is: A, \$8.33 million; B, \$5.83 million; C, \$5.83 million (point S in fig. 3). In this case, the Shapley value is not in the core.

The Pairwise Comparisons Principle

One might suppose that there is only one way the parties to a negotiation can be treated equally. Yet the preceding discussion shows there is an almost dizzying variety of ways equal treatment may be interpreted in the context of cost allocation. How can we make sense out of these rival definitions of equality? One way to narrow down the list is to look for further properties that an allocation method should satisfy. There is now a rich literature on the axiomatic foundations of cost allocation, and the more important theoretical methods (the nucleolus and Shapley value) can be characterized by very appealing properties. A detailed discussion of this literature would take us too far afield.[5] There is one criterion, however, that merits discussion here because it has important applications to other problems of fair division. The idea is first to choose the criterion of fairness that seems most appropriate when there are just two claimants, then extend it to multiparty situations by insisting that the allocation satisfy the criterion for every *pair* of claimants.

> *Pairwise comparisons principle.* An allocation among a group of claimants is fair if it treats every pair of claimants fairly relative to some two-party criterion of fair division.[6]

The pairwise comparisons principle simplifies the analysis of fairness by breaking it into two parts: a decision about what fairness means in the two-party case, and a criterion for extending the concept to more than two parties.

To illustrate the application of this idea to cost allocation, consider two parties (e.g., two towns) who must decide how to divide a certain joint cost c. We assume that c is less than the sum of the stand-alone costs of the parties, $c_1 + c_2$, so that the potential savings $s = c_1 + c_2 - c$ are positive. We shall also assume that the parties are to be treated equally. In this case equal division, the Shapley value, the nucleolus, the kernel, and the alternate cost avoided method *all* boil down to the same thing, namely, the parties are situated in the middle of the bargaining range defined by their stand-alone costs.

---

5. For a survey of this literature see Young 1985.

6. This condition is known in the fair division literature as "pairwise consistency." It was proposed by Harsanyi (1959) for bargaining problems, by Balinski and Young (1982) for apportionment problems, and by Aumann and Maschler (1985) for "bankruptcy" problems. The idea has several alternative formulations in cooperative game theory. See Young (forthcoming) for a more complete discussion.

Now suppose that we want to extend this solution to situations involving more than two parties. Suppose further that we want the solution to be in the core whenever the core is nonempty. The pairwise comparisons principle then says that *every two claimants should be in the middle of their bargaining range, as defined by the core constraints.* As we have seen, the nucleolus has this property, as does any solution that is in the intersection of the kernel with the core.[7] These solutions are "fair" in the sense that they treat the parties equally *given* the bounds imposed by their stand-alone costs.

Inheritance

As a problem of fair division, cost allocation is relatively simple because it concerns one divisible good, namely, money. Matters become more complex when there are several goods at stake that the claimants value differently. Equal division may be fair, but it is not necessarily efficient. Is it possible to treat the claimants both fairly and efficiently?

To be concrete, consider a group of heirs who are left equal shares of an estate that consists of various goods. Each good is assumed to be perfectly divisible. The straightforward solution is to give each heir an equal portion of the goods, but if the heirs have different tastes, then they will be able to do better by trading goods that they like less for goods that they like more. The end result might be an unequal distribution that they all prefer to dividing the estate equally. The issue, then, is which of these unequal, but preferred, distributions "inherits" the fairness of equal division.

One solution, of course, would be to allocate equal portions to the heirs and then let them trade. In theory, they should be able to strike a bargain that makes some or all of them better off, and none of them worse off, than the initial allocation. The difficulty is that, typically, there will be a wide range of bargains with this property. Which one of them will the bargainers actually agree to? On the one hand they may simply haggle, making proposals and counterproposals until one of them accedes to the other's demand. Alternatively, they may look for some criterion of distribution that both of them can agree to in principle. The latter is often more fruitful than outright haggling because it is less likely to result in injured feelings, protracted delays, or, possibly, a complete breakdown in the negotiations.

Example. Alistair and Beatrice have been left equal shares of their parents' estate. The property consists of $200,000 in cash and 100 acres of

---

7. The nucleolus, the kernel, and the Shapley value can all be axiomatically characterized by extensions of the pairwise comparisons principle. See Sobolev 1975; Peleg 1986, 1987; Hart and Mas-Colell 1987.

land. Beatrice married into money but has a sentimental attachment to the land. Alistair is a threadbare intellectual who has little income and no interest in land except for the money that it will fetch at auction. Beatrice would be indifferent between receiving all of the land or a payment of $300,000. Alistair is indifferent between receiving all of the land or a payment of $100,000, which is the amount that he believes it would bring in a sale. We shall assume that both heirs have fixed trade-off rates between money and land, that is, Alistair values each acre of land at $1,000, while Beatrice values each acre of land at $3,000.

If each is awarded half of the land and half of the money, then the distribution could certainly be called "fair." The problem is that there are other divisions that both of them would prefer. If Alistair takes all of the money and Beatrice all of the land, for example, then both of them would be better off.

A division is *efficient* if there is no other division that makes one or both parties strictly better off and neither of them worse off. It is efficient to give Alistair all of the money and Beatrice all of the land. But in what sense is it fair? In the next two sections I shall look at various answers to this question from a normative standpoint. Then I shall look at the same question from a procedural standpoint.

Egalitarian Solutions

One way of treating the heirs fairly is to give them portions that have "comparable" value. But how can their different value systems be compared? One solution would be to choose a reference commodity, such as money, and divide the estate so that each heir considers his or her portion to be equivalent in value to the same amount of money. For example, if Alistair is given $200,000 plus 25 acres, and Beatrice 75 acres, then each values his or her portion at $225,000. This solution is *egalitarian* with money as the *standard of value*.

Of course, it matters which commodity (or bundle of commodities) is chosen to be the standard of value. Suppose that, instead of money, we take the estate itself as the standard. In this case, the value of a given portion (to a particular individual) is defined to be the *fraction* of the whole estate that the individual considers to be equally desirable to that portion. For example, Alistair is indifferent between all of the land and one-third of the land plus one-third of the money, so he values the land equivalently to one-third of the whole estate.

For each possible division of the estate, we may compute the value that each party attaches to his or her portion using the estate as the standard of

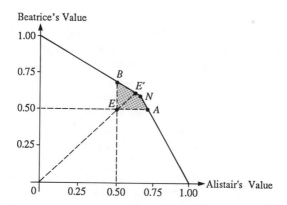

Fig. 4. The bargaining set for the inheritance problem

comparison.[8] This yields the set of payoff combinations shown in figure 4. For example, if Alistair gets all of the money and Beatrice all of the land, then Alistair values his portion equivalently with two-thirds of the whole estate, and Beatrice values her portion at three-fifths of the whole estate. Hence this division is represented by the point N = ($\frac{2}{3}$, $\frac{3}{5}$). Equal division is represented by the point E = ($\frac{1}{2}$, $\frac{1}{2}$), and so forth. We also allow for the possibility that some of the estate is not distributed to the heirs at all (perhaps because it is paid out in lawyers' fees). For example, the origin represents the situation in which neither heir receives anything.

Since the two heirs can always divide the estate equally if all else fails, the only plausible candidates for a negotiated solution are those that *dominate equal division* in the sense that both are at least as well off as they would be under equal division. The set of allocations with this property corresponds to the shaded region in figure 4. The northeastern boundary of this region represents all divisions that are both efficient and dominate equal division. The egalitarian divisions correspond to a 45-degree line from the origin, and the unique point E' where it intersects the boundary represents an egalitarian division that is efficient, namely, $187,500 for Alistair and $12,500 plus all of the land for Beatrice. This has the property that each heir considers his or her portion to be equivalent in value to five-eighths of the whole estate (point E' in fig. 4). Note that this distribution is strictly better than equal division for both parties.

More generally, when the estate is taken to be the standard of value, then it is always possible to divide the goods efficiently so that: (1) all claimants

8. I assume throughout that individuals' utility functions are continuous and strictly increasing, so this notion is well-defined.

value their portions equally; (2) each considers his portion to be at least as valuable as an equal split of all of the goods. This is not necessarily the case if another commodity is used, however. For example, the division that gives each heir equal money value is $200,000 plus 25 acres to Alistair and 75 acres to Beatrice. But Beatrice would prefer to have half of the whole estate ($100,000 plus 50 acres).

The egalitarian criterion generalizes to any number of claimants as follows. Choose a standard of value, that is, a fixed bundle of goods. A division of property is *egalitarian* with respect to this standard if each claimant considers his portion to be equivalent in value to the same fraction of the fixed bundle.[9]

The Nash Solution

A second possible solution to the problem of fair division is to ask for a distribution that maximizes the total utility of the claimants instead of one that gives them equal utility. This is the *utilitarian criterion* of distributive justice. As before, the answer depends on how the utility or value functions are calibrated. Suppose, for example, that utility is equated with money value. Then Beatrice would get all of the land because she places a higher money value on each acre than Alistair does. Moreover, since they value the money equally (dollar for dollar), the distribution of the money does not affect total utility. Hence, it is perfectly consistent with the utilitarian criterion that Beatrice receive all of the money too. This outcome can hardly be called fair, however.

A more defensible approach is to compare the relative, rather than the absolute, changes in utility that result from different distributions of the goods. Consider the situation in which Alistair gets $100,000 and Beatrice gets $100,000 plus all of the land. Transferring some of the money from Beatrice to Alistair does not increase total utility (measured in money terms) because each dollar has equal "value" to both of them. Note, however, that Alistair's utility increases by a larger *percentage* than Beatrice's utility decreases. Hence, we could argue that such a transfer ought to be made. This argument suggests, in fact, that all of the money should be given to Alistair, because every dollar taken from Beatrice and given to Alistair increases his utility by more (in percentage terms) than her utility decreases.

Consider, then, the situation in which Alistair gets all of the money and Beatrice all of the land. If we were to transfer one acre of land from Beatrice to Alistair, then the latter's utility would increase by $1,000/200,000 = 0.5$

---

9. This concept is due to Pazner and Schmeidler 1974. A similar solution concept in bargaining theory was suggested by Raiffa (1953) and axiomatized by Kalai and Smorodinsky (1975).

percent while the former's would decrease by 3,000/300,000 = 1.0 percent, so the above argument suggests that the transfer should not be made. We have therefore found a distribution of money and land such that every redistribution causes one claimant's utility to decrease by a larger percentage than the other claimant's increases.

More generally, suppose that the goods are divisible and the claimants' utility functions are concave. Then the goods can be distributed among the two claimants so that every redistribution causes one claimant's utility to decrease by a larger percentage than the other's increases. The utility payoffs associated with such a distribution are called the *Nash solution* (point N in fig. 4). The Nash solution establishes a form of parity between the claimants as measured by their relative rates of gain in utility.[10] It can also be justified by a set of general bargaining principles that the parties might agee to in advance (Nash 1950). Finally, it is the equilibrim outcome of a bargaining procedure that places both claimants on an equal footing, as we shall see in a subsequent section.

Divide and Choose

We now shift the focus from end-state notions of fairness to procedural ideas of fairness. If the negotiators cannot agree on a formula for dividing the goods, could they perhaps agree on a procedure for conducting the negotiations that is expected to lead to a fair outcome?

One familiar device for dividing a piece of property fairly is to let one person divide it into two parts and to let the other have first choice. By the toss of a coin, one of the two claimants is declared to be divider. Say that it is Alistair. He divides the estate into two portions, and Beatrice chooses whichever portion she prefers. We shall assume, as before, that the value of any combination of land and money equals the value of the land plus the value of the money (i.e., the value functions are additive). Under these circumstances both parties can guarantee themselves portions that dominate equal division. Beatrice can assure herself of such a portion by selecting the piece that she prefers no matter what division Alistair makes. Alistair can assure himself of such a portion by dividing the estate into two equal shares, so it does not matter which Beatrice selects.

However, the divider can do strictly better than equal division if he or she knows the chooser's tastes, and both of them act rationally. Suppose, for example, that Alistair is divider and that he creates the following two portions.

---

10. The Nash solution is computed by maximizing the product of the claimants' utilities.

I. 16 acres + $200,000   II. 84 acres

Assuming that Beatrice cares only about the value of her own portion, she will choose portion II. This leaves Alistair with all of the money and some of the land, which is substantially better for him than receiving a half share of both goods. It corresponds (give or take an acre) to point *A* in figure 4, which is the point where Alistair maximizes his utility given that Beatrice's utility equals one-half.

Suppose, instead, that Beatrice is divider. If she knows Alistair's tastes, then she might arrange the following choice.

I. $150,001   II. 100 acres + $49,999

Alistair will choose portion I, and Beatrice will realize a large surplus from portion II. This division corresponds (give or take a dollar) to point *B* in figure 4, which is the point where Beatrice maximizes the value of her portion, given that Alistair values his portion at one-half of the whole estate.

It appears, then, that the divider may enjoy a substantial advantage if he or she knows the chooser's tastes. It seems reasonable to ask whether there is some modification of the divide-and-choose procedure that puts the parties on a more equal footing. In the next two sections I shall consider two such modifications.

Bidding to Be Divider

One way to equalize the roles of divider and chooser is to auction off the right to be divider. By allowing the claimants to bid for the privilege, the "rent" attached to being divider is competed away and divider and chooser are placed on an equal footing.[11] The bidding process works as follows.

Step 1. Each heir "bids" a fraction between zero and one.
Step 2. The heir who bids the largest fraction becomes divider. (If they bid the same fraction, then one of them, say the elder, is designated to be divider.) The divider creates two portions, one designated for himself and the other designated for the chooser.
Step 3. The chooser accepts or rejects her designated portion. If she rejects, then she gets to take the fraction of the goods that *she* bid, and the divider takes the remainder.

---

11. This idea is due to Crawford 1979. See also Demange 1984.

I illustrate this idea using the above example. Suppose that Beatrice bids three-fifths and Alistair bids two-thirds. Alistair wins the bid. He then divides the goods into two portions, one designated for Beatrice and one for himself. If Beatrice finds that her portion is equivalent in value to at least three-fifths of the estate (in her estimation), then she should choose it. Otherwise, she should reject the division and claim three-fifths of the land and three-fifths of the money. It turns out that Alistair can make Beatrice an offer that she will accept (and is still attractive for him), namely:

Alistair: $200,000,   Beatrice: 100 acres.

Beatrice's portion represents exactly three-fifths of the estate's value to her, so she has nothing to lose by choosing it, and he retains a portion worth two-thirds of the estate to himself.

Beatrice, however, can do better by bidding more. For example, if she bids just under two-thirds, say .65, Alistair must create a portion that *she* values at .65 of the whole estate, or else he risks getting only .35 of the estate. The portion 100 acres plus $25,000 has this property. But this leaves him with only $175,000, which he values at substantially less than two-thirds of the whole. If he were to bid slightly less than Beatrice, say .64, then she would become divider and be forced to offer him a portion worth .64, and so forth. It can be shown that, in equilibrium, both bid five-eighths, and the division is:

Alistair: $187,500,   Beatrice: 100 acres + $12,500.

In general, the equilibrium outcome of this game is that both parties bid the same fraction of the estate, and the resulting division is efficient. In other words, bidding to be divider implements an efficient, egalitarian solution with the estate as the standard of value. Thus we have constructed a formal procedure or mechanism that leads to a fair and efficient outcome, provided that the parties know each other's preferences and act rationally based on this knowledge.

Offer Counteroffer

Another way of putting the parties on a more or less equal footing is to allow the privilege of being divider to alternate between them. As before, we toss a coin to determine who goes first. Say that it is Alistair. On the first day of the negotiations, he proposes a division, with one piece designated for himself and the other for Beatrice. She can either accept or reject the proposal. If she rejects it, then on the following day she gets to make a proposal, which he either accepts or rejects, and so forth. The offers and counteroffers alternate in this way on succeeding days until someone accepts. This is called the *offer-counteroffer procedure*. It treats the parties more even-handedly than divide and choose, because the chooser is given the power to reject the other's division and become divider.

There is the potential difficulty, of course, that offers and counteroffers could go on indefinitely with no resolution. For example, Alistair could propose that he receive the whole estate whenever he is divider, and Beatrice could do the same. On the other hand, they might not follow such a strategy if they are impatient to get the goods.

Alternatively, we could suppose that there is a small probability $p > 0$ that the negotiations will break down for each day that passes without a settlement. If the value of an offer tomorrow would be v, then the prospect of such an offer has an expected utility today of only $(1-p)v$, because the probability is p that the negotiations will not resume tomorrow. The risk of breakdown encourages the parties to compromise rather than persist in making unreasonable demands.

The most sensible strategy, in fact, is for the person who goes first to make an offer that tempts the other to accept right away. Suppose, for example, that on the first day Alistair offers Beatrice a division that has utility u to himself and v to her. She is then faced with a choice: if she refuses, then she can make a proposal on the second day that is better for her, but there is a risk that the negotiations will break down in the meantime. Suppose that she plans to make a proposal on day two that has utility u' to him and v' to her, where $u' < u$ and $v' > v$. Because she has to wait a day to make her proposal, its present value is only rv' for her and ru' for him, where $r = 1 - p$. So she is willing to accept his offer of v now provided that $v \geq rv'$.

This reasoning assumes, of course, that Alistair actually will accept her offer on day two. If he does not, then the negotiations will be protracted even further, and the present value of her counteroffer will be even less than rv'. To induce Alistair to accept her offer of u' on day two, he must find it at least as attractive as waiting until day three to renew his own offer of u. Therefore it must be the case that $u' \geq ru$. In equilibrium these two conditions are satisfied as equalities: $u' = ru$, and $v = rv'$.[12] In this case Beatrice might as well accept Alistair's offer on the first day, because the cost of delay equals any advantage she would get by waiting until the second day to make an alternative proposal.

The situation is illustrated in figure 5 with a discount rate of $r = 0.9$. In

---

12. By "equilibrium" I mean a subgame perfect equilibrium. See Rubinstein 1982 and Binmore and Dasgupta 1987.

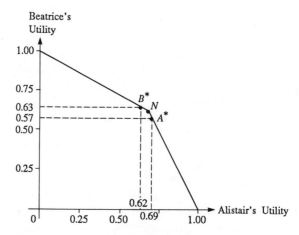

Fig. 5. The equilibrium to offer-counteroffer and its relation to the Nash solution

this case, the *unique* equilibrium is for Alistair to offer Beatrice approximately 94.5 acres on the first day and to keep the money and remaining land for himself (point A^* in the figure). Her counteroffer would be to offer Alistair approximately $185,000 and keep the land and remaining money for herself (point B^*). With a discount rate of 0.9 it is not worth waiting, however, so she accepts his offer.

Of course, if Beatrice went first, then the outcome would be B^*, which is somewhat more favorable to her. If the probability of breakdown between rounds is very small, however, then A^* and B^* will be very close, so there is no substantial advantage in going first. It will also be noted that A^* and B^* are quite close to the Nash solution N. This is a general result (Binmore and Dasgupta 1987):

> If the probability of breakdown between rounds is small, then the equilibrium outcome of the offer-counteroffer procedure is close to the Nash solution.

Thus the Nash solution can be understood as the outcome of a game that gives the parties equal control over process, and that mimics the give-and-take of actual bargaining.

Fairness and Equality

In this chapter, I have argued that fairness in distributive bargaining entails some form of equal treatment. It does not necessarily mean that the parties are entitled to absolutely equal amounts, however. Departures from equality may be called for when the negotiators have different opportunities, abilities, needs, or tastes. Such differences, which are almost inevitable in real applications, mean that fairness is a subtle and nuanced idea that often admits of more than one interpretation.

While one may dispute which interpretation is most appropriate in a given set of circumstances, however, framing negotiations in terms of fairness principles represents an advance over mere haggling for several reasons. First, there are relatively few concepts of fair treatment that are credible in any given situation, and this fact helps to focus the negotiations. Second, an agreement based on fairness principles is not likely to generate grudges. The outcome does not rest on the cleverness of the parties, their bargaining ability, or their willpower, so it is unlikely that anyone feels bested or "had." This enhances the durability of the agreement. Third, a negotiation based on explicitly formulated principles can serve as a guide to future negotiators in similar situations. It establishes a precedent, and this in itself has significant social value.

A question that I have not addressed is what fairness means in a larger, social sense. Is the distribution of opportunities and goods in society just? If not, what should be done to rectify it without sacrificing initiative and enterprise on the part of individuals? Such questions have been the subject of much debate among contemporary philosophers, and they are far from being definitively answered.[13] Fortunately, many practical problems of fair division can be successfully analyzed without resolving the issue of social justice in the large. In cost sharing, inheritance, and other problems of this sort, the issue is not how to rectify inequities in the social order. The immediate question is how to divide a specific benefit (or burden) among a group of persons given that they have legitimate differences that entitle them to different amounts. Concepts of fairness can be a useful guideline for negotiating such divisions, for they create shared expectations in the minds of the disputants that make the business of negotiating more efficient and more amicable.

REFERENCES

Aumann, R. J., and M. Maschler. 1985. "Game-Theoretic Analysis of a Bankruptcy Problem from the Talmud." *Journal of Economic Theory* 36:195–213.
Balinski, M. L., and H. P. Young. 1982. *Fair Representation*. New Haven: Yale University Press.

---

13. Rawls1971; Nozick 1974; and Walzer 1983 provide a spectrum of opinion on this topic.

Binmore, K., and P. Dasgupta. 1987. *The Economics of Bargaining*. Oxford: Basil Blackwell.

Crawford, V. 1979. "A Procedure of Generating Pareto-Efficient Egalitarian-Equivalent Allocations." *Econometrica* 47:49–60.

Demange, G. 1984. "Implementing Efficient Egalitarian Equivalent Allocations." *Econometrica* 52:1167–77.

Farrand, M., ed. 1911. *The Records of the Federal Convention of 1787*. New Haven: Yale University Press.

Harsanyi, J. 1959. "A Bargaining Model for the *n*-Person Game." In *Contributions to the Theory of Games*, vol. 4, ed. A. W. Tucker and D. Luce. Annals of Mathematics Studies no. 40. Princeton: Princeton University Press.

Hart, H. L. A., and A. M. Honore. 1959. *Causation in the Law*. Oxford: Clarendon Press.

Hart, S., and A. Mas-Colell. "Potential, Value, and Consistency." *Econometrica* 57:589–614.

James, L. D., and R. R. Lee. 1971. *Economics of Water Resource Planning*. New York: McGraw-Hill.

Kalai, E., and M. Smorodinsky. 1975. "Other Solutions to Nash's Bargaining Problem." *Econometrica* 43:510–18.

Maschler, M., and M. Davis. 1965. "The Kernel of a Cooperative Game." *Naval Research Logistics Quarterly* 12:223–59.

Nash, J. 1950. "The Bargaining Problem." *Econometrica* 18:155–62.

Nozick, R. 1974. *Anarchy, State, and Utopia*. New York: Basic Books.

Pazner, E. A., and D. Schmeidler. 1974. "A Difficulty in the Concept of Fairness." *Review of Economic Studies* 41:441–43.

Peleg, B. 1986. "On the Reduced Game Property and Its Converse." *International Journal of Game Theory* 15:187–200.

Peleg, B. 1987. "On the Reduced Game Property and Its Converse: A Correction." *International Journal of Game Theory* 16:290.

Raiffa, H. 1953. "Arbitration Schemes for General Two-Person Games." *Annals of Mathematics Studies*. Princeton: Princeton University Press.

Rawls, J. 1971. *A Theory of Justice*. Cambridge, Mass.: Belknap Press.

Rubinstein, A. 1982. "Perfect Equilibrium in a Bargaining Model." *Econometrica* 50:97–109.

Schelling, T. 1960. *The Strategy of Conflict*. Cambridge, Mass.: Harvard University Press.

Schmeidler, D. 1969. "The Nucleolus of a Characteristic Function Game." *SIAM Journal on Applied Mathematics* 17:1163–70.

Sen, A. 1970. *Collective Choice and Social Welfare*. San Francisco: Holden Day.

Shapley, L. S. 1953. "A Value for *N*-Person Games." In *Contributions to the Theory of Games*, vol. 2, ed. H. Kuhn and A. W. Tucker. Annals of Mathematics Studies no. 40. Princeton: Princeton University Press.

Sobolev, A. I. 1975. "The Characterization of Optimality Principles in Cooperative Games by Functional Equations." In *Matematischeskie Metody v Socialnix Naukax*, Proceedings of the Seminar, Issue 6, ed. N. N. Voroby'ev, 94–151. Vilnius: Academy of Sciences of the Lithuanian SSR.

Straffin, P. J., and J. Heaney. 1981. "Game Theory and the Tennessee Valley Authority." *International Journal of Game Theory* 10:35–43.

Thomson, W. 1989. "The Consistency Principle." University of Rochester. Typescript.

Walzer, M. 1983. *Spheres of Justice*. New York: Basic Books.

Young, H. P., ed. 1985. *Cost Allocation: Methods, Principles, Applications*. Amsterdam: North-Holland.

Young, H. P. Forthcoming. *Equity*. Princeton: Princeton University Press.

CHAPTER 3

Arbitration Procedures

Steven J. Brams, D. Marc Kilgour, and Samuel Merrill III

Arbitration is defined as "the hearing and determination of a case in controversy by a person chosen by the parties or appointed under statutory authority.[1] By this definition, not only do the parties to a dispute submit their differences to the judgment of an arbitrator, but there is also the "determination" of an outcome: the dispute does not end in impasse; there is a resolution that both parties are obliged to accept. This was true in biblical times, too:

> If a case is too baffling for you to decide, be it a controversy over homicide, civil law, or assault—matters of dispute in your courts—you shall promptly repair to the place which the LORD your God will have chosen, and appear before the levitical priests, or the magistrate in charge at the time, and present your problem. . . . You shall carry out the verdict that is announced to you. (Deut. 17:8–10)

Thus, arbitration has a venerable history.

We restrict our analysis to "interest" arbitration, or arbitration between parties with different interests, such as labor and management over wages. "Grievance" or "rights" arbitration, by comparison, refers to the interpretation of the privileges or rights allowed the parties under an existing contract (e.g., what an employer is obligated to do to ensure worker safety). Also, we limit consideration to disputes that involve only two parties, in which one party wants more of something and the other party less. Two-party disputes, in fact, constitute the great bulk of cases settled by interest arbitration.

We thank Colin Day, Barry O'Neill, Peyton Young, and referees for their valuable comments on earlier drafts of this chapter. This chapter is a substantially modified and abbreviated version of chapter 3 of *Negotiation Games: Applying Game Theory to Bargaining and Arbitration,* by Steven J. Brams (New York and London: Routledge, 1990). Reprinted by permission of Routledge, Chapman and Hall, Inc.

1. *Webster's Ninth New Collegiate Dictionary,* 1983.

If the parties to a dispute cannot reach a settlement on their own, arbitration may be mandated by law. The usual rationale for mandating arbitration is that the external costs (i.e., those to parties not involved) of, for example, a strike by police officers or firefighters are so great that imposing a settlement is preferable to imposing such external costs on the public.

Of course, the fact that a dispute will be arbitrated if two sides are not able to settle will affect the prior negotiations of the parties. If there is no requirement that arbitration be used as a last resort, the disputants must consider the possibility of an impasse, such as a prolonged strike, if they do not settle. On the other hand, if arbitration is mandatory should negotiations break down, the parties must consider the possibility of an imposed settlement, which may or may not be to their liking. In the event that arbitration is used, the issue of what kind of settlement will be selected depends critically on the arbitration procedure.

Although the dictionary definition of arbitration is silent on *how* a settlement is determined, traditionally the arbitrator is free to render any judgment, which is what we call *conventional arbitration*. In recent years, however, a number of different procedures have been proposed that do not give the arbitrator free rein in selecting a settlement. For example, one procedure now in common use, *final-offer arbitration* (FOA), restricts the arbitrator's choices to one or the other of the so-called final offers made by the two sides. Although this procedure does not induce the two sides to converge by making the same offers—as some of its proponents had hoped—it does give them an incentive to settle on their own, lest the arbitrator choose an "extreme" offer of the other side. Other procedures give the two sides more of an incentive to converge, but not necessarily to the settlement preferred by the arbitrator.

If we are to design procedures intelligently, we must model these strategic effects. But good design also requires empirical testing and normative evaluation. At this stage, a comparison of the theoretical predictions of the arbitration models with experience is possible only for two procedures (conventional arbitration and FOA), because the other procedures to be discussed are untried. On the other hand, controlled experiments with the other procedures are possible and, in fact, have been conducted in the case of a procedure we call multistage FOA (Neale and Bazerman 1987).

Our analysis of different procedures indicates that there is no perfect procedure: trade-offs are inevitable. Thus, for example, there is no procedure that simultaneously induces the parties to converge on their own (so an arbitrated settlement need never be imposed), mirrors the settlement preferred by the arbitrator (which presumably helps to ensure its fairness), and forecloses the possibility of an extreme settlement (by encouraging both sides to compromise if not converge). Our task will be to compare and evaluate some of the most promising procedures and the trade-offs they entail.

With the exception of conventional arbitration, which tends to lead to exaggerated claims, all the arbitration procedures force the disputants to compromise between attempting to match the arbitrator's judgment and pushing for their own best offers, but they do this in varying degrees. Some procedures induce the disputants to home in on the arbitrator's preferred settlement, whereas others either do not promote such convergence or induce convergence to some other point. It seems that only the threat of an unfavorable settlement can reduce posturing and get the parties to make concessions and offers that converge, yet the convergence may not be to the arbitrator's position. Indeed, as we shall suggest, convergence may not even be desirable.

What one considers desirable, from a normative perspective, depends on the kind of behavior that one believes an arbitration procedure should encourage in the settlement of disputes. We offer some prescriptions, based on different criteria, in the concluding section.

Conventional Arbitration

Under the most commonly used form of interest arbitration, conventional arbitration, an arbitrator acceptable to both sides of a dispute specifies a settlement that is binding on the parties. It would appear to work well when the arbitrator is knowledgeable about the issues and impartial, so any judgment he or she renders is considered fair.

In practice, however, conventional arbitration suffers from several disadvantages (Bloom 1986; Neale and Bazerman 1987). The most important is that the arbitrator's judgment may not be independent of the two sides' positions. For example, if the arbitrator tends to split the difference between these positions, each side will have an incentive to make an extreme demand and not budge from it (Farber 1981).[2]

Of course, it may not pay to exaggerate too much, because arbitrators tend to devalue positions that seem outlandish (Bazerman and Farber 1985). Nevertheless, conventional arbitration does not provide much incentive for the parties to reconcile their differences.

There is a related problem with conventional arbitration—it may have a chilling effect on the negotiations that precede the arbitration, especially if there is the perception that the arbitrator may be swayed by exaggerated

---

2. This problem does not afflict FOA: the players' optimal offers are not affected as long as the arbitrator bases his or her choice, in part, on these offers. True, an arbitrator's partial split-the-difference philosophy will shift his or her position toward the midpoint of the two offers, but this position—as long as it also reflects the arbitrator's independent views—will remain nearer the offer that the arbitrator actually prefers. Hence, the arbitrator will still choose this offer, robbing the players of an incentive to alter their strategies (e.g., by making exaggerated claims) even if these have *some* influence on the arbitrator's position.

claims. After all, why should parties negotiate seriously if, by taking extreme positions, they can use these positions to bolster their claims in the subsequent arbitration? But more than just "setting up" an arbitrator, a party may decide to derail a negotiated settlement if it believes it can obtain a better outcome in arbitration.

The extent to which an arbitration procedure encourages serious bargaining—and promotes convergence toward a negotiated settlement—is one of the principal criteria we use in evaluating different procedures. Conventional arbitration does not do well on this criterion insofar as there is any kind of averaging by the arbitrator that favors the party that is more extreme.

Final-Offer Arbitration (FOA)

FOA was proposed in Stevens 1966, though it had been informally discussed earlier (see Stern et al. 1975, 113n.7). In the last 25 years, it has gained widespread attention and use.

Under FOA, each party submits its final offer for settlement to an arbitrator, who must choose one final offer or the other. The offer chosen by the arbitrator determines the settlement. Unlike conventional arbitration, the arbitrator is not permitted to split the difference, or compromise the offers of each side in any other way. One side or the other "wins" by having its offer chosen.

Proponents of FOA have argued that it forces the two sides to converge, eliminating the need for a settlement imposed by the arbitrator, as under conventional arbitration. This is how one analyst described the reasoning underlying the convergence argument:

> If the arbitrator or panel was permitted to select only one or the other of the parties' final offers, with no power to make a choice anywhere in between, it was expected that the logic of the procedure would force negotiating parties to continue moving closer together in search of a position that would be most likely to receive neutral sympathy. Ultimately, so the argument went, they would come so close together that they would almost inevitably find their own settlement. (Rehmus 1979, 218)

Of course, if the two sides do not converge or come close to converging, the arbitrator will be forced to pick between two possibly extreme offers. Hence, the value of FOA depends on its ability to induce a *negotiated* settlement, under the threat of a possibly onerous settlement if one loses under FOA.

In effect, the two parties play a guessing game with each other about where the arbitrator stands, trying to offer a settlement that is favorable to themselves and, at the same time, does not deviate too much from the judgment of the arbitrator. A number of theorists have modeled these trade-offs,[3] which we shall analyze with a simple game-theoretic model. We will then compare the theoretical predictions of the model with empirical data from major league baseball and public-employee disputes.

A Model of FOA

FOA can be modeled as a two-person game, wherein each party tries to make a more competitive offer than the other. The game is *constant-sum,* because the gains by one side are exactly balanced by the losses of the other, making the sum of the payoffs to both sides a constant.

We assume that the players have only incomplete information about what the arbitrator thinks is a fair settlement. In the model, this means that the players do not know the arbitrator's preferred settlement but view it as a range of possibilities, some possibly more likely than others. This information is *common knowledge*—both players know it, each knows that the other knows it, and so on.

The players may acquire this knowledge from a variety of sources. If the arbitrator has a prior record, this may be informative, as well as guidelines to which the arbitrator may be required to adhere. Information on previous settlements of disputes in the same area may also narrow the range of likely choices of the arbitrator. In addition, each side will assess the quality of the arguments presented by both sides to try to ascertain in which direction the arbitrator might be pulled.

We do not assume that the players, in taking account of these different factors, will be able to second-guess the arbitrator exactly. Instead, we assume that they develop a common perception, described by a probability distribution, about a range of possible settlements. This distribution gives the relative likelihood that different settlements will be preferred by the arbitrator. Thus, the model incorporates uncertainty; this uncertainty is viewed identically by both players and is common knowledge.[4]

---

3. See, for example, Farber 1980; Chatterjee 1981; Crawford 1982; Brams and Merrill 1983 and 1986; and Wittman 1986. For a model of both conventional and final-offer arbitration, wherein the arbitrator seeks to maximize his or her expected utility based on the offers of the two sides and inferences about their private information (e.g., reservation prices), see Gibbons 1988. In modeling FOA, Samuelson (1989) also assumes the players possess private information in a game of incomplete information; McCall (1990) assumes that the union negotiator has information superior to that of the rank and file in a principal-agent model of FOA.

4. In a model of combined arbitration (to be discussed later), Brams and Merrill (1986) relax the common knowledge assumption: the players may have different distributions over the arbitrator's preferences.

To simplify the analysis, we focus on one simple distribution to illustrate how the optimal strategies of the two parties can be computed under FOA. Additionally, we assume that the dispute is over a single quantifiable issue, such as a wage scale or cost-of-living adjustment, though models of FOA have been developed that allow for more than one issue (Wittman 1986).

The two disputants begin by making simultaneous final offers; the arbitrator then chooses one or the other.[5] Let a and b denote the final offers of a "low" bidder A and a "high" bidder B, respectively. A, for example, might be management, which wants to keep the wage scale as low as possible, and B labor, which wants higher wages.

Let x denote the arbitrator's preferred settlement. Under FOA, if x is closer to a, the settlement is a; if x is closer to b, the settlement is b; if x is equidistant from a and b, the settlement is a or b with equal probability; and if $a = b$, the settlement is the common value. We do not assume that the players know x but only that the players' beliefs about x are common knowledge and can be represented by some probability distribution. This distribution describes how likely, in the players' eyes, the arbitrator will favor one settlement versus another.

For example, assume that all settlements are equally likely—that is, the players think that x is equally likely to fall anywhere in a specified interval. Management and labor might agree, for example, that the arbitrator is likely to favor a wage increase x of between \$0 and \$1, and that every value of x in that interval has the same chance of occurring. This assumption about the distribution of x is given by the uniform density function $f(x) = 1, 0 \leq x \leq 1$, which means that the relative likelihood, $f(x)$, of any x in the interval from 0 to 1 is the same for all x (see fig. 1).

On the other hand, one might assume that the arbitrator is more likely to be closer to the midpoint of the interval, $1/2$, than the endpoints, 0 or 1. Because the uniform density function is very easy to work with, however, we use it here to illustrate the calculation of the optimal strategies of the players. Later we shall note the effects of other densities on players' optimal strategies.

We begin by defining the expected settlement, $F(a,b)$, which may be interpreted as the payoff that A wants to minimize and B wants to maximize. If $a \geq b$, the final offers converge or crisscross (i.e., A's offer equals or exceeds B's offer). In this case, the settlement is simply equal to the common offer if $a = b$, or the offer closer to the arbitrator if $a > b$. Henceforth we assume for FOA that this is not the case and concentrate on the expected settlement in the case of nonconvergence.

---

5. If the arbitrator is influenced by the final offers, the results we will describe still hold, as shown in the exchange between Rabow (1985) and Brams and Merrill (1985) and explained in note 2.

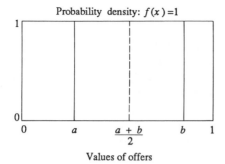

Probability density: $f(x) = 1$

Values of offers

Fig. 1. Final offers of A (*a*) and B (*b*) for uniform distribution

In the latter case,

$$F(a,b) = a[Pr(x \text{ is closer to } a)] + b[Pr(x \text{ is closer to } b)],$$

where *Pr* indicates the probability of the event inside the brackets. As illustrated in figure 1, *a* will be closer to *x* if *x* is between 0 and $(a + b)/2$, which will occur with probability $(a + b)/2$. (This probability is simply the area of the rectangle, extending from 0 to the midpoint of the offers of A and B, with height equal to the value of the density function, 1, between these points.) Likewise, B will be closer to *x* with probability $1 - (a + b)/2$. Hence,

$$F(a,b) = a[(a + b)/2 - 0] + b[1 - (a + b)/2]$$
$$= (a^2 + 2b - b^2)/2.$$

Using calculus, it is easy to show that A minimizes $F(a,b)$ by choosing $a = 0$; similarly, B maximizes $F(a,b)$ by choosing $b = 1$.[6] These strategy choices simultaneously minimize (for A) and maximize (for B) the expected settlement and constitute the *solution* of this two-person, constant-sum game. These strategy choices imply that $F(0,1) = 1/2$, which is the *value* of the

---

6. Differentiating $F(a,b)$ with respect to *a* and *b*,

$$\frac{\partial F}{\partial a} = a; \frac{\partial F}{\partial b} = 1 - b,$$

and setting the derivatives equal to zero, yields $a = 0$ and $b = 1$, which are a minimum and a maximum, respectively, because

$$\frac{\partial^2 F}{\partial a^2} = 1 > 0; \frac{\partial^2 F}{\partial b^2} = -1 < 0.$$

game, or the settlement that each player can ensure for itself whatever the other player does.[7]

In fact, no matter what strategy B chooses, A's best response is $a = 0$. Similarly, no matter what strategy A chooses, B's best response is $b = 1$. That is, $a = 0$ is a *dominant strategy* in that it is A's best response to any choice of B in the interval from 0 to 1; similarly, $b = 1$ is a dominant strategy for B. If either player deviates from its dominant strategy, he or she cannot do better and may do worse (see note 7), which makes the outcome an equilibrium. For example, if A chooses $a = 0$, but B chooses $b \neq 1$, $F(a,b) < \frac{1}{2}$, so B, who wants to maximize $F(a,b)$, is hurt by this choice.

It may seem strange that it is the endpoints, 0 and 1, of the interval that are the optimal strategies of A and B, respectively. After all, these strategies are divergent, contrary to the view expressed earlier that FOA will induce each side to approach its adversary in order to maximize the chances of having its offer selected.

The flaw in the earlier reasoning is that, although each player increases the probability that its offer will be chosen by moving toward the midpoint of the distribution, this gain in probability is more than offset by the loss in potential payoff it suffers by compromising its final offer. The net effect is to push the players to the extremities of the distribution, not to pull them toward the center.

But what if there were "more probability" in the center—say, the density function were unimodal (i.e., had one peak or mode) and symmetric (i.e., had the same shape on each side of the mode)? Under certain conditions, the concentration of area around the center helps, but rarely by very much. For example, the optimal strategies of A and B for the well-known normal distribution are more than two standard deviations apart (2.51 to be exact), which means that 80 percent of the area under this density lies between the optimal positions of A on the left and B on the right (Brams and Merrill 1983), as shown in figure 2. The fact that there is an 80 percent probability that the arbitrator will prefer a less extreme settlement than would be chosen under FOA illustrates, as in the uniform case, how FOA induces one-sided settlements.

For other distributions, a player's optimal strategy may not even lie inside the interval of possible values of x, resulting in an even greater divergence of offers than that illustrated for the uniform distribution. Optimal strategies for still other distributions—including discrete distributions, in which the number of possible offers is finite—may be "mixed" (involving randomized choices between two "pure," or specific, strategies) or may not exist.

---

7. This value is the best possible for each player in the sense that, if $a = 0$, $F(0,b) \leq \frac{1}{2}$, so the minimizer guarantees the settlement is never more than $\frac{1}{2}$; and if $b = 1$, $F(a,1) \geq \frac{1}{2}$, so the maximizer guarantees the settlement is never less than $\frac{1}{2}$.

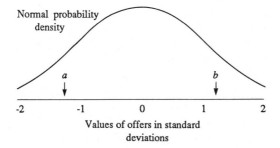

Fig. 2. Optimal FOA strategies of A (*a*) and B (*b*) for normal distribution

Necessary and sufficient conditions have been found for the existence of different kinds of optimal strategies, which tend to be quite sensitive to the specific distribution assumed over the arbitrator's preferences (Brams and Merrill 1983). But for essentially all continuous distributions, there is never convergence of the optimal final offers (e.g., to the median). Quite the contrary: optimal final offers tend more to be divergent than convergent, often separated by two or more standard deviations.

But is this necessarily bad? According to Stern et al. (1975, 3), the divergence in final offers "increases the pressure on the parties to take realistic bargaining positions and to settle their dispute through direct negotiations without use of arbitration." Presumably, a reasonable settlement on which the players could agree would be the value of the game under FOA ($^1/_2$ in our earlier example), which would obviate the risk of an unfavorable extreme outcome.

FOA in Major League Baseball

Negotiated settlements are, in fact, the norm in major league baseball, in which FOA has been used to settle salary disputes between the teams and players since 1975. Of the 111 major league players who filed for arbitration in 1988, 93 (84 percent) negotiated contracts before FOA was actually used (Chass 1988). As one baseball arbitrator put it, "I'm starting to feel like the atomic bomb. The deterrent effect of me as an arbitrator is enough" (Cronin 1989, quoting Stephen B. Goldberg).

Evidently, it is the likelihood of divergent final offers under FOA that puts pressure on the disputants to settle on their own, discouraging the actual use of FOA.[8] Brams and Merrill (1983, 940) called this the *paradox of arbitration,* arguing that "it takes a procedure like FOA, which implements a

---

8. Because there has been no use of conventional arbitration in major league baseball, however, we cannot compare the proportion of negotiated settlements under the two different procedures.

biased outcome, to get the two sides to abandon it, bargain seriously, and settle their differences on their own."[9]

Despite the fact that the vast majority of settlements in baseball are negotiated, 303 cases went to arbitration between 1975 and 1989. The scorecard reads 165 FOA victories for the teams and 138 for the players (Chass 1990), suggesting that the players are somewhat more aggressive in their demands and, consequently, less likely to win. By contrast, labor union leaders, who have constituents as well as themselves to satisfy, tend to be more conservative, as we will show in the next section.

Another factor may be at work in the case of baseball—the enormous overall increase in recent baseball salaries (thanks to a major television contract), which alleviates the cost of losing. Thus, even the players who went to arbitration and lost made remarkable gains in 1989, averaging incredible 110 percent average salary increases over 1988. By contrast, the FOA winners averaged 135 percent increases, whereas those who negotiated their salaries (84 percent of the total, the same as in 1988) had average increases of 98 percent (Chass 1990). Manifestly, the players who used FOA had stronger cases for big increases than those who negotiated settlements, but perhaps the most striking fact is that average salaries approximately doubled in one year. With that kind of increase, how much risk is there in "losing" under FOA?

FOA in Public-Employee Disputes: The Importance of Winning

As of 1981, FOA was used to settle public-employee disputes in ten states (Freeman 1986).[10] Although FOA leads to more negotiated settlements than conventional arbitration in such disputes (Freeman 1986), the risk of losing under FOA has not led to its demise. Instead, players (usually labor) have adopted certain strategies to minimize this risk, depending on how they view the consequences of winning and losing under FOA.

To understand these strategies, suppose that one or both players under FOA derives value from winning per se (e.g., because of the psychic reward from having its offer chosen), above and beyond the gain from the settlement that the arbitrator selects. We model such a situation, in which winning adds independent value to the settlement under FOA, by assuming that the "perceived" settlement is adjusted downward if A wins (so A benefits) and upward if B wins (so B benefits).

---

9. On the other hand, an arbitration procedure that induces convergence may also be good, because it facilitates the closing of the final gap that might separate two sides. We discuss such procedures later.

10. FOA has also been used in bidding competitions on U.S. Defense Department contracts (Carrington 1988; Halloran 1988).

Call this adjustment a *bonus*. A labor negotiator in a wage dispute, for example, may be more satisfied with, say, a 5 percent raise in the pay rate if that settlement is his or her own final offer than if it were management's. By the same token, to management the mere fact that labor's offer is chosen may make it less attractive.

There are various reasons why disputants may put added value on winning. One reason may be cultural—it is said, for example, that Americans prize winning more than other nationalities. Another may derive from the psychic needs of certain individuals, who, because of insecurities, seek affirmation of their positions.

We suspect, however, that bonuses are at least as much role related as tied to subjective feelings or cultural values. Consider the different roles of labor and management in work disputes. There are several reasons—some admittedly speculative—why labor's bonus might exceed management's, although our subsequent conclusions in no way depend on such a relationship. The rank and file, on whose votes labor leaders depend, tend to be caught up in the euphoria of winning or the frustration of losing a settlement, whereas the people to whom management is responsible (e.g., shareholders or taxpayers) are usually more remote. A string of losses may be fatal to a labor negotiator's position as a union leader. Management negotiators are likely to have less personal stakes in the appearance of victory and focus more on the possible long-run consequences of appearing weak. Labor negotiation is only one, albeit an important one, of the concerns of management.

Assume that bonuses for winning—in addition to the value of the settlement—may accrue to one or both parties in a dispute and need not be equal. When only one player derives a bonus from winning and both players are aware of this (i.e., the bonus is common knowledge), then the player that derives the bonus will be forced toward the position of the one that does not.[11] Say this is labor (B); then B will choose a lower *b* than is optimal according to our previous calculation.

By contrast, the player (A) who derives no bonus will tend to move away from B by lowering its offer, *a*, from what was previously optimal. In other words, concessions by one player (B) do not elicit concessions by the other (A). Quite the opposite: both players, instead of moving toward each other, move leftward or rightward together—in this case, leftward by making lower offers, hurting the player who receives the bonus (B).[12]

---

11. See Brams and Merrill 1991a. Similarly, Wittman (1986) demonstrated that a risk-averse player, who prefers moderate settlements to risky lotteries, will move toward its adversary. To be risk-averse, in fact, is another way of saying that winning less with greater certainty provides a player with a bonus.

12. In analyzing "optimum retorts," Raiffa (1982, 114–15) also showed that the best response of one player to another's shift toward the center was to move farther away.

It is the players' common knowledge of the bonus that allows the player who cares more about winning to be exploited by the player who does not, shifting the equilibrium settlement in the latter's favor. Clearly, it would be in the interest of the party deriving the bonus to hide its bonus—if that were possible—to induce movement by the adversary toward its position rather than away from it.

Such attempts at cover-up are surely made ("we will never surrender"), but they, like bonuses, are often difficult to detect. Nevertheless, it may still be possible to infer which party derives the bonus from the positions that two parties take and some estimate of where the arbitrator stands.

To illustrate this calculation, we turn to a study by Ashenfelter and Bloom (1984) of 423 arbitration cases involving salary disputes between police unions and local governments in New Jersey during 1978–80. Of these cases, 324 were conducted under FOA and 99 under conventional arbitration. Of the 324 FOA settlements, more than two-thirds (69 percent) were awarded to labor.

Ashenfelter and Bloom (1984) argue that not only were the FOA decisions impartial but also that the arbitrators used the same standards as under conventional arbitration, which is a finding independently supported by Farber and Bazerman (1986). Ashenfelter and Bloom (1984, 123) indicate, however, that under FOA

> the parties may not typically position themselves equally distant from, and on opposite sides of, the arbitrator's preferred award. This might happen either because unions have a more conservative view of what arbitrators will allow, or because unions may be more fearful of taking a risk of loss than are employers.

Although the first explanation cannot be ruled out (we know of no attitudinal data to test it), the data on offers and settlements allow a test of the second explanation.

To begin with, assume that risk-averse players, because they fear losing, place a higher value on winning. Thus, in the New Jersey FOA cases, Brams and Merrill (1991a) postulated that labor, but not management, perceived itself to receive a bonus from winning. In fact, the data strongly indicate that labor's final offers under FOA, which averaged a 7.9 percent increase in total compensation, more closely approximated arbitrator choices (7.5 percent under conventional arbitration) than management's final offers, which averaged 5.7 percent.

Using Ashenfelter and Bloom's (1984) estimates for the mean and standard deviation of this distribution, Brams and Merrill (1991a) computed labor and management's optimal final offers, both with and without a labor bonus.

The hypothesis that labor received no bonus was shown to be untenable. On the other hand, a hypothesized bonus for labor equivalent to about a 4 percent increase in compensation explained well the actual final offers.

But labor, by increasing its probability of winning, may have paid dearly by decreasing the expected value of the settlement. If there were no bonus for labor, our model shows that the average settlement would have been an 8.0 percent increase, whereas the actual average settlement was a 7.4 percent increase, which, in relative terms, is an 8.0 percent loss to labor.

Variants of FOA That Induce Convergence

Recently, several variations on FOA have been proposed that tend to bring two parties together, sometimes immediately and sometimes in stages.[13]

Combined arbitration (Brams 1986; Brams and Merrill 1986) mixes conventional arbitration and FOA in such a way that both sides are motivated to make the same final offer, provided that they believe that the arbitrator is more likely to favor a middle, rather than an extreme, position.[14] This hybrid procedure works as follows.

 i) The two parties submit their final offers (*a* and *b*) at the same time that the arbitrator records his or her choice of a fair settlement (*x*).
 ii) If the arbitrator's choice falls *between* the two final offers (and the offers do not crisscross), then the offer closer to the arbitrator's choice becomes the settlement. Thus, FOA is used in the case of

---

13. The list in the text is not exhaustive. For example, *Bonus FOA*, proposed by Brams and Merrill (1991a), gives the winner under FOA a bonus, equal to the gap between the two final offers, for having its offer accepted by the arbitrator. This bonus is paid by the loser to the winner; it is an *external* reward that is part of the procedure—unlike the *internal* bonus discussed previously, which we interpreted to accrue from the pride or satisfaction of winning.

As an illustration of Bonus FOA, assume management's optimal offer is 4 percent and labor's is 6 percent. If labor wins, the settlement is 8 (= 6 + 2) percent, whereas if management wins, the settlement is 2 (= 4 − 2) percent.

Because the stakes of winning and losing are higher under Bonus FOA than under FOA, Bonus FOA provides a greater incentive than does FOA for the parties to approach each other, decreasing the gap separating their optimal offers under FOA by a factor of two-thirds. But once the bonus is added to or subtracted from the offers, depending on who wins, the settlement is exactly the same as under FOA. Thus, if the optimal offers of the two players under FOA are 2 and 8 percent, then under Bonus FOA they would be 4 and 6 percent, making 2 percent and 8 percent the only possible settlements. By comparison, the variants of FOA discussed here lead to less lopsided settlements, as may two new procedures (Brams and Merrill 1991b), not discussed here, that allow the players to choose the mean of their final offers—either simultaneously or sequentially—before the arbitrator makes a choice.

14. More precisely, they will converge to the median of the arbitrator's probability distribution if it is unimodal and symmetric.

ascending offers *a–x–b,* with *a* or *b* the settlement, depending on which is closer to *x.*

iii) If the arbitrator's choice falls *outside* the two final offers (and the offers are not identical, nor do they crisscross), then the arbitrator's choice is the settlement. Thus, conventional arbitration is used in the case of ascending offers *a–b–x* or *x–a–b,* with *x* the settlement in each case.

iv) If the offers are identical, then the common offer is the settlement. If the offers crisscross (i.e., the minimizer's offer is greater than the maximizer's offer), then the offer closer to the arbitrator's choice is the settlement, as under FOA.

Note that rule iii allows for the imposition of the arbitrator's judgment—and, consequently, a settlement more extreme than the final offers of either side. It is especially this rule that induces the parties to converge absolutely, because each party is "protected" on its side by a more extreme arbitrator who favors it. This protection motivates both parties not just to move toward each other—as under Bonus FOA (see n. 13)—but to make identical final offers.

Two-stage FOA (Brams, Kilgour, and Weber 1991) allows the initial loser under FOA to respond with a counteroffer. If closer to the arbitrator's judgment, the loser's counteroffer is averaged with the winner's original offer and becomes the settlement; if the winner's original offer remains closer than the counteroffer, then the original offer becomes the settlement.

To illustrate this procedure, consider how it might work in major league baseball, where T = team (assumed to have a female owner), P = player (assumed to be male), and A = arbitrator (for balance, we leave open the question of gender).

1. T proposes a salary of $1M and P proposes $1.3M; both offers are made public. A thinks $1.1M is fair, but this choice is not announced. (It may be recorded for later reference to permit subsequent verification that A's actions were consistent with his or her judgment.)

2. A selects T as the *initial winner* because she is closer to A's ideal of $1.1M than P is.

3. P gets a second chance, after being told that T is the initial winner. Knowing that A's ideal must be between $1M and $1.15M (because T's $1M is closer to A's ideal than P's $1.3M), P makes a counteroffer of $1.15M, which is made public.

4. P becomes the *new winner* because his counteroffer of $1.15M is now closer to A's ideal of $1.1M than is T's winning original offer of $1M. The settlement under two-stage FOA is the average of the initial and new winning offers: ($1M + $1.15M)/2 = $1.075M.

Multistage FOA (Brams, Kilgour, and Weber 1991) is similar to two-stage FOA, except that the sequence of offers and counteroffers is not limited to two stages but continues until one side wins twice in a row. We can illustrate multistage FOA by continuing our earlier example. After *P* becomes the new winner under two-stage FOA, instead of there being a settlement, *T* under multistage FOA would now have an opportunity to make her own counteroffer—knowing that *P* won (temporarily) with his counteroffer of $1.15M—and the process might unfold as follows.

4'. *P* becomes the *new winner* because his counteroffer of $1.15M is now closer to *A*'s ideal of $1.1M than is *T*'s winning original offer of $1M.

5. *T* makes a counteroffer of $1.06M, which is closer to *A*'s $1.1M than *P*'s $1.15M, so *T* becomes the new winner.

6. *P* responds with a new counteroffer of $1.12M, which is closer to *A*'s $1.1M than *T*'s $1.06M.

7. *T* responds with a new counteroffer of $1.07M, which is *not* closer to *A*'s $1.1M than *P*'s $1.12M. Hence, *P*'s $1.12M becomes the settlement because he won twice in a row.

In comparison to the settlement under two-stage FOA ($1.075M), the settlement of $1.12M under multistage FOA is slightly closer to *A*'s ideal of $1.1M in this hypothetical example. We emphasize that this example is illustrative of the use of two-stage and multistage FOA, not optimal offers under these procedures, which are given in Brams, Kilgour, and Weber (1991) and Brams (1990, chap. 3).

Both two-stage FOA and multistage FOA lead to convergence of a very different kind from combined arbitration: the two sides approach the arbitrator, wherever he or she is located, rather than the perceived median (from which the arbitrator may be quite distant). We shall compare the rationales of each in the concluding section.

Although both sequential procedures tend to produce less extreme settlements than FOA, two-stage FOA is simpler and seems to perform as well as multistage FOA in many situations. However, it truncates to two rounds the give-and-take aspect of bargaining that occurs in many real-life situations.

The continuing opportunity that players have to learn from the feedback they receive, and revise their offers accordingly, may be a virtue in arbitration as well as bargaining. On the other hand, two-stage FOA avoids the indefinite termination of multistage FOA and has similar convergence properties.

If near convergence to the arbitrator's position under two-stage or multistage FOA seems desirable, why, one might ask, not use conventional arbitration? After all, it would absolutely eliminate any discrepancy between the settlement and the arbitrator's position.

The apparent reason for using one of the sequential procedures is that it induces the players to converge on their own. Consequently, the settlement is not imposed, although the players' convergence is very much driven by the perceived position of the arbitrator after the first stage.

If convergence means *forcing* two parties to accept a settlement contrary to their interests, it would not seem to be a laudable goal. But when the lack of a settlement in, for example, a public-employee strike jeopardizes public health or safety, one might reasonably argue that public consequences should take precedence over private interests: arbitration *should* be able to override any impasse in the negotiations. Even in private disputes, an arbitrated settlement may be appealing because it saves the parties the costs of a prolonged conflict (e.g., a strike) that could bankrupt both of them.

It would seem preferable that the parties reach an agreement on their own—even if driven to do so by an arbitration procedure—than have an arbitrator impose it on them. Judging from the high number of agreements reached in major league baseball without resorting to FOA, the threat of implementing FOA seems to foster negotiated settlements.

Compared with FOA, which tends not to induce convergence, the optimal offers under the procedures described in this section induce greater compromises by the players. But which procedure is best? We address this question in the concluding section by showing how an answer depends on the criteria by which the different procedures are evaluated.

Summary and Conclusions

FOA and its variants force the parties to make some compromises, lest they be hurt by demanding too much. In contrast, under conventional arbitration, the disputants are often motivated to posture and make preposterous demands, leading to divergence rather than convergence, especially if the arbitrator is likely to split the difference between the claims of the two sides.

Next to conventional arbitration, FOA is the least satisfactory in inducing convergence, unless the parties derive internal bonuses from winning independent of the value of the settlement itself. But if only one party derives an internal bonus, and both parties are aware of it, the party receiving the bonus is hurt in the settlement because its greater receptivity to compromise induces its adversary to toughen its stance and concede less.

The upshot is that the more compromising party, while enhancing its chances of having its offer selected under FOA, does so at the expense of lowering its expected payoff when the parties choose their equilibrium strategies. As seen in the police arbitration disputes in New Jersey, the unions were the exploited party, receiving an average 8 percent less in relative pay increases than they might have achieved with less conservative final offers, even though they won more than two-thirds of the settlements under FOA.

In comparison, in major league baseball the teams have won more FOA cases than the players, but we suggested that this is because the players represent only themselves and do not have to worry, like labor leaders, about appeasing constituents. Also, even losing under FOA has reaped the baseball players huge salary increases recently, affording them the opportunity, by being less timid, to risk failure and still come out substantially ahead.

In selecting an arbitration procedure, the choice depends on what kind of convergence, if any, one deems most desirable. If it is convergence to the median of the arbitrator's probability distribution, then combined arbitration seems best equipped to move players there. If it is convergence to what the arbitrator considers fair, then two-stage or multistage FOA seems best, even if it is a position different from the median of the arbitrator's distribution (as the players perceive it).

One's faith in the perceived median as a compromise, versus one's faith in the arbitrator's judgment, will be the determinant of whether one regards combined arbitration, or either two-stage or multistage FOA, as the better of the convergence-inducing arbitration procedures for settling disputes. The choice between these alternatives may be summarized in the following fashion.

—Combined arbitration, more than any other procedure, compels the parties themselves to bargain prior to its use because it carries the greatest risk for the players of an extreme settlement; the arbitrator's distribution provides them with an orientation, and its median becomes a focal point for agreement.

—Two-stage and multistage FOA, more than other procedures, tend to draw the parties toward the arbitrator by introducing the possibility of learning in successive stages, but never at the cost of imposing the arbitrator's judgment upon them (as can occur under combined arbitration if the parties fail to converge).

These are the two sets of procedures we find most attractive in fostering convergence. But we leave which is more equitable unresolved, because this determination rests on a normative judgment about what kind of convergence—to the median or the arbitrator's position—one seeks to promote.

A case can be made, we believe, for each kind. One would want to approach the arbitrator if he or she were viewed as being completely impartial and more capable than anyone else of finding an equitable settlement. The median would be more attractive if the players had less faith in the arbitrator's fairness and more in their common perception of what he or she would be most likely to choose—namely, a compromise in the middle (if the distribution is symmetric and unimodal). The former view (arbitrator the best judge) would favor one of the sequential procedures, whereas the latter view (players the best judges) would support combined arbitration.

At the same time, we believe, a case can be made for FOA. The fact that it may lead to extreme settlements tends to encourage serious bargaining and negotiated settlements before FOA is used, as has been the case in major league baseball. But when negotiated settlements are harder to reach, as has been true in public-employee disputes, the procedures with more convergence-inducing properties deserve to be considered.

They are, to be sure, untried, but their attractive theoretical properties commend them for experimentation, especially in situations in which the use of conventional arbitration or FOA has become routine instead of a last resort. When even FOA fails to stimulate serious bargaining, arbitration procedures like combined arbitration and two-stage or multistage FOA seem called for to induce the parties to make greater concessions and strike their own compromises.

REFERENCES

Ashenfelter, O., and D. E. Bloom. 1984. "Models of Arbitrator Behavior: Theory and Evidence." *American Economic Review* 74:111–25.

Bazerman, M. H., and H. S. Farber. 1985. "Arbitrator Decision Making: When Are Final Offers Important?" *Industrial and Labor Relations* 39:76–89.

Bloom, D. E. 1986. "Empirical Models of Arbitrator Behavior under Conventional Arbitration." *Review of Economic Statistics* 68:578–85.

Brams, S. J. 1986. "New, Improved Final-Offer Arbitration." *New York Times,* August 9.

Brams, S. J. 1990. *Negotiation Games: Applying Game Theory to Bargaining and Arbitration.* New York: Routledge.

Brams, S. J., D. M. Kilgour, and S. Weber. 1991. "Sequential Arbitration Procedures." In *Systematic Analysis in Dispute Resolution,* ed. S. S. Nagel and M. K. Mills. Westport, Conn.: Quorum. Forthcoming.

Brams, S. J., and S. Merrill III. 1983. "Equilibrium Strategies for Final-Offer Arbitration: There Is No Median Convergence." *Management Science* 29:927–41.

Brams, S. J., and S. Merrill III. 1985. "Response to Rabow." *Management Science* 31:375–76.

Brams, S. J., and S. Merrill III. 1986. "Binding versus Final-Offer Arbitration: A Combination Is Best." *Management Science* 32:1346–55.

Brams, S. J., and S. Merrill III. 1991a. "Final-Offer Arbitration with a Bonus." *European Journal of Political Economy* 7:79–92.

Brams, S. J., and S. Merrill III. 1991b. "Arbitration Procedures with the Possibility of Compromise." New York University, Department of Politics. Photocopy.

Carrington, T. 1988. "Pentagon Halts Multiple Submissions of 'Best and Final Offers' by Contractors." *Wall Street Journal,* July 26.

Chass, M. 1988. "Arbitration: In Settlements, Size Counts." *New York Times,* February 21.

Chass, M. 1990. "Players Big Winners as Arbitration Ends." *New York Times,* February 22.

Chatterjee, K. 1981. "Comparison of Arbitration Procedures: Models with Complete and Incomplete Information." *IEEE Transactions: Systems, Man, Cybernetics* SMC-11:101–9.

Crawford, V. P. 1982. "A Comment on Farber's Analysis of Final-Offer Arbitration." *Journal of Conflict Resolution* 26:157–60.

Cronin, B. 1989. "The Umpire Strikes Back." *Northwestern Perspective* 2:2–7.

Farber, H. S. 1980. "An Analysis of Final-Offer Arbitration." *Journal of Conflict Resolution* 24:683–705.

Farber, H. S. 1981. "Splitting-the-Difference in Interest Arbitration." *Industrial and Labor Relations Review* 35:70–77.

Farber, H. S., and M. H. Bazerman. 1986. "The General Basis of Arbitrator Behavior: An Empirical Analysis of Conventional and Final-Offer Arbitration." *Econometrica* 54:1503–28.

Freeman, R. B. 1986. "Unionism Comes to the Public Sector." *Journal of Economic Literature* 24:41–86.

Gibbons, R. 1988. "Learning in Equilibrium Models of Arbitration." *American Economic Review* 78:896–912.

Halloran, R. 1988. "Honesty Called 'Impossible' in Pentagon Bidding System." *New York Times,* July 28.

McCall, B. P. 1990. "Interest Arbitration and the Incentive to Bargain: A Principal-Agent Approach." *Journal of Conflict Resolution* 34:151–67.

Neale, M. A., and M. H. Bazerman. 1987. "Progressive Approximation Final-Offer Arbitration: Matching the Goals of a Conflict Domain." *International Journal of Management* 4:30–37.

Rabow, G. 1985. "Response to 'Equilibrium Strategies for Final-Offer Arbitration: There Is No Median Convergence.'" *Management Science* 31:374–75.

Raiffa, H. 1982. *The Art and Science of Negotiation.* Cambridge, Mass. Harvard University Press.

Rehmus, C. M. 1979. "Interest Arbitration." In *Portrait of a Process: Collective Negotiations in Public Employment,* ed. Public Employment Relations Services. Ft. Washington, Penn.: Labor Relations Press.

Samuelson, William F. 1989. "Final-Offer Arbitration under Incomplete Information." School of Management, Boston University. Photocopy.

Stern, J. L., C. M. Rehmus, J. J. Loewenberg, H. Kasper, and B. D. Dennis. 1975. *Final-Offer Arbitration: The Effects on Public Safety Employee Bargaining.* Lexington, Mass.: D. C. Heath.

Stevens, C. M. 1966. "Is Compulsory Arbitration Compatible with Bargaining?" *Industrial Relations* 5:38–52.

Wittman, D. 1986. "Final-Offer Arbitration." *Management Science* 32:1551–61.

CHAPTER 4

Analysis of Incentives in Bargaining and Mediation

Roger B. Myerson

Much of the difficulty of bargaining derives from the fact that the individual parties in a dispute generally have different information. Thus, an individual negotiator may try to behave inscrutably to conceal his (or her) information, or he may signal to try to convey some information to other individuals. Also, he may disbelieve or distrust the signals conveyed by others. In general, each individual must try to learn about his opponents and must try to influence what they believe. The theory of games can provide powerful analytical techniques for understanding these issues and coping with them more effectively. In this chapter, I survey some of these techniques, emphasizing their application to the problem of designing effective mediation procedures.

The method of game theory is to try to understand issues in bargaining by studying hypothetical situations in which the structure of individuals' incentives and information are specified precisely and quantitatively. Such examples may be unrealistically simple in many respects, but we can hope to gain important insights as long as the key issues that we want to understand are well represented. Of course, this is the method of analysis in any field of inquiry: to pose one's questions in the context of a simplified model in which many (irrelevant) details of reality are ignored. Thus, although we may never hope to be involved in a situation in which people's positions are as clearly defined as those studied by game theorists, we can still hope to understand real bargaining situations better by studying these hypothetical examples.

In the game-theoretic analysis of such examples, it is generally assumed that players in any game will behave rationally (each attempting to maximize his own payoff from the game) and intelligently (so that a game theorist never assumes that he understands the game better than the players in it). These assumptions may be quite limiting in circumstances when foolish behavior by some parties can be systematically predicted. However, there are many bargaining situations in which assuming that people will behave rationally and intelligently is at least a reasonable working assumption for gaining basic insights into the problem. Furthermore, game theory has shown that much behavior that might at first seem irrational or foolish can, indeed, be explained by rational decision making. For example, one of the goals of this chapter is to show that there may be bargaining situations in which rational, intelligent individuals may fail to reach an agreement in bargaining, even though potential agreements exist that would be mutually beneficial. That is, disagreement or failure to realize mutually beneficial opportunities is not necessarily evidence of irrationality or foolishness.

In this chapter, I consider one simple example that can serve to illustrate many of the most important insights that can be gained from game-theoretic analysis of bargaining. Specifically, I consider a single seller and a single potential buyer who are trying to agree on a price for some unique and indivisible object. We assume that this object may be worth either $0 or $80 to the seller, and it may be worth either $20 or $100 to the buyer. When bargaining begins, each individual knows his or her own value for the object, but thinks that the other individual's value is equally likely to be either of the two possible numbers. Thus, we may think of the two individuals' values as being independent random variables, such that each of the four possible combinations of values has probability .25. For simplicity, we assume that neither individual has any opportunity to trade this object with anyone else.

In the terminology of game theory, the information that an individual has at the beginning of the game, which others do not know, is called his *type*. In this example, each individual has two possible types: one for each of the two values that he or she might have for the object. We may say that the seller's type is *strong* if the object is worth $80 to him, since he then has relatively less need to trade than might otherwise be expected. On the other hand, we may say that the seller's type is *weak* if the object is worth $0 to him, since he would then be relatively more eager to accept any given offer from the buyer. Similarly, in our terminology, the buyer's type is *strong* if the object is worth $20 to her, since she then really cannot be compelled to pay any higher price; her type is *weak* if the object is worth $100 to her, since she then has relatively more price flexibility than might otherwise be expected. We may anticipate that, in bargaining, each individual may try to convince the other that he or she is strong, even when he or she is weak, to force the other to accept a more favorable price. However, no trade can occur unless at least one individual concedes that he or she is weak, since there are no mutually acceptable prices between the two strong types. The probability that mutually acceptable prices actually do exist is very large (.75), so potential gains from trade probably do exist, but the temptation of both parties to bluff may make it hard to realize these potential gains. Thus, although this is a simple example, it can illustrate (and, I hope, clarify) many of the important problems and dilemmas that arise because different individuals have different information.

To begin to analyze this example, we must begin by recognizing what the results of our analysis should be. Specifically, we must recognize that we cannot simply determine the probability that the object will be traded and (if so) at what price, because these probabilities and prices should depend on the individuals' values for the object, which we do not know. Instead, we must try to determine the *plan* (or rule) by which the price and the probability of trade will depend on the values of the object to the two individuals. Such a trading plan can be presented in a matrix, showing the *probability* of trade and the *price* if the trade occurs, for each of the four possible combinations of values that the two individuals might have for the object.

The first theory that one might be tempted to apply to this example is the theory of "splitting the difference," which suggests that, if the buyer's value for the object is higher than the seller's, then they should agree to trade at a price halfway between their respective values, and, if the seller's value is higher, then they should not trade. For this example, this theory can be represented by matrix 1.

Buyer's Value

		$20	$100
Seller's Value	$80	(0, *)	(1, $90)
	$0	(1, $10)	(1, $50)

Matrix 1. The split-the-difference plan

Here and in each of the subsequent matrices, for each of the four possible combinations of values, the probability of trade is shown first and the price of the object if trade occurs is shown second. (The asterisk indicates that the price-if-trade cannot be defined when the probability of trade is zero.)

Unfortunately, the trading plan in matrix 1 cannot be the correct description of how the two rational individuals would trade in this situation. To see why, suppose that the seller's value is actually $0 (although the buyer does not know this). Matrix 1 says that he will either sell for $50 if the buyer is also weak, or for $10 if the buyer is strong, so that the weak seller's expected gains under this plan are $(.5 \times 50) + (.5 \times 10) = \$30$. On the other hand, if he bluffs and pretends that his value for the object is $80, instead of revealing his true $0 value, then he will not sell if the buyer is strong, but he will sell for $90 if the buyer is weak. The weak seller's expected gains from bluffing would be $.5 \times 90 = \$45$. Thus, we cannot expect that the weak type of seller would trade according to the plan shown in matrix 1, since he could get a higher expected gain by following a different bluffing strategy ($45 > $30).

(For simplicity, we are assuming here that both individuals are risk neutral, so that each seeks to maximize his or her expected gains from trade.)

Incentive Constraints and Mediation

Now that we have shown that the trading plan in matrix 1 cannot be implemented, let us see how to find the plans that actually can be implemented. To do this, we suppose that the buyer and seller have agreed to let a mediator help coordinate their bargaining process. This mediator may plan to use a procedure of the following form. First, the mediator will go to each individual separately and ask for a confidential report stating his or her value for the object. (In this simple example, the mediator can insist that each individual should report one of his or her two possible values, since anything else would obviously be a lie.) For simplicity, let us suppose (for now) that this mediator wants to implement a trading plan that treats the two parties symmetrically, in some sense. We may suppose that if both individuals concede that they are weak, then the mediator will definitely recommend that they should trade (since the range of mutually acceptable prices is as large as can be), and that the price should then be $50 (halfway between $0 and $100). If they both claim to be strong (values of $20 to the buyer and $80 to the seller), then the mediator should not recommend trading, since no mutually acceptable prices can be found. If one individual claims to be strong and the other reports that he or she is weak, then things are a bit more complicated, because their positions are not so clearly symmetric. So, for now, let us avoid specifying exact numbers for these cases. Let q denote the probability that the mediator would recommend trading if the buyer reported that she was strong and the seller reported that he was weak, and let y denote the expected price (presumably between $0 and $20, the seller's and buyer's values in this case) that the mediator would have the buyer pay if trading were recommended. For symmetry, we may suppose that q would also be the probability of trading if the seller reported that he was strong and the buyer reported that she was weak, and that $100 - y$ would be the expected price if trade occurred in this case. (In each case, y is the profit that a weak individual would get in trading with a strong individual, whether the weak individual is the buyer or the seller.) Then the mediator's trading plan is summarized in matrix 2.

Buyer's Value

		$20	$100
Seller's Value	$80	(0, *)	$(q, \$100-y)$
	$0	$(q, \$y)$	(1, $50)

Matrix 2.   A general symmetric trading plan

For this plan to be feasible, y and q must be chosen to satisfy two basic inequalities. First, we need

$$y \leq 20 \qquad (1)$$

to assure that the strong type of each individual is getting nonnegative expected gains from trade, since either individual could refuse to participate in the plan (and thus not trade at all) if he or she expected to lose by such participation. A second inequality comes from the need to give a weak individual some incentive to concede that he or she is weak. In this trading plan, a weak individual (say, the seller with value \$0 for the object) gets expected gains from trade equal to $(.5 \times 50) + (.5 \times q \times y)$ if he reports his type honestly (assuming that the buyer will also report honestly to the mediator); but if he claims to be strong then he gets an expected gain of $(.5 \times q) \times (100 - y)$. Thus, to give the weak types an incentive to report honestly, we need

$$(.5 \times 50) + (.5 \times q \times y) \geq (.5 \times q) \times (100 - y), \qquad (2)$$

or, equivalently,

$$q \leq 25/(50 - y). \qquad (3)$$

These constraints are called *incentive constraints,* because they are constraints on the trading plan that are derived from the need to give each individual an incentive to participate honestly according to the plan. Analysis of incentive constraints can provide important insights into the structure of competitive situations. In this example, the incentive constraints imply, among other things, that q cannot be greater than $25/(50 - 20) = .833$. This maximal level of q is achieved by letting $y = 20$, which gives the trading plan shown in matrix 3.

Buyer's Value

		\$20	\$100
Seller's Value	\$80	(0, *)	(.833, \$80)
	\$0	(.833, \$20)	(1, \$50)

Matrix 3. An incentive-efficient trading plan

In this plan, if one individual claims to be strong and the other claims to be weak, then, with probability .833, the mediator may recommend that trade occur at the strong individual's value for the object; and, with probability

.167, the mediator may recommend that no trade take place, even though the mediator knows that there exists a range of prices that would be acceptable to both parties. If both claim to be strong, then no trade is recommended. If both claim to be weak, then trade is surely recommended at a price of $50.

Thus, in a feasible trading plan, the probability of the buyer getting the object cannot be greater than $(.25 \times 1) + (.25 \times .833) + (.25 \times .833) + (.25 \times 0) = .667$, which is strictly less than the probability (.750) that the object is worth more to the buyer than the seller. That is, in any feasible trading plan, the mediator must anticipate that, with some positive probability (at least .750 $- .667 = .083$), the seller may fail to sell the object even though it is actually worth more to the buyer. It is impossible for a mediator to guarantee that the object will always go to the person who values it most.

This sweeping conclusion may require a bit more justification. We have not considered trading plans in which the two individuals are treated asymmetrically, nor have we considered the possibilities of random prices, trade between two strong individuals, or failure to trade between two weak individuals. However, this argument can be extended to prove that trading plans with these features still cannot achieve any higher probability of trade than .667 if they satisfy the relevant incentive constraints. The incentive constraints become a bit more complicated to write when such general plans are considered (because there are more variables to consider), but the analysis remains essentially the same.

A deeper objection might be raised, however. If the mediator simply did not worry about making the individuals want to report their type honestly, could the probability of trade be increased above what can be achieved with trading plans that induce honest behavior? The answer to this question is No, because of an important and general argument known as the *revelation principle*.

To understand the revelation principle, we must begin by reviewing the basic concept of equilibrium in game theory. Given any game, let us say that a *scenario* is any complete theory of how the players may behave in the game, specifying what moves each player would choose (and with what probability, if two or more moves are considered possible) at each stage in the game, for each possible state of the player's information. An *equilibrium* of a game is a scenario such that no player could ever expect to do better by unilaterally deviating from the predictions of the scenario, if the player believed that everyone else would always behave according to the scenario. That is, if a scenario is not an equilibrium, then there is some point in the game where the scenario predicts that a player will make a move that would clearly be a mistake, in terms of the player's own interests and information, if the scenario is understood. Although people do sometimes make mistakes, game theorists recognize that almost any kind of bargaining outcome could be explained under an assumption that negotiators simply behave foolishly. To avoid this assumption, then, we must suppose instead that players' behavior in a game will follow some scenario that is an equilibrium.

When a mediator chooses a mediation plan (or trading plan), the mediator is essentially creating a game that the other parties must play. They choose their strategies for sending messages and signals in the framework defined by the mediator, and for deciding under what circumstances they will accept the mediator's ultimate recommendations (if such decisions are not binding). We say that a mediation plan is *incentive compatible* if it would be an equilibrium for all parties to report all their private information honestly to the mediator and to accept the mediator's final recommendations, when everyone understands that the mediator is using this plan. The incentive constraints that I have discussed are the mathematical conditions that an incentive-compatible plan must satisfy. In general, for each individual who is involved in the mediation and for any ordered pair of his or her possible information types, there is an *informational incentive constraint* that asserts that, if the player were actually the first type and if everyone else was expected to be honest, then the player should not expect to do better by dishonestly reporting the second type than by honestly reporting the first (and actual) type to the mediator. Also, for each possible type of each individual, there is a *participational incentive constraint* that asserts that the player should not expect to gain by refusing to participate in the mediation plan at all when this is his or her type. Each of these constraints can be expressed as a simple mathematical inequality. In the analysis of our example, it was sufficient for us to consider just one participational incentive constraint (1), and one informational incentive constraint (2).

The *revelation principle* asserts that, given any mediation plan that a mediator could design, and given any equilibrium that describes how the parties will behave (perhaps dishonestly) in the game that this mediation plan defines, there is an equivalent incentive-compatible plan in which the outcome (under honest behavior) is always the same as in the given equilibrium of the given mediation plan. (Notice that a mediation plan could include "just letting them haggle face to face.") The proof of this result is simple. For any given equilibrium of any given mediation plan, an equivalent incentive-compatible plan can be constructed as follows. First, the mediator asks each individual to confidentially report all of his or her relevant private information (that is, the player's type, in our game-theoretic terminology). Then the mediator calculates the communication and bargaining moves that would have been used by each individual with his or her reported information under his or her strategy for communicating and bargaining in the given equilibrium. Then the mediator computes (or simulates, if there is any randomness involved) the outcome or agreement that would have been derived from these bargaining moves under the rules of the given mediation plan. This outcome is the final agreement that the mediator actually recommends in the new plan. If any individual could ever expect to gain by lying to the mediator (or by not participating) in the new plan, then that individual could have expected to gain by effectively lying to himself (or by deciding to not participate) before implementing his given equilibrium strategy in the given plan (since the mediator in the new plan is, in effect, implementing that given strategy for the player); but this cannot happen in a rational equilibrium.

Thus, the revelation principle assures us that we can restrict ourselves to considering incentive-compatible mediation plans without any loss of generality. (The revelation principle could be restated as: "without loss of generality, we can assume that the mediator makes honesty the best policy.") This is important, not just because honesty is important per se, but because the set of incentive-compatible mediation plans is much easier to analyze than the set of possible equilibria of all possible mediation plans. In our example and, indeed, in a very general class of situations, the analysis of the relevant incentive constraints is mathematically straightforward and gives a clear characterization of all incentive-compatible mediation plans. Thus, in our example, we were able to compute that the highest probability of trade generated by any incentive-compatible plan is .667. Now, by the revelation principle, we can conclude that it is impossible for any plan involving dishonest behavior in equilibrium to generate a probability of trade that is higher than .667.

To further appreciate the power of the revelation principle, let us consider what would happen if a mediator tried to violate it and increase the probability of trade. Specifically, let us suppose that the mediator's plan is to implement the "split-the-difference" trading plan shown in matrix 1. When the mediator asks the two individuals to report their values and uses these reports to determine the price of the object according to the split-the-difference plan, the mediator creates a game in which honesty is not an equilibrium (as we have already observed). There are, however, three other equilibria of this game. In one equilibrium, the seller always reports his value honestly but the buyer always claims that her value is $20 (even if it is really $100), so that the object is either sold for $10 or not at all. In another equilibrium, the buyer always reports her value honestly but the seller always claims that his value is $80, so that the object is either sold for $90 or not at all. In the third equilibrium, each individual lies with probability .60 if the player is weak and is honest otherwise. With each of these equilibria, the trading plan from matrix 1 becomes equivalent to a different incentive-compatible plan, as shown in matrices 4, 5, and 6. (When the price is random, I show the expected price if trade occurs between the given types.)

Most impartial arbitrators or mediators would probably consider mediation plans described in matrices 4, 5, and 6 to be very undesirable. Matrix 4

Buyer's Value

		$20	$100
	$80	(0, *)	(0, *)
Seller's Value			
	$0	(1, $10)	(1, $10)

Matrix 4. A trading plan that is equivalent to an equilibrium of the split-the-difference game

Buyer's Value

		$20	$100
	$80	(0, *)	(1, $90)
Seller's Value			
	$0	(0, *)	(1, $90)

Matrix 5. A trading plan that is equivalent to an equilibrium of the split-the-difference game

Buyer's Value

		$20	$100
	$80	(0, *)	(.4, $90)
Seller's Value			
	$0	(.4, $10)	(.64, $50)

Matrix 6. A trading plan that is equivalent to a randomized equilibrium of the split-the-difference game

seems biased unfairly against the seller, and matrix 5 seems biased unfairly against the buyer. Matrix 6 treats the two individuals more symmetrically, but it is very inefficient, because the probability of trade in this plan is only $(.25 \times .4) + (.25 \times 4) + (.25 \times .64) = .36$; agreement to trade is unlikely in this plan.

Thus, in general, it may be better for a mediator to respect the incentive constraints and try to find a plan that satisfies these constraints at the lowest social cost (according to whatever social-cost criterion he or she uses) than for the mediator to try to ignore the incentive constraints. When a mediator ignores the incentive constraints, he or she must · expect that the cost of satisfying these incentive constraints will not go away, but instead will be derived from the strategies of misrepresentation and bluffing that the various parties will use. If only one party bluffs, as in the first two equilibria discussed above, then the result may be to transform a seemingly fair plan into one that is very unfair to the nonmanipulating individual (as in matrices 4 and 5). If both parties bluff, then the result may be that agreement is rarely reached at all, as in matrix 6.

The revelation principle assures us that any trading plan that can be implemented by any bargaining procedure, including unmediated face-to-face bargaining, can also be implemented by a mediator who gives the parties no incentive to lie. On the other hand, many plans that can be implemented by such a mediator cannot be implemented by unmediated bargaining (in which the parties must talk directly to each other, rather than to a mediator). For example, consider the plan shown in matrix 3. Because the price depends on the information types of both parties, they would need to share their information with each other before a final price was agreed on, if they were to implement this trading plan by unmediated bargaining. But, under this trading plan, either individual, if his or her type was weak, would want to pretend that he or she was strong once he or she got any information from the other individual suggesting that the probability that the other individual was weak was greater than .5. For example, if the buyer announced her type first and revealed that she was weak, in an attempt to implement matrix 3 without any mediation, then the seller would prefer to claim that the object was worth $80 to him, even if it were really worth $0 (because selling for $50 gives lower expected gains to the seller than selling for $80 with probability .833, when the object is $0 to him). So this trading plan, which maximizes the probability of trade, can only be implemented with some kind of mediation. Thus, this analysis shows the importance of using mediation in bargaining. Mediation maximizes the set of feasible trading plans, because it allows each individual to reveal his or her information without reducing other individuals' incentive to reveal their information as well.

Selecting an Efficient Plan

Some incentive-compatible trading plans (such as in matrix 6) may be clearly inefficient, in the sense that there are other incentive-compatible plans (such as in matrix 7) that all the parties would obviously prefer. We say that an incentive-compatible trading plan is *incentive-efficient* (or simply, *efficient*) if there does not exist any other incentive-compatible plan that gives a higher expected payoff to every possible type of every individual involved. Incentive-efficiency is the basic welfare criterion that a mediator should try to satisfy if the mediator is to serve his or her clients well. To appreciate the importance of this remark, compare it to the more naive criterion of guaranteeing that the parties should never miss an opportunity to make a mutually advantageous trade; such a criterion would be impossible to satisfy in situations like this example. As we have seen, trying to pretend that these incentive constraints do not exist or can be costlessly satisfied, as in matrix 1, may just create a worse situation, as in matrices 4–6. It is generally better to accept the incentive constraints and analyze them with a goal of finding the least costly way of satisfying them.

At the time of bargaining (in this example), each party already knows how much the object is worth to him or her, so he or she really cares only about the expected payoffs for his or her true type. However, a mediator does not know these private informational types when the mediator is formulating a mediation plan, so the mediator can be sure that a change in the plan would be considered an improvement by all parties only if every possible type of every individual would consider it an improvement. This is why the incentive-efficiency criterion should involve checking to make sure that there is no way to make all possible types of all individuals better off.

To characterize the incentive-efficient plans for this example, where there are two individuals, each of whom has two possible types, we have four expected payoffs to compute. Let S_0 denote the expected payoff to the seller if he is weak, let S_{80} denote the expected payoff to the strong seller, let B_{100} denote the expected payoff to the weak buyer, and let B_{20} denote the expected payoff to the strong buyer. For the plans shown in matrix 2, these expected payoffs are

$$S_0 = B_{100} = (.5 \times 50) + (.5 \times q \times y);$$

$$S_{80} = B_{20} = (.5 \times q) \times (20 - y).$$

Using a mathematical technique called linear programming, one can analyze the incentive constraints for this example and prove that any incentive-compatible plan that satisfies the equation

$$(3 \times S_0) + (5 \times S_{80}) + (3 \times B_{100}) + (5 \times B_{20}) = 200 \tag{4}$$

must be incentive-efficient. It is straightforward to check that the plans in matrix 2 are incentive-efficient if and only if

$$q = 25/(50 - y), \tag{5}$$

which is the maximum feasible value for the probability q, given the price y. It can be shown that the plans in matrices 4, 5, and 6 are not incentive-efficient, and they generate expected payoffs that do not satisfy equation (4).

The question still remains: Which incentive-efficient plan should a mediator actually implement? A further criterion that an impartial mediator may want to satisfy is *interpersonal equity* (that is, giving each party gains from an agreement that are, in some sense, commensurate with what that party is contributing to the other parties in the agreement). Game theorists have sought to develop a general mathematical theory of equity in games for many years with some incomplete success. (Concepts like the Shapley value and Nash bargaining-solution have been defined for this purpose. For an introduction to these ideas, see for example Shubik 1983; Young 1988; or Myerson 1991.) In this special example, however, we can define interpersonal equity without such general theories. The buyer and seller have a clear symmetry of position (notice how their possible values are symmetrically arrayed around $50), so an interpersonally equitable mediation plan should have the symmetric structure shown in matrix 2. Thus, the plans shown in matrices 4 and 5 can be ruled out as inequitable. The efficient and equitable mediation plans are those shown in matrix 2, when $q = 25/(50 - y)$ and y is not greater than 20.

This still leaves an infinite number of efficient and equitable mediation plans. One of them, corresponding to $y = 20$, is shown in matrix 3. Two more, corresponding to $y = 10$ and $y = 0$ respectively, are shown in matrices 7 and 8.

Buyer's Value

		$20	$100
Seller's Value	$80	(0, *)	(.625, $90)
	$0	(.625, $10)	(1, $50)

Matrix 7. An incentive-efficient trading plan

Buyer's Value

		$20	$100
Seller's Value	$80	(0, *)	(.5, $100)
	$0	(.5, $0)	(1, $50)

Matrix 8. An incentive-efficient trading plan

These equitable and efficient plans differ in what they offer the weak and strong types of each individual. Among these plans, the strong types of both individuals get the highest expected payoffs in matrix 8 (where $S_{80} = B_{20} = 5$), and they get the lowest expected payoffs in matrix 3 (where $S_{80} = B_{20} =$

0). On the other hand, the weak types get the highest expected payoffs in matrix 3 (where $S_0 = B_{100} = 33.3$), and they get the lowest expected payoffs in matrix 8 (where $S_0 = B_{100} = 25$). Thus, choosing among these efficient and equitable plans involves making some kind of *intertype compromise,* as well as interpersonal compromise. We must ask: Is it better to use a mediation plan that favors the strong types (matrix 8), one that favors the weak types (matrix 3), or something in between (matrix 7)?

One way to resolve this question is to assume that the individuals themselves should be able to negotiate its answer. There is good reason to believe that such negotiations would result in a plan that favors the strong types, as in matrix 8. To see why, notice that all of these efficient and equitable plans lose their incentive compatibility if one party learns that the other party is weak. (As we have seen, it is generally better to claim that you are strong if you know that your opponent is weak.) Thus, to avoid giving the impression of weakness, each individual would be likely to take the negotiating position favored by his or her strong type in these premediation negotiations, even if he or she was actually weak. That is, arguing for the plan in matrix 8 is the best *inscrutable* tactic for an individual who does not want to seem weak.

To see this another way, notice that, if the buyer were convinced that the seller were strong (having value $80), then the buyer probably would be willing to accept a plan like that in matrix 5, where a take-it-or-leave-it price is set at $90. That is, a price of $90 would seem quite equitable to the buyer if she were sure that the object was worth $80 to the seller. Thus, before the mediation plan is fixed, the seller would like to do everything possible to convince the buyer that he (the seller) is strong. One way that the seller might do this is to reject the services of a mediator who proposed to implement one of the plans from matrix 3 or matrix 7. That is, a mediator who proposed to use a plan that was relatively more favorable to the weak types might be exposed to a "mediator-bashing" tactic, where one party attacks the currently proposed mediation plan as a way to signal something about his or her type to the other party. Plans like matrix 8, which favor the strong types, are most likely to be stable against such mediator-bashing tactics.

Cost of Time in Bargaining

In the preceding analysis, we have not explicitly considered the role of time in bargaining. One might argue that, when the object has not been traded, the seller and buyer should continue bargaining as long as they believe that there is any positive probability of finding a mutually beneficial trade, so that the buyer should eventually get the object if it is worth more to her than to the seller. This argument, if true, would seem to contradict our conclusion that there must be a positive probability of the seller keeping the object when it is actually worth more to the buyer. In fact, there is no contradiction, because the preceding analysis has been based on an assumption that a trade must occur now or never. If we drop this assumption, *delay of trade* may replace *failure to trade* as the costly signal or threat that provides the incentive to make concessions. However, the total expected signaling costs are not generally decreased by the possibility of future bargaining. In fact, as I now show, total signaling costs may actually be increased because the possibility of future bargaining may reduce individuals' incentives to make serious offers at any given time.

To properly analyze this issue, we need to make some specific assumptions about how the two individuals (seller and buyer) in our example would feel about the prospect of trading at a later time. Let us assume that the object of bargaining is durable, so that it can be sold at any time. To account for the cost of time, let us suppose (to be specific) that there is a 10 percent annual interest rate. Thus, a dollar to be earned at some time t years in the future is worth less than a dollar earned now, because a dollar now could be invested at the 10 percent interest rate to generate more than a dollar in t years. In fact, when the possibility or reinvesting interest income is taken into account, a dollar earned t years in the future is worth only $e^{-.1t}$ dollars now, where $e \approx 2.718$ is a mathematical constant.

With such discounting of future gains, consider a simple open-ended bargaining game. In this game, the seller and buyer each make some initial price demand, which will remain constant over time until one of the two individuals concedes, at which time trade will occur at the price demanded by the other individual. To be specific, suppose that initially the seller demands a price of \$90 and the buyer demands \$10. The strong type of each individual (with value \$80 or \$20) would be unwilling to accept the other's demand, but the weak type (with value \$0 or \$100) would prefer to accept it than to never trade at all. A weak individual might not want to immediately accept the other's demand, however, in hopes that his or her own demand might be accepted instead, if the other individual is weak. In the equilibrium of this bargaining game, neither individual ever knows when the other might concede, because the weak type of each individual would decide randomly how long to wait for the other's concession.

To see how the probabilities of concession are determined in this equilibrium, let s be a very small number (like $1/365$). Suppose that, at some time, a weak seller is trying to decide whether to concede immediately or to go on waiting another fraction s of a year. Let $p(s)$ denote the probability that the buyer will concede to the seller's demand during such a time interval of length s. If the seller decides to wait for this interval of length s before conceding, then at the end of the interval he may get either \$90 (from the buyer's concession) with probability $p(s)$, or \$10 (from the seller's own concession at the end) with probability $1 - p(s)$. On the other hand, if the seller concedes to the buyer's demand now, then the seller gets \$10 immediately, which will be worth approximately $\$10 \times (1 + .1 \times s)$ at the end of the same time interval of length s, when it is invested at the 10 percent rate. (This formula is only approximate because I am ignoring, for now, the small compound interest correction.) Thus, to make the weak seller indifferent between conceding immediately and waiting s years more (so that the seller is willing to let his own concession time be randomly determined), we need

$$[90 \times p(s)] + \{10 \times [1 - p(s)]\} \approx 10 \times (1 + .1 \times s),$$

and so

$$p(s) \approx s/80. \tag{6}$$

(Here, $\approx$ means "is approximately equal to," and this approximation is very good as long as s is small.) A similar argument from the buyer's viewpoint shows that the probability of a concession by the seller during this period must also satisfy (6). According to this formula, at any time in this bargaining game, the probability of a concession by either individual must be only $(1/365)/80 \approx 0.000034$ during the next day of bargaining, or only about $1/80$ during the next year. If the probability of one individual conceding were higher than this, then the other individual would surely choose to wait. If the probability of one individual conceding were lower than this, then the weak type of the other individual would surely choose to concede immediately.

Exact formulas for the probability of a concession during any given period can be computed from relation (6), using integral calculus. These formulas show that it may take up to 55.4 years for a weak individual to finally make a concession in this open-ended bargaining game. The expected time until someone finally concedes to the other's demand is 24.5 years if only one individual is weak, and is 15.4 years if both individuals are weak. (To be exact, if an individual is weak, then the probability in equilibrium that he or she would choose to concede sometime during the first t years of this bargaining process is $2 \times (1 - e^{-t/80})$, for any number t between 0 and 55.4. When $t = 55.4$, this probability equals one.)

Because of the discounted value of future profits, each individual would be indifferent between the following two alternatives: (i) trading at some given price after waiting t years; and (ii) trading at this given price now, with probability $e^{-.1t}$, or never trading, with probability $1 - e^{-.1t}$. If we let T denote the random time when someone finally accepts the other's demand in this equilibrium of our bargaining game, then the expected value of the quantity $e^{-.1T}$ is .222 if only one individual is weak, and it is .356 if both

Buyer's Value

		$20	$100
Seller's Value	$80	(0, *)	(.222, $90)
	$0	(.222, $10)	(.356, $50)

Matrix 9.   A trading plan that is equivalent to an equilibrium of an open-ended bargaining game

individuals are weak. (These numbers can be computed from the probability formula in the preceding paragraph, using integral calculus.) Thus, this equilibrium of our open-ended bargaining game is equivalent to a trading plan, shown in matrix 9, in which trade is supposed to occur either now or never. (Here, as before, the probability of trade and the expected price if trade occurs are shown in each cell. The expected price of $50 in the cell where both are weak is the average of the two possible prices $10 and $90, which are then equally likely, depending on who concedes first.) Each type of each individual gets the same expected present-discounted value of gains from trade in this now-or-never trading plan as in the equilibrium of our open-ended bargaining game with initial demands of $90 and $10.

The trading plan in matrix 9 satisfies all the incentive constraints implied by the revelation principle. Furthermore, it is clearly worse for both individuals than the incentive-compatible trading plan shown in matrix 6, for example. More generally, as long as both individuals use the same interest rate for discounting future profits, any equilibrium of any open-ended bargaining game must be equivalent to some now-or-never trading plan that satisfies all the incentive constraints that I have discussed. In this sense, open-ended bargaining cannot help the individuals to avoid the cost of satisfying the incentive constraints, and may actually make matters worse.

If we generalize our open-ended bargaining game to allow each individual to choose his or her initial demand (instead of arbitrarily assuming that these demands are $10 and $90), then there are many more equilibria to be considered. In particular, for any y between $0 and $20, there is an equilibrium in which the buyer's initial demand is y and the seller's initial demand is $100 - y$. If y is very close to zero, then the expected time before the first concession in this equilibrium is very large, and the expected present-discounted values of gains from trade are very close to zero; so we may refer to this as a *standoff equilibrium*. In such a standoff equilibrium neither individual has much incentive to concede at any time, because the other's demand is so extreme. Furthermore, in such an equilibrium, neither individual wants to switch to a less extreme demand, because he or she fears that he or she would then be perceived as surely being weak and would then be expected (by the other player) to fully concede soon, so that a less extreme demand would not elicit any more rapid concession from the other individual.

Such standoff equilibria may actually be very useful to a mediator, because they offer a way to nullify the effect of future bargaining opportunities and, thus, to achieve trading plans like the one in matrix 8, rather than the one in matrix 9. If a mediator can persuade the buyer and seller to focus on playing a standoff equilibrium in all bargaining that might follow *after* the current mediation efforts, then trade may essentially be "now or never" for the two individuals, as we previously assumed. That is, a mediator may be able to effectively prevent postmediation bargaining by suggesting that, if a trade is not recommended, then any effort to reopen bargaining with further price offers should be taken as a sign of weakness, and that an individual who is thus revealed to be weak should also be expected to quickly concede to all further demands. Thus, the analysis in the earlier sections of this chapter, where we assumed that trade must occur now or never and will not occur at all if the mediator recommends against trading, may also accurately characterize what can be accomplished by a mediator in situations where the buyer and seller actually have open-ended opportunities to continue bargaining.

Conclusions

The analysis of this example has led us through many of the basic issues that arise in practical mediation. This analysis may be extended to more complicated examples, provided that the structure of all individuals' preferences and information is given in some well-quantified form (see, for example, Myerson 1984; Hurwicz, Schmeidler, and Sonnenschein 1985; Roth 1985). A more difficult task is applying this kind of analysis to real situations where people's preferences and information are not so easily given any simple quantitative representation. In such situations, it may be impossible to come up with a simple quantitative "solution" like matrix 8, but the insights generated by our analysis of quantitative examples may still be applied. The general insights discussed in this chapter may be summarized as follows.

When the various parties in bargaining have private information, communicating separately with a mediator in confidential caucuses may help them to achieve better outcomes, because each party can reveal information to a mediator without reducing other parties' incentives to reveal their information. This statement is based on the assumption that the mediator will keep the parties' revelations confidential until final recommendations are made.

After an initial session in which the parties introduce the mediator to the structure of the problem, the mediator should think analytically about the "mediation plan" that describes how his or her final recommendations will depend on the information that the parties will confidentially reveal to him or her. In particular, the mediator should think about mediation plans that are "incentive compatible" in the sense that they would not give any party an incentive to lie about information that the mediator solicits. If a mediator uses a mediation plan that seems equitable and efficient but is not incentive compatible, then rational and intelligent parties may pervert the plan by lying in a way that may lead, with high probability, to unfair agreements or even disagreement. Furthermore, any equilibrium of any bargaining game can be simulated by an equivalent incentive-compatible mediation plan, so a mediator loses no power by restricting himself or herself to incentive-compatible plans.

To avoid mediator-bashing tactics by bargainers who want to convince each other of the strength of their positions, a mediator may have to choose a mediation plan that is better for a party whose private information actually puts that party in a stronger position than other parties might suspect.

There may be some situations in which no incentive-compatible mediation plan, and no rational equilibrium of any bargaining game, could guarantee that the parties would reach a mutually beneficial agreement whenever such an agreement exists. That is, costly disagreement is not necessarily a result of irrational behavior by bargainers. On the contrary, a positive probability of costly disagreement may be necessary to give a rational bargainer some incentive to admit the weakness of his or her position when he or she actually *is* weak. Thus, the appropriate question for an analytical mediator is not how to guarantee that the best possible agreement will always be reached, but, rather, it is how to formulate a mediation plan that will maximize the parties' expected benefits from agreement without creating incentives for them to lie in confidential caucuses or to engage in mediator bashing.

A choice among mediation plans is a decision under uncertainty that involves compromise between different parties, as well as compromise between the interests of the different possible types of any one party. There generally is not an incentive-compatible mediation plan that would be best for all types of all parties.

When two parties bargain without any deadlines, they may get trapped in a standoff equilibrium, in which bargaining drags on so long as to virtually nullify the value of the agreements that might eventually be achieved. In such a standoff equilibrium, each party insists on an extreme demand and is afraid to moderate its demand, lest such moderation be taken as a sign of weakness and of imminent acceptance of the other party's extreme demand. Because these demands are so extreme, each party is willing to wait a very long time, in hopes of getting his or her own demand accepted, rather than immediately conceding to reach an agreement at the other party's demand.

A mediator may try to exploit the possibility of standoff equilibria in postmediation bargaining to induce the various parties to accept whatever recommendation may be suggested, provided that this recommendation is not worse for any party than bargaining indefinitely without agreement. That is, a mediator may encourage the parties to accept his or her recommendations by suggesting that any party who attempted to negotiate an agreement different from the mediator's recommendation would be perceived by the other parties as actually being in a weak position and prepared to give away almost everything in subsequent bargaining.

BIBLIOGRAPHY

Hurwicz, L., D. Schmeidler, and H. Sonnenschein, eds. 1985. *Social Goals and Social Organization.* Cambridge: Cambridge University Press.

Myerson, R. B. 1984. "Two-Person Bargaining Problems with Incomplete Information." *Econometrica* 52:461–87.

Myerson, R. B. 1991. *Game Theory: Analysis of Conflict.* Cambridge, Mass.: Harvard University Press.

Roth, A. E., ed. 1985. *Game-Theoretic Models of Bargaining.* Cambridge: Cambridge University Press.

Shubik, M. 1983. *Game Theory in the Social Sciences: Concepts and Solutions.* Cambridge, Mass.: MIT Press.

Young, H. P. 1988. "Fair Division." Working paper. Brookings Institution. Photocopy.

CHAPTER 5

Conflictual Moves in Bargaining: Warnings, Threats, Escalations, and Ultimatums

Barry O'Neill

In July, 1964, Undersecretary of State George Ball tried to dissuade Lyndon Johnson from sending U.S. ground forces to Vietnam en masse. Johnson intended to pressure the North Vietnamese to end the war on his terms, but Ball feared that escalation would become an autonomous force, impelling both sides to higher and higher levels of violence. "Once on a tiger's back," his memo argued, "we cannot be sure of picking a place to dismount" (Ball 1972).

This chapter looks at the coercive side of bargaining: delaying, warning, threatening, escalating, and issuing ultimatums. It describes a series of simplified situations where bargainers must decide whether to use these tactics. The rules are stated precisely enough that game-theoretical logic will determine the best move, and we can then compare what the theory advises with what real bargainers might do. Any major difference tells us something about the bargainers' mental processes or goals. The models use only elementary mathematics, simple probability, linear equations, and graphs, and can be read independently of one another.

A main theme will be Ball's worry: Is choosing a conflictual move really like climbing onto a tiger? Can skillful negotiators use coercive ploys to their advantage, or do such moves sweep them into a more bitter conflict? Smoke (1977) notes that, during the debate on the Vietnam War, one's grammar often reflected one's political persuasion: some worried about the "war escalating," an intransitive verb suggesting no control, others about whether the United States should "escalate the war." The issue is: Is escalation a tool that bargainers control or a force that controls them?

Since game models usually assume foresight, one might expect them to lean toward the "useful tool" viewpoint, but several examples here suggest the

I wrote this chapter, in part, while a visiting scholar at the School of Public Affairs, University of Maryland, with support from an SSRC/MacArthur Foundation Fellowship in International Security. Peyton Young's and Ken Binmore's suggestions are appreciated.

opposite. They show that some situations are innately perverse and even sensible bargainers will do poorly. Other examples imply that certain tactics would succeed in principle, but finding the right move lies beyond the calculating powers of mortal negotiators.

The goal of the analysis is a set of concepts that lets us think straight about these problems. The point is not to calculate best strategies in real situations. The difference between immediate "cookbook" application and theoretical insight is evident from recent U.S. history. The works of Thomas Schelling (1960) and Daniel Ellsberg ([1961] 1975) were widely read for their analyses of threats and escalation, but U.S. officials who tried to set foreign policy according to these writings generated some notable failures. Schelling's ideas about competitive risk taking, waging war as a form of negotiation, and escalating to show resolve came to permeate U.S. nuclear strategic theory, and his memos on Vietnam went up to President Kennedy and other high officials (e.g., Schelling [1961] 1988). The methods were reasonably successful in the 1961 Berlin crisis and the 1962 Cuban missile crisis, but Lyndon Johnson's gradual escalation in Vietnam became a disaster. Ellsberg's theory that leaders might gain from projecting an image of recklessness was taken up by Richard Nixon and his national security advisor, Henry Kissinger, who intensified U.S. bombing of North Vietnam to support their demands at the Paris peace conference. This was their so-called madman theory (Haldeman 1975, 98). Kissinger told Nixon that Ellsberg was the man who had taught him the most about bargaining, but this praise upset Ellsberg, who had then come to oppose the war. He claimed that he had never expected to see these Machiavellian abstractions applied by a U.S. president (Hersh 1983). (Some authors who discuss the strategy of escalation in Vietnam are Brodie 1971; Thies 1980; Kaplan 1983.)

The moral is that formal structures are only guides to thinking. They are too simple to determine real decisions and must be subordinated to wise judgment. In my view, if formal studies continued for a thousand years, they would not replace the intuition of a good negotiator. Models are important for a different reason: bargaining involves more than intuition, and people carry rough theories in their heads about how to conduct and respond to coercion. These theories complement intuition and guide the individual's strategy, but they are largely unconsidered and sometimes self-contradictory. The goal of the modeling, here, is to find a consistent set of concepts to analyze bargaining moves.

Types of Conflictual Moves

First, I will state some definitions that distinguish escalation, threats, warnings, ultimatums, and delays within the context of bargaining. A *bargaining situation* involves two or more parties who can make and accept offers, who can compromise with each other, and who can achieve mutual gains. (This definition leaves open the possibility that the parties can make other moves in addition to the offers, coercive moves, for example.) An *escalation* is a new and stronger action, an intensification or widening of the conflict, aimed at promoting the escalator's gain from an agreement at the expense of the other's. This definition contains the fuzzy terms *stronger, intensification,* and *widening.* The word is, in fact, vague in everyday usage, but within each model it will be clear which moves qualify as escalations. Typically, an escalation means applying a more severe sanction to the other, but it could involve widening your demands or making some other conflictual move. *Delaying tactics* have the same goal as escalatory moves, but they are passive—one side simply withholds negotiation or agreement. A *warning* is a communication to the other side, pointing out that if it violates your wishes the resulting situation will induce you to harm them. Here, a *threat* is defined as a signal-and-commitment, sent usually (but not necessarily) through language, that the sender will take a certain action harmful to the adversary if the latter does not comply with some demand. You might threaten to make a certain escalatory move, or to cause a delay, or to perform some deed at some later time should the negotiations end in failure. Threats differ from warnings in that the very act of making the threat establishes a commitment, or at least is meant to do so. The threat itself gives the threatener the incentive to carry it out conditional on noncompliance. Threats are attempts to commit oneself, whereas pure warnings simply call attention to incentives that would have arisen anyway, that would motivate one to do this or that given the other's undesired action. An *ultimatum* is a species of threat, namely, to end the bargaining if a certain "last offer" is not accepted.

Further types of coercive moves involve simply *demonstrating* one's abilities, setting deadlines, and *bridge burning,* setting up mechanisms that make certain future actions unprofitable. As an example of a demonstration, Goldhamer (1981) mentions a practice of Chinese bowmen before an engagement of stepping forward from the assembled troops to display feats of archery to the enemy. More recently along these lines, Nikita Khrushchev proposed a guided missile targeting contest in which the United States and USSR would fire long-range missiles, unarmed, at some specified target, with radars monitoring their flights to prevent cheating (*New York Times,* November 16, 1957). He made this unusual challenge at a time when the Soviet Union was concerned that its rivals view it as having a reliable deterrent.

An example of bridge burning is Herman Kahn's story (1965) of teenagers playing highway chicken. As you speed toward the other car, a strategist's advice might be to throw your steering wheel out the window, to visibly give up control. Of course, you hope that you will not see the other's steering wheel simultaneously flying out the window. Bridge burning differs from threatening in that the new constraints on the bridge burner flow from some act that is not itself the signal to the other side. Of course, the opponent had better learn about the action. In Stanley Kubrick's ingenious movie *Dr. Strangelove,* the Soviet government hardwired its missiles to retaliate after a nuclear explosion, but decided to postpone the announcement of the change until the yearly celebration of the October Revolution. The result was Armageddon. Bridge burning also differs from threatening in that it can support a promise, not just a negative sanction. For example, a promise of nonaggression could be backed up by actual destruction of weapons. I will not say more about bridge burning or demonstrating since their dynamics are close to threats and warnings, respectively.

Deadlines became prominent in the confrontation between Iraq and the United States over Kuwait. The Bush administration set midnight January 15, 1991, as the last time that Iraq could leave Kuwait without risking aerial attack, and later declared a noon February 23 deadline after which the United States would invade with ground troops. If the U.S. goal was to induce Iraqi compliance, the technique failed both times. The reasons are instructive. First, the reverse implication of setting these deadlines was that the United States would *not* attack *before* the stated times. This may have been the operative part of the threat as far as the Iraqi government was concerned and may have induced Iraq to postpone any concessions at least until the last minute. The dates chosen were arbitrary, creations of the deadline setter, so that giving in to them then would have made Iraq appear subservient, and exacted extra loss of face beyond making the compromise per se. In both cases, the United States attacked almost immediately after the deadlines passed. However, it had not threatened an immediate attack; citing the need for military surprise, its statements had left the timing uncertain. Thus the threats had left open Iraqi possible hopes to negotiate a solution soon after the deadlines but before an attack. All in all, introducing the deadline technique probably hindered a negotiated settlement.

Usually, coercive moves have two purposes, singly or in combination: an *informational* goal of telling the other something, and a *functional* goal of changing the objective situation to your advantage. The informational purpose involves showing what you are able to do, or what you are willing to do, and therefore, in a sense, who you are. An example of a functional escalatory move is a *bargaining chip,* a policy that you implement just to be able to give it up in exchange for a better agreement.

Those escalations that have some functional purpose can be grouped into several categories. Some increase the rate of damage to the other side during the negotiation, like working-to-rule in a labor-management dispute. Some cause damage to the other party *afterward,* in case of no agreement. Some escalatory moves increase the risk of a breakdown in the negotiations. An example would be two warring countries who have negotiated a ceasefire but deliberately violate it to induce concessions from the other. Here, prolonging negotiations costs nothing; in fact, it would be fine if the governments bargained forever. The motive pushing each to an agreement is the fear that the ceasefire might collapse.

Threats often face the problem of credibility, an issue treated lucidly by Schelling (1960). If a threat is a signal-with-commitment, the message may get through but the commitment aspect may not come off. You may warn the other that you will end the bargaining unless they concede, but if they refuse, what motivates you to follow through on your threat? If the other recognizes your disincentive, your threat is empty. To solve a credibility problem, you might accompany the threat with bridge burning or project a reputation for always wanting to follow through on any threat, as if that were your personal principle.

The examples that follow try to show how the various moves are different and how they fulfill their functions in bargaining.

Threats

The *Blackmailer's Fallacy* (Rapoport 1964) illustrates a puzzling error that one can avoid with a coherent set of concepts. An art connoisseur values a painting at $100, and everyone knows that fact. A thief steals it, but is unable to sell it elsewhere. Attaching no value to it, the thief wants money from the collector in exchange for the painting's return. The thief demands $99 and is confident that the connoisseur will accept, since paying will put the latter $1 ahead. The connoisseur, however, makes a final offer of $1 and is sure that the thief will accept, based on the same logic that the other will be $1 ahead. Each holds fast and the painting is never returned.

Each seems to be reasoning correctly based on the other's actual costs and benefits, but their logic must be wrong since their expectations of success never come true. The reader might try to articulate just where their logic went wrong. At first we could suppose that each was incorrect in assuming rationality on the other's part, but just how and where was the other irrational, and what is the valid argument?

Example 1: Complete Information and a Fixed, Credible Threat

For a proper treatment of the blackmailer's problem, we use a simple version of a model by Raiffa (1953), which is related to the approach of Nash (1953). It will prove worthwhile to be somewhat abstract in stating the blackmailer's problem, and so we specify a bargaining situation by two elements: first, each agreement's pair of benefits from the various agreements the bargainers can make, and second, the pair of benefits the bargainers would receive if there were no agreement. The list of agreements is labeled A. Each agreement in A is associated with a pair of numbers, the values of that agreement to each of the bargainers. Thus, list A generates S, the set of benefit levels the bargainers can reach by agreement. The benefits in case of no agreement are the $D = (d_B, d_C)$, standing for the disagreement outcome for the blackmailer and the connoisseur. The context here involves *complete information* in that both bargainers know the situation they are in; they know all the moves available and the outcomes and benefits that would follow. If, for example, the thief did not know the connoisseur's value for the painting and vice versa, the analysis would be quite different. (Roger Myerson discusses incomplete information bargaining in chap. 4 of this volume.)

To clarify the meaning of S, A, and D, we will construct them for the blackmailer's problem. First dealing with D, we are free to set the zero point of the benefit scale at any convenient value. Our choice of a zero will not alter Raiffa's recommended solution, as it turns out. We specify it as their benefits if the painting is never returned, so $d_B = d_C = \$0$. To determine A and S, we will assume that benefit level is measured simply by money value. Note that if the painting is returned free, the connoisseur will be $100 ahead. Thus the pair ($0, $100) is in S. So is ($100, $0) and, indeed, every pair of positive numbers that add up to $100. Such pairs represent all possible payments from the connoisseur to the thief up to $100. Still more pairs of numbers are in S, since it is conceivable that the two could agree on the return of the painting for a payment, and then throw some of their money away. That would be foolish, of course, but our definition of S admits all *possible* outcomes, and therefore we include in S all pairs of benefits that sum to less than or equal to $100. The pair D is shown in figure 1. The set S is all points on or southwest of the $-45°$ line in that figure.

The solution by Raiffa's approach is that they choose a payment where the gains from agreeing are equal, and where no other agreement is better for both. This means starting at the point d_B, d_C in figure 1, and drawing a straight line at 45° up to the northeast border of S. The intersection of the line and the border is the solution. If it is designated (b^*, c^*), the gains from agreeing will be $b^* - d_B$ and $c^* - d_B$; they will be equal since the line is at 45°, and not improvable for both players together since the solution is at the edge of S. Solving $b^* - d_B = c^* - d_B$, with $b^* + c^* = \$100$ and $d_B = \$0$, $d_C = \$0$, yields $b^* = c^* = \$50$.

This procedure seems "fair," but is fairness the proper criterion here? Some would argue that in bargaining, fairness is as important as power, but

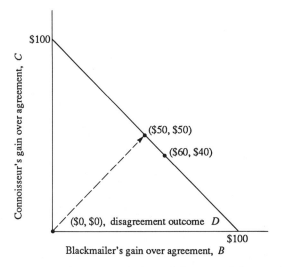

Fig. 1. A balanced threat, an unbalanced threat, and the equal-gains-from-agreement principle

the approach here will try to justify the solution on the basis of power. The equal-gains-from-agreement method can indeed be given a power-based rationale, using the following idea of "balanced threats." Suppose, as shown in figure 1, that *B* demands $60, implying that *C* will receive $40. Given *C* holds firm, *B* is facing a loss of $50 when weighing the alternatives of holding firm versus accepting *C*'s offer of $50. However, *C* is facing a loss of only $40 from declining versus accepting, should *B* hold firm. The former being greater, *B*'s threat to hold firm does not "balance" *C*'s threat, and, it might be argued, is less credible for that reason. To make *B*'s threat more credible, *B* must reduce the demand. When both ask for $50, their threats are balanced.

This argument seems a tortuous route to an obvious solution: just split the gains equally. After all, the situation is symmetrical in that each can expect from $0 to $100. The point of the longer rationale is that it can be applied even to situations that are not symmetric. For example, suppose the thief could sell the painting for $20. The equal-gains argument can still be used, and recommends a $60 payment from the connoisseur. Each would then gain $40 from an agreement over a disagreement. Alternatively, suppose the thief is an honest taxpayer, so that each dollar earned will become 70 cents. This induces a frontier of the agreement that slopes at a different angle than figure 1, a straight line from ($70, $0) to ($0, $100), as in figure 2. The symmetry of the situation is gone, but the equal-gains principle still gives an answer. If the connoisseur pays x, then equating their gains gives $.7x = 100 - x$, implying a ransom of $58.82, and their gains of $41.18.

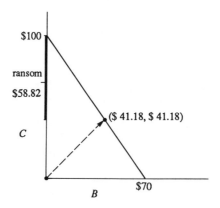

Fig. 2.   The equal-gains principle when one side's gains are discounted

Example 2: Complete Information and Credible
Variable Threats

In example 1, the threat was *fixed,* in the sense that failing to agree meant the bargainers simply walked away; neither had a repertoire of different retaliatory actions. Suppose a situation includes several disagreement outcomes. This is called the *variable threats* case, in the sense there are several alternatives, each leading to a different disagreement outcome. Assume it is the blackmailer who gets to choose which disagreement outcome would result. The equal-gains argument would then tell the blackmailer which one to choose: to make the threat that gives him the greatest benefit when the equal-gains argument is applied to select an agreement. Suppose, for example, that the blackmailer could either destroy the painting, yielding each $0, or fence it for $30, producing as a side consequence the possibility that the piece might eventually end up back in the connoisseur's hands. The connoisseur assesses the likelihood of this event and judges the prospect to be worth $20. If the blackmailer chose the latter threat, that of selling the painting, the disagreement point would be $d_B = \$30$, $d_C = \$20$, and the equation requiring equal gains would become $b^* - d_B = c^* - d_B$, with $b^* + c^* = \$100$, yielding $b^* = \$55$, $c^* = \$45$ (fig. 3 depicts the situation). Since the $55 ransom from a threat to sell the painting beats $50 from a threat to destroy it, the blackmailer should threaten to sell it rather than destroy it. Even though that move is not as frightening to the connoisseur, it improves the thief's agreement share.

The equal-gains principle implies the following rule for choosing threats: make whichever threats puts you furthest ahead of the other, were that threat to be carried out. That is, threaten *as if* your interests were directly opposed

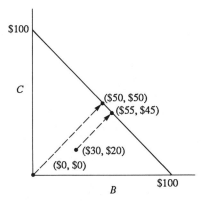

Fig. 3. The thief's choice between two threats

should there come no agreement. Although this rule follows logically from the model, and seems to predict behavior in the laboratory quite well (O'Neill 1977), it may not be wise to use it in practice. It fits with the model's assumption that agreement will surely be achieved, but this is obviously not true in practice. It would call for making a threat that would bring disaster to both, as long as that threat gives you the greatest relative advantage in a disagreement. Threatening *as if* you and the opponent had opposing interests is dangerous when there is less than complete knowledge of each concerning what the other wants. Often the other may be watching your negotiating behavior to judge whether you really want an agreement. Good advice for bargainers is to keep the issue of sincerity off the table, but threats chosen for the damage they do to the other may prompt distrust of one's sincerity, and undermine the other's willingness to compromise.

There are strong social norms against an explicit threat, and violating them infuses the target with new attitudes and utilities beyond the motives inherent in the objective situation. These new goals are competitive and may block agreement. An individual under an ultimatum is likely to stiffen, since acquiescing means a loss of face. In reality, reassurances may be more effective than threatening, and a threatened party may become willing to compromise only after the threat is withdrawn. One might say that the trick of bargaining is to keep both pairs of eyes on their original goals. Strong threats undermine this. The norms against strong threats are not surprising, given that otherwise, according to example 2, draconian threats would be made in everyday conflicts. (An experimental literature in social psychology discusses the dangers of threats; see, for example, Kelley 1965.)

The threatener's dilemmas are: How can I commit myself to a threat without putting it on the record? More generally, how can I make a threat where I would lose face by backing away from it, but the other would not lose face by complying with it? "Veiling" the threat may help lessen the other's negative reaction—if a threat is not explicit, giving in means less loss of face. However, this tactic clashes with the goal of credibility; explicitness seems necessary for an effective commitment since ambiguity would allow the threatener to back out more easily. Another dodge is to phrase the threat as if one were not really its agent, to claim "my hands are tied."

In international affairs, these dilemmas have bothered the large powers all the more since the invention of the atomic bomb. There is a clear credibility problem in the threat to use nuclear weapons to gain some political advantage or keep the status quo. For example, NATO's traditional policy, that it might start a nuclear war should the Eastern bloc invade with conventional forces, seems hard to believe considering the consequent losses. Veiling has been one method of bolstering credibility. Not spelling out one's actions makes their unpalatability less obvious. During the 1973 Middle East War, the Soviet Union appeared to be planning to dispatch forces to rescue the Egyptian army, and Henry Kissinger warned that this action might cause "incalculable consequences" (Blechman and Hart 1983). There was no explicit promise of retaliation or mention of any specific action; the phrasing did not make the United States the agent of harm, but sounded more like a misfortune would descend from the skies. The threat was not sent at the height of the crisis, but delayed until tensions seemed to be easing, as if it were too dangerous to make earlier. An unusually sharp threat for one directed at an ally was John Foster Dulles's 1953 statement that the French Parliament had better vote to join European defense, or the United States would make an "agonizing reappraisal" of its role in Europe. Again, consequences were not spelled out.

Other threats have been strictly nonverbal, thereby avoiding questions of detail. During the 1962 Cuban missile crisis, the United States tried to signal its resolve by dispersing its bombers to local airports, ordering alerts without the use of secret codes, and having its missile submarines exchange targeting plans "in the clear."

An alternative to veiling a threat in vagueness is to inject self-contradiction. In 1957, Khrushchev announced plans to sign a treaty with East Germany that might have ended Western occupation rights in Berlin. Eisenhower responded with a series of inconsistent announcements following the lines that the United States would have to fight over Berlin *and* that war would be pointless as it would preserve no one's freedom (Betts 1987). The threat was there somewhere, but muddied, deliberately and cleverly in the view of Eisenhower's admirers.

Is a vague threat just a hollow one? Were these uses of vagueness and self-contradiction smart ways to induce compliance or pointless gestures? The fact that the crises were resolved is only weak evidence on the value of a vague threat, since the crisis might have subsided anyway. In spite of the abstract arguments for the importance of commitment, national leaders seem to want enough room to back away. This issue of partial credibility is taken up in the next example.

Example 3: Partially Credible, Fixed Threats

In this example, threats are only partially credible, in the sense that in response to noncompliance, the makers will not want to carry them out and they will perhaps not be forced to; that is, they are able to commit themselves, but only with some probability. Some uncertain external circumstance determines whether each threatener will have to follow through (this model is a specific version of Crawford's approach [1982]).

How could a negotiator set up a situation where an uncertain future event ends the interaction? A union leader might claim that, having announced a commitment to a wage demand, he or she will be voted out by the membership if the demand is not met. International negotiators may call for a concession and assert that, if it is denied, their government will become disillusioned and withdraw from the talks. Later events will reveal whether their severe predictions were really correct. Sometimes the determinants of commitment are internal to the negotiator. I may announce a threat, but not know myself what I would do. Only when I am in the situation do I find out how stubborn I am.

These threats are ultimatums: Accept this, my last offer, or I will end the bargaining. The concept of ultimatum, as defined here, is more than just the offer that happens to be one's last. Issuing an ultimatum means that one is deliberately *making* the offer one's last, so we stress that here the negotiator demand is triggering the constituency's hard line. This usage is different from that of the ultimatum bargaining experimental literature, which uses the looser definition (Guth and Tietz 1988).

Example 3 extends the analysis of the conflict between the blackmailer and the connoisseur. The bargainers there had, in effect, $100 to divide between them, so we can talk as if they were dividing a pot rather than paying and taking ransom. At the first stage, each demands a certain share: B's demand is labelled b and C's is labelled c. Each declares that the negotiations will be terminated if the other does not grant them that much. The announcements are simultaneous. When they hear each other's demand, they may find that it has precluded their own (demands are *incompatible* if they sum to more than $100). At that point they might wish to continue negotiating rather than leave with $0, but each one's threat to leave will be imposed with respective probabilities p and q. These latter constitute their "commitment probabilities" or "threat credibilities." Each one's probability is known to both.

The rules state that, if the demands are compatible, each receives the amount demanded plus half the surplus. If the demands are incompatible, then they learn whether their previous threats will be enforced. If one's threat is solid and the other's is not, then the latter can back down from its demand and accept the other's offer. It will certainly take this opportunity. If neither threat has to be implemented, then each party gets $50; if both have to be implemented, they get $0.

Given these rules, a participant will ask: How much should I demand at the first stage, given our two threat credibilities? How can I exploit my full power and not end up with incompatible demands, implemented threats, and a failed negotiation? The decision is subtle, here, because each one's optimal move depends on what it expects the other to do. In this context of think and doublethink, we apply the game-theoretical idea of a *Nash equilibrium*. Here it means a pair of strategies, one for B and one for C, such that B has no incentive to abandon its assigned strategy if it expects the other to use its assigned strategy, and similarly for C. If any regular way of settling has evolved for this particular type of negotiation, then it should specify an equilibrium. Thus, because a settlement procedure gives B a specific expectation about what C will do, B will make an optimal choice given C's move, and the same can be said for C's strategizing about B and they both know the situation. Only for an equilibrium are the responses best against each other.

The rationale for a Nash equilibrium is quite different from the solutions of examples 1 and 2. Previously, the argument was that threats should balance. This logic is plausible, but it is hard to generalize to solve other situations. The equilibrium concept is generalizable, and it will be used for all subsequent examples. The equilibrium argument is not in conflict with the balanced threat rationale, since the latter solution is one equilibrium of the game. Given the other demands $50, neither player is tempted to deviate from demanding $50 for fear of either reducing its share or causing a disagreement.

In the present example, only certain pairs of strategies are Nash equilibria, and the task is to find them. If an equilibrium involves B demanding b and C demanding c, B's demand must be a best possible one in the light of c and vice versa. Therefore, for a given c there are only two possible moves for $B:$ demand $100 - c$ or demand $100. Don't demand less than $100 - c$, since that would leave an unclaimed surplus, and if you decide to demand more than $100 - c$, incompatibility is certain, so you might as well ask for everything and hope that C's ultimatum will collapse. (Strictly speaking, B should ask for slightly less than everything to give C some small incentive to accept, but we can approximate B's demand as $100.) Applying this logic to both bargainers, there will be, at most, two types of equilibria: both will either demand $100, the *confrontation equilibrium,* or there will be some b such that the demands are b and $100 - b$, the *compromise equilibrium*. Other pairs are not candidates for equilibria.

Let us check these types of outcomes to see whether they represent equilibria. The pair of demands ($100, $100), will be a Nash equilibrium for any values of p and q, since neither bargainer alone can gain by asking for less, given that the other wants $100. To test compromise demands (b, $100 $- b$) to see if they form an equilibrium, we ask two questions: (1) will B be content to demand b rather than $100 (which is the most tempting alternative), given that B believes C will demand $100 - b$; and (2) will C be content to demand $1 - b$ rather than $100, given that C knows that B will demand b? If both answers are yes, then (b, $100 - b$) is a Nash equilibrium.

For illustration, we can look at the case of commitment probabilities $p = q = .30$. To answer (1), B's question whether to demand only b or to demand all $100: by demanding b, B will receive that amount. By switching to demand $100, B will get $100 if B's threat is solid and C's is not; B will receive b if C's is solid and B's is not; B will receive $50 if neither threat is solid; and B will receive $0 if both threats are solid. Thus, B's expected payoff from demanding $100 is contingent on four possible events, and to calculate it we must include the probabilities of each of the four. The respective probabilities are $p(1 - q) = .21$, $(1 - p)q = .21$, $(1 - p)(1 - q) = .49$, and $pq = .09$. Thus, B's expected gain from switching will be $(.21 \times $100) + (.21 \times $b) + (.49 \times $50) = $45.50 + .21$b$. B will be content to demand b if this latter is no greater than b. This holds as long as $b \geq 57.60. C's question (2), whether to demand only $1 - b$ or switch to demand all $100 can be answered similarly: the result is that C will stay at the compromise equilibrium as long as $b \leq 42.40. However, no values of b satisfy both of these inequalities, so there are no compromise equilibria when $p = q = .30$.

Only the confrontation equilibrium exists. Bargainers demand everything and hope that only their threat will stand. The confrontation equilibrium gives each one, on the average, $45.50, since, with probability $.30 \times .30 = .09$, both threats stand and one bargainer, say B, gets nothing; with probability $.30 \times .70 = .21$ the other's threat stands and B gets nothing; with probability $.70 \times .30 = .21$, B's alone stands and B gets $100; and, with probability $.70 \times .70 = .49$, neither threat stands and B gets $50. Weighting the payoffs by their probabilities and adding gives $45.50.

The pair sometimes fail to make a deal (with probability .09), an interesting consequence since one would expect that sensible individuals would take an opportunity for gain. However, each made a threat not knowing for sure whether they or the other would yield. Their problem was not lack of rationality but lack of information.

What are the equilibria for other values of p and q? Do compromise

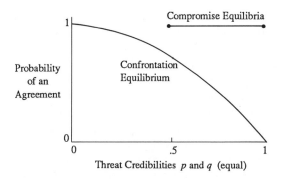

Fig. 4. Probability of agreement from the compromise and confrontation equilibria, as a function of the credibility of the two threats

equilibria sometimes exist? Do the bargainers benefit by having more credible threats? Suppose B boosts its commitment power from $p = .30$ to $.40$, with C having $q = .30$ as before. The previous calculations indicate that both will demand $100 and get expected payoffs of $49 and $39, respectively. The increase in B's commitment power has helped B and hurt C, as one might expect. Although the no-gain outcome is more frequent, more often than before B stands firm when C backs down, and B gets the whole prize. However if *both* have a higher commitment power, $p = q = .40$, again there is only the confrontation equilibrium at which both have an expected payoff of $42, worse than the case of $p = q = .30$. The higher commitment probabilities mean they are just as demanding but more likely to stand fast, and this change hurts them.

We have seen that threats of low credibility can cause waste. When p and q rise, still kept equal to each other, the confrontation equilibrium becomes bleaker, more wasteful. However, a new opportunity appears when p and q pass $.50$. Compromise equilibria become possible. More credible threats make demands for the whole pot so dangerous that players are no longer tempted away from a compromise. A range of compromise equilibria arise, and the equal $50 = $50 split is always one of them. Figure 4 shows the probability of reaching an agreement, given the two types of equilibria as a function of the threat credibilities.

For higher values of p and q, the game has more than one equilibrium. Which will the bargainers choose? The accepted philosophy views this question as outside game theory. It depends on details of the history and the context of the bargaining. Game-theoretical reasoning shows that if the model reflects the players' goals and knowledge and if they expect a specific outcome, that outcome must be an equilibrium, but theory is silent about which equilibrium it will be. But an interesting result here is that a compromise equilibrium appears when threats become more credible and frighten players away from risking a conflict.

Example 4: Escalation Due to a Preemptive Advantage

Consider two people in a dispute that can be settled by negotiation, where each can try to pressure the other by filing a lawsuit. The other can then file a countersuit, but the effect will be reduced, we assume, just because that move comes second. It is clearly a move made in reaction and less a statement of determination. This example postulates that filing second is not worth it; if the other goes first, you should just give up. Assume then that each has an opportunity to file, and that the two sides have to simultaneously choose whether to do so. If both hold back and let the opportunity pass, we assume they cannot or will not use the move later. Filing the suit is assumed to be costly to the user. Some plausible net payoffs (the gain derived from the settlement minus the cost of filing) are shown in matrix 1, where the prize to be shared is $100 and the cost of filing a suit is $30.

	Refrain	File Suit
Refrain	50, 50	0, 70
File Suit	70, 0	35, 35

Matrix 1. The decision on filing a suit

The rows correspond to one side's choices of refraining from escalating or going ahead, and the columns are the other's choices. The cells give the Row- and Column-chooser's payoffs at each outcome. If neither moves, they share a prize of $100 equally, producing 50, 50 in that cell. One who files alone receives $100 minus a cost of $30, yielding the cells 70, 0 and 0, 70. If they both try to file, we posit that only one will succeed in doing it first and the other will see that party's success and back off. (It would have been more precise to label the move "*Try* to File Suit First.") If both try, each has an equal chance of being first so they can expect 35, the mean of 0 and 70.

This game has the strategic structure of the notorious Prisoner's Dilemma. An escalatory move will help no matter what the other does, that is, whether the other chooses Refrain or File, so the only equilibrium involves both bargainers escalating. Here, 50 each was possible, but they end up with 35 each. The other 20 was wasted. Some writers have stated that inefficiency from rational negotiators requires that they be uncertain about their situation, but this claim is wrong. Although incomplete information led to waste in example 3, it is not a precondition for it, as this example shows. Here, the preemptive advantage inherent in the situation, not any deficit in the bargainers' rationality or information, caused the inefficiency.

Changing the input numbers can change the strategic situation. Increasing the lawyer's fee from $30 to $60 gives matrix 2.

	Refrain	File Suit
Refrain	50, 50	0, 40
File Suit	40, 0	20, 20

Matrix 2.   Filing a more costly suit

This game is more interesting than the last one because it has two equilibria, one where both refrain and another where both file. (To check that both 50, 50 and 20, 20 are equilibria, note that each player is optimizing by using its equilibrium move given it is expecting the other's equilibrium move.) So, increasing lawyer's fee has opened up a hope for efficiency, just as increasing threat credibility did in example 3. But it is only a possibility; bargainers may continue to waste resources. This type of game, called a *Stag Hunt* by virtue of the ordering of its payoffs, illustrates the concept of mutual trust. Only players who trust each other to some degree will choose the better equilibrium. The Stag Hunt is different in this regard from the Prisoner's Dilemma of previous matrix 1. Trusting the other in a Prisoner's Dilemma would be foolish, assuming that the payoffs in the matrix really constitute the other's goals. The adversary will surely file suit no matter what you do. But here, trust is consistent with rationality, and so is mistrust. The example shows that trust is a separate concept from rationality, neither required or ruled out by its logic.

At the File/File equilibrium outcome, each party reasons "I prefer the refrain outcome over all others, but if one of us is going to file suit, it had better be me." A lone filer gets 40, while 0 goes to the adversary. Although there are two equilibria, one of them is unstable, vulnerable to worries that the other will deviate. Perhaps the other's reason for deviating is worry about you, but, nonetheless, one equilibrium is shaky, and unfortunately it is the better of the two.

Example 5: Escalation Due to Asymmetry
in Escalatory Levels

The next example illustrates another way that escalatory moves can entrap a bargainer. Unlike the preemptive advantage analysis in example 4, this entrapping feature is embodied not in a single move, but in the whole pattern of moves available to both players. The lesson will be that their sets of moves should be similar, in the sense that each side should have a corresponding response to the other, or they may lose control.

The *dollar auction* (Shubik 1971) is a simple model of bidding up in an auction, certainly a type of escalation but not really negotiation. We shall describe it, first, in its original auction form, and then modify it into a model of negotiation. Two individuals take turns making bids. Whoever makes the higher bid in the end will win $1. To make the rules specific, assume the bids must be in units of nickels and that each bidder must either drop out or raise the last bid by at least a nickel. When one drops out the other wins the dollar but, unlike a normal auction, the rules require that the winner and the loser both pay their respective last bids. For example, if they have bid up to 20 and 25 cents, and the first drops out, the dollar goes to the second, and the auctioneer collects a total of 45 cents.

When this game is played in classroom demonstrations and psychological experiments, the students bid up and up as if they were riding George Ball's tiger. The dollar auction may hold a clue about why real escalation takes control of the actors. Often, neither bidder will drop out for fear of wasting the investment up to that point, which (by the rules) must be paid whether one wins or loses the dollar. If they reach bids of 90 and 95 cents, for example, the lower bidder will be tempted to raise to $1 in hopes of losing nothing, rather than losing 90 cents. This logic still applies when the bids pass $1. Bidders continue to raise in hopes of collecting the dollar to offset their losses.

The dollar auction can be solved for the best playing strategy. That strategy is a function of the money the two players have available to bid (O'Neill 1986; Leininger 1989). Optimal play would see the first party offering an amount between 0 and $1, calculated by a certain complex formula, and the other not bidding at all. One constructs the tree of all moves, countermoves, countercountermoves, etc., and then, starting at the end, reasons backward from using expectations of future moves to determine the best choice for the present. The solution formula is unintuitive, however. This tree extends out to astronomical numbers of final nodes, and no one could expect human beings to carry out such a calculation. Further, the reasoning is valid only if one knows the other is using this foresight. In reality, no one will figure just when they should rationally drop out, and we are left with an escalatory trap. Even if real bidders could calculate how to maximize their monetary gains, experiments indicate that, after a few bids, their goals change, and they acquire a taste for winning the dollar per se, partially ignoring the money spent to get it. They would be willing to take a loss just to prevent the other from gaining the prize (Teger 1980; Brockner and Rubin 1985). So, even though superintelligent, unemotional players would not lose money, real players fall into the trap. In this regard, the dollar auction is fundamentally different than the Prisoner's Dilemma trap of example 4, which ensnares the rational.

As stated, the model is an auction, but it can portray negotiation. The bids are interpreted as levels of escalation, and we assume that whoever is ahead in the escalation will be able to get more favorable terms when negotiation ends the conflict. Going to the higher levels entails paying irretrievable costs, for example, wages lost in a wider strike. Reinterpreted as a bargaining model, the dollar auction is entrapping because each side must stay below or surpass the other in escalation; neither can compromise by matching the last move and then settling on equal terms.

A mismatch of available escalatory moves can arise in various ways. One way is the existence of a preemptive advantage of the type described in example 4. If the other's jump to a certain level makes that level ineffective for the other, you cannot match the other's level and expect an equal settlement. The rules will impel the bargainers upward, like bidders in the dollar auction.

Another way to preclude exact matches of levels is simply to arrange levels of escalation that do not correspond from one side to the other. When one side escalates, the other would have to stay lower or jump higher than the first. This arrangement would hinder compromises and produce an "escalatory updraft." This is typical in conflicts; usually the set of possible escalations involve discrete jumps that cannot be adjusted to match the other side's move. In an extreme case, the sides might have moves that are so different that they cannot be compared; for a given state of the conflict there might be no way to judge which had escalated to a higher level.

The same problem would arise if the two sides had different perceptions about what are equal escalatory levels, or if sides could not observe clearly each other's choice of level. Neither will know that they are at equal positions and that it is time to compromise. At the beginning of World War II, for example, deliberate bombing of civilian populations was widely regarded as an atrocity and avoided by both sides. However, whether a certain bombing attack on civilians was deliberate or accidental was not observable to the victim, and this factor contributed to the collapse of moral restraint. Liddell Hart (1946, quoted in Freedman 1983) commented tersely that "inaccuracy of weapon-aim fostered inhumanity of war-aim."

The conclusion is that preemptive advantage, asymmetry, incomparability, unobservability, or lack of natural matching of levels adds to the danger of escalation. Parties should try to set up situations that avoid them or should take special care in pushing their cause.

Delays

Delays may be more acceptable as coercive moves than escalations or threats because holding back seems less actively hostile. On the other hand, they can sometimes raise doubts about whether you really want an agreement and sap the other's motivation to compromise.

One strain of research treats them as signals about one's goals. Delayers hurt themselves to prove to the other party how much they want a favorable agreement. Models of this kind have been discussed by Sobel and Takahashi (1983; summarized by Sutton 1986), and by Cramton (1987 and 1990). Cramton and Tracy (1990) model the choice of engaging in a strike versus simply delaying the signing of a contract, and compare their predictions with data on 2,600 contract negotiations. Green and Laffont (1988) attribute a constructive purpose to delays. Delays do not cost the bargainers directly, but if both delay too long the negotiations will end. Each is uncertain whether an agreement is really worth it, but each holds some relevant knowledge on this question, which is signaled back and forth by each party's eagerness or reserve in putting an agreement off. The risk that negotiations will end gives these delays their credibility as signals. Some game-theoretical models on delays and strikes are surveyed by Kennan and Wilson (1989) and Osborne and Rubinstein (1990).

Conclusion

A theme of this chapter is the issue of when aggressive moves will help and when they will engender an upward spiral of conflict. Threats can be dangerous because they can cause the other to lose face and trigger a response of inflexibility. Some situations are innate traps that induce bargainers to escalate. Delaying may raise questions about one's sincerity. A skilled bargainer is sensitive to the norms of bargaining within a culture.

In general, escalation, delays, and threats are difficult to manage because they call on us to predict the other's response. Prediction is harder for those moves that essentially cast our fate to the wind. In his memo, Ball claimed prediction becomes more difficult when the escalatory moves are more forceful, "It is in the nature of escalation that each move passes the option to the other side, while at the same time the party which seems to be losing will be tempted to keep raising the ante. To the extent that the response to the move can be controlled, that move is probably ineffective. If the move is effective it may not be possible to control—or accurately anticipate—the response" (1972, 46). To anticipate the other's responses, one must put oneself in an adversary's shoes, but this ability can vanish quickly when a conflict intensifies.

REFERENCES

Ball, George, W. 1972. "Top Secret: The Prophecy the President Rejected." (Reprint of a memo, October 5, 1964.) *Atlantic Monthly,* 43–46.

Betts, Richard. 1987. *Nuclear Blackmail and the Nuclear Balance.* Washington: Brookings Institution.

Blechman, Barry, and Douglas Hart. 1983. "The Political Utility of Nuclear Weapons." *International Security* 7:132–56.

Brockner, Joel, and Jeffrey Rubin. 1985. *Entrapment in Escalating Conflict: A Social-Psychological Analysis.* New York: Springer-Verlag.

Brodie, Bernard. 1971. "Why We Were So (Strategically) Wrong." *Foreign Policy* 5:151–62.

Cramton, Peter. 1987. "Strategic Delay in Bargaining with Two-sided Uncertainty." School of Organization and Management working paper, Yale University. Photocopy.

Cramton, Peter. 1990. "Dynamic Bargaining with Transaction Costs." School of Organization and Management working paper, Yale University. Photocopy.

Cramton, Peter, and Joseph Tracy. 1990. "Strikes and Delays in Wage Bargaining: Theory and Data." School of Organization and Management working paper, Yale University. Photocopy.

Crawford, Vincent. 1982. "A Theory of Disagreement in Bargaining." *Econometrica* 50:607–37.

Ellsberg, Daniel. [1961] 1975. "The Theory and Practice of Blackmail." Reprinted in *Bargaining: Formal Theories of Negotiation,* ed. Oran Young. Urbana: University of Illinois Press.

Goldhamer, Joan, ed. 1981. "Reality and Belief in Military Affairs: An Inventory of Additional Material in the File of Herbert Goldhamer." RAND Corporation, N-1726.

Green, Jerry, and Jean-Jacques Laffont. 1988. "International Agreements through Sequential Unanimity Games." Department of Economics, Harvard University. Mimeo.

Guth, Werner, and Reinhard Tietz. 1988. "Ultimatum Bargaining Behavior—A Survey." Working paper no. 21, Zentrum für interdisziplinare Forschung, Bielefeld University.

Haldeman, H. R. 1975. *The End of Power.* New York: Doubleday.

Hersh, Seymour. 1983. *The Price of Power: Kissinger in the Nixon White House.* New York: Summit.

Kahn, Herman. 1965. *On Escalation: Metaphors and Scenarios.* Rev. ed. Baltimore: Penguin Books.

Kaplan, Fred. 1983. *The Wizards of Armageddon.* New York: Simon and Schuster.

Kelley, Harold H. 1965. "Experimental Studies of Threats in Interpersonal Negotiations." *Journal of Conflict Resolution* 9:79–105.

Kennan, John, and Robert Wilson. 1989. "Strategic Bargaining Models and the Interpretation of Strike Data." *Journal of Applied Econometrics* 4:S87–130.

Leininger, Wolfgang. 1989. "Escalation and Cooperation in Conflict Situations: The Dollar Auction Revisited." *Journal of Conflict Resolution* 33:231–54.

Liddell Hart, B. H. 1946. *The Revolution in Warfare.* London: Faber and Faber.

Nash, John. 1953. "Two-Person Cooperative Games." *Econometrica* 21:128–40.

O'Neill, Barry. 1977. "Variable-Threat Bargaining: A Test of the Raiffa-Nash Theory." Ph.D. diss. University of Michigan.

O'Neill, Barry. 1986. "International Escalation and the Dollar Auction." *Journal of Conflict Resolution* 30:33–50.

Osborne, Martin, and Ariel Rubinstein. 1990. *Bargaining and Markets.* Boston: Academic Press.

Raiffa, Howard. 1953. "Arbitration Schemes for Generalized Two-Person Games." In *Contributions to the Theory of Games.* Vol. 2, ed. H. W. Kuhn and A. W. Tucker. Annals of Mathematics Studies no. 28. Princeton: Princeton University Press.

Rapoport, Anatol. 1964. *Strategy and Conscience.* New York: Harper and Row.

Schelling, Thomas. 1960. *The Strategy of Conflict.* Cambridge, Mass.: Harvard University Press.

Schelling, Thomas. [1961] 1988. "Nuclear Strategy and the Berlin Crisis." Reprinted in *The Development of American Nuclear Strategy,* ed. Marc Trachtenberg. New York: Garland.

Shubik, Martin. 1971. "The Dollar Auction Game: A Paradox in Noncooperative Behavior and Escalation." *Journal of Conflict Resolution* 15:545–47.

Smoke, Richard. 1977. *War: Controlling Escalation.* Cambridge, Mass.: Harvard University Press.

Sobel, Joel, and Ichiro Takahashi. 1983. "A Multistage Model of Bargaining." *Review of Economic Studies* 50:411–26.

Sutton, John. 1986. "Noncooperative Bargaining Theory: An Introduction." *Review of Economic Studies* 53:709–24.

Teger, Alan. 1980. *Too Much Invested to Quit.* New York: Pergammon Press.

Thies, Wallace. 1980. *When Governments Collide.* Berkeley: University of California Press.

CHAPTER 6

Negotiator Rationality and Negotiator Cognition: The Interactive Roles of Prescriptive and Descriptive Research

Max H. Bazerman and Margaret A. Neale

As of 1980, the field of negotiation could be dichotomized into two components: economic models of rational agents, which could serve as prescriptions in a rational world, and behavioral models describing the actual behavior of negotiators. Researchers from these two approaches did not generally talk to each other, and neither had much influence on practitioners.

Economic models of negotiation tend to assume rationality and focus on the outcome that should emerge from these rational actions by both (or all) parties. The most well-developed component of this economic school of thought is game theory, which focuses on the mathematical analysis of rational behavior under a specified set of conditions facing each party (the game). Economic models focus on the prediction of whether or not an agreement will be reached and, if one were reached, the specific nature of that agreement. Under full information, if an agreement zone exists, economic models predict that an agreement will occur. Under incomplete information, Myerson and Satterthwaite (1983) have shown that rational actors may fail to reach an agreement despite the existence of an agreement zone. In addition, economic models predict that the agreement that will occur under full information will be Pareto optimal. That is, there will be no alternative joint resolution that would be preferable to both parties (Zeuthen 1930; Nash 1950; Cross 1969; Farber 1981).

If economic models provided fully accurate *descriptions* of the outcomes that occur in negotiation (which many economic theorists claim), there would be no need to write this chapter. In fact, there would be no need to make a

The research was supported by a National Science Foundation grant to Peyton Young and Howard Raiffa and by the Dispute Resolution Research Center at Northwestern University.

distinction between descriptive and prescriptive models, since the economic model would offer a perfect description. There is empirical evidence that actual negotiator behavior does not conform to the rationality postulated in these models. First, behavioral decision research shows that individuals deviate from rationality in systematic and predictable ways (Kahneman, Slovic, and Tversky 1982; Nisbett and Ross 1982; Dawes 1988). More specific to the negotiation context, ample evidence exists that deviations from rationality in individual decisions result in the failure to reach negotiated agreements despite the existence of an agreement zone, and agreements that are reached are often Pareto inefficient (Neale and Bazerman 1985a; Bazerman 1986). The fact that these deviations from rationality are systematic is important in critiquing the limitations of economic models. For if these deviations were random, the prescriptions offered by economic models might still be optimal, even if the descriptive value of the models would be reduced. However, as we will later argue, the systematic nature of the deviations requires changes in the optimal prescriptions that can be offered to a negotiator. Traditional descriptive research focused on structural determinants of negotiated outcomes, such as differential information/payoffs, the effects of the surrounding characteristics of the negotiation (e.g., the form of third-party intervention that would be in effect if the parties failed to reach agreement; see Kochan 1980), and individual differences among negotiators (e.g., interpersonal orientation; see Rubin and Brown 1975).

These descriptive theories have a number of limitations, however. First, they typically describe components of the negotiation that are relatively fixed. Because the negotiator does not often have the ability to change the structural characteristics of the negotiation (i.e., the relative power of the negotiators) or the personality characteristics (i.e., the level of Machiavellianism of an opponent), he or she can only adapt to the situation and the opponent as presented.

Second, such theories offer description without a basis (e.g., the goal of acting rationally) for offering prescription. Thus, they offer no baseline from which to evaluate the performance of a negotiator. Without such an evaluative anchor, it is very difficult to determine exactly how might one "do better." Third, empirically, they explain little of the actual variation that occurs in negotiation (Neale and Bazerman 1991). We believe that a descriptive model of negotiation would be more useful if such a model offered negotiators useful information about decisions that are still facing the negotiator, if the information could be used directly for making optimal prescriptions, and if the model could predict the outcomes of negotiation more accurately. We will argue that a behavioral decision research approach to negotiation offers such attributes as these.

Prescriptive and Descriptive Decision Models of Negotiation—the 1980s

One argument that emerges from the previous discussion is the need for prescriptions that more realistically consider limitations to rationality. Raiffa (1982) has outlined such an approach in his asymmetrically prescriptive/descriptive approach to negotiation. He suggests that prescriptive advice to negotiators should be based on an understanding of the actual decision processes of the opponent, rather than by assuming that the other party is fully rational. Lax and Sebenius (1986) develop this approach by offering tactical advice for negotiators, primarily in the managerial context. Applebaum (1987) has addressed the use of the asymmetrically prescriptive/descriptive approach for dealing with contexts in which a key task of the negotiator is to collect information from the other side.

This line of research has created a framework for thinking rationally in a less-than-fully-rational world. The work has a pattern of showing how to take a variety of negotiation contexts and identifying how decision analysis can be used to develop rational prescriptions for negotiator behavior. A strong argument can be made that this approach leads to better prescriptions than those offered by the traditional models of rational decision making. However, the superiority of this approach has not been the subject of rigorous empirical investigation, although it has been used to gain insight into a variety of salient, real-world problems (Raiffa 1982; Lax and Sebenius 1986).

Raiffa's work represents a key turning point in negotiation research for a number of reasons. First, in the context of developing a prescriptive model, he explicitly realizes the importance of developing accurate descriptions of the opponents—rather than assuming them to be fully rational. Second, his realization that negotiators need advice implicitly acknowledges that negotiators do not intuitively follow purely rational strategies. Most important, he initiated the dialogue between researchers advocating prescriptive and descriptive models. His work outlines the need for descriptive models that allow the focal negotiator to better anticipate the likely behavior of the opponent. In addition, we argue that a central focus of the decision analyst should be to realize that focal negotiators may have decision biases that limit their ability to follow prescriptive advice.

Our research addresses several questions that are raised by the asymmetric prescriptive/descriptive approach. If the other side (or the focal negotiator) does not act fully rationally, what systematic departures from rationality can be predicted? Building on work in behavioral decision making, we and our colleagues have endeavored to specify the deviations from rationality that can be expected in negotiations. We will survey a number of these effects, but since this material is reviewed elsewhere (Bazerman 1986; Bazerman and Carroll 1987; Neale and Northcraft 1990b), we will limit our discussion to a short review of each deviation from rationality.

Ignoring the Cognitions of Others

Rational models imply that negotiators fully and rationally consider the decisions of the opponent negotiator in formulating their own strategy. In fact, one of the most valuable aspects of game theory is its emphasis on an explicit consideration of the decisions of the opponent (Myerson in this volume). Despite the obvious importance of considering the strategy of a competitor, we argue that a fundamental impediment to rational decision making in competitive situations is the failure of the competitive actor to incorporate the decision processes of the opponent (Samuelson and Bazerman 1985; Bazerman and Carroll 1987; Neale and Northcraft 1990a; Neale and Bazerman 1991). Actors tend to simplify their decision task by ignoring the *contingent decision processes* of competitive others. They assume a particular future action by the opponent (e.g., based on a most likely course of action or based on an expected value assessment), rather than realizing that the opponent's behavior is contingent on a variety of factors.

Acquiring a Company (example 1) shows a modified version of one of the examples used by Samuelson and Bazerman (1985). In this problem, potential acquirers only know that the company is equally likely to be worth any value between $0 and $100 and that, whatever its value, it is worth 50 percent more to the acquirer than to the target owner. The target owner knows the exact value and will accept any bid at or above that value. What should the acquirer bid?

The most common response (90 of 123 subjects) found by Samuelson and Bazerman (1985) was in the $50–$75 range. The simple (naive) logic that accounts for this result can be stated as follows.

> The value of the firm is uncertain, but its expected value to the target is $50/share. The expected value of the firm to me is $75/share. Thus, I can make a reasonable profit by offering some price slightly in excess of $50/share. I offer $60/share (or $51/share).

This logic would be rational if the target was also uninformed about the value of the firm. However, an informed target will only accept offers if they are profitable, which a subject can assess through the appropriate conditional logic or through the use of a simple example.

In the following exercise you will represent Company A (the acquiror), which is currently considering acquiring Company T (the target) by means of a tender offer. You plan to tender in cash for 100% of Company T's shares but are unsure how high a price to offer. The main complication is this: the value of Company T depends directly on the outcome of a major oil exploration project it is currently undertaking. Indeed, the very viability of Company T depends on the exploration outcome. If the project fails, the company under current management will be worth nothing--$0/share. But if the project succeeds, the value of the company under current management could be as high as $100/share. All share values between $0 and $100 are considered equally likely. By all estimates, the company will be worth considerably more in the hands of Company A than under current management. In fact, whatever the ultimate value under current management, the company will be worth fifty percent more under the management of A than under Company T. If the project fails, the company is worth $0/share under either management. If the exploration project generates a $50/share value under current management, the value under Company A is $75/share. Similarly, a $100/share value under Company T implies a $150/share value under Company A, and so on.

The board of directors of Company A has asked you to determine the price they should offer for Company T's shares. This offer must be made now, before the outcome of the drilling project is known. From all indications, Company T would be happy to be acquired by Company A, provided it is at a profitable price. Moreover, Company T wishes to avoid, at all cost, the potential of a takeover bid by any other firm. You expect Company T to delay a decision on your bid until the results of the project are in, then accept or reject your offer before the news of the drilling results reaches the press.

Thus, you (Company A) will not know the results of the exploration project when submitting your price offer, but Company T will know the results when deciding whether or not to accept your offer. In addition, Company T is expected to accept any offer by Company A that is greater than the (per share) value of the company under current management.

As the representative of Company A, you are deliberating over price offers in the range $0/share (this is tantamount to making no offer at all) to $150/share. What price offer per share would you tender for Company T's stock?

My Tender Price is: $_____ per share.

Example 1. Acquiring a company

Suppose that I make an offer of $60/share. If it is accepted, then the firm must be worth between $0 and $60/share. The average value of the firm to the target when my offer is accepted is $30/share, and $45/share to me. My profit has the expected value of $45 − $60, or −$15/share when my offer is accepted.

It is easy to generalize this reasoning to the conclusion that, when an offer is accepted, the acquirer will obtain a company that is worth 25 percent less than the amount that it will pay for that company. Thus, the best action is to make no offer at all, $0/share. However, fewer than 10 percent of the subjects offer $0/share in this problem, even though it requires minimal analytical skill.

This tendency to ignore information that is available by considering the decisions of opponent negotiators is consistent with research on the winner's curse in an auction context. Research has shown that "winning bidders" often find that they have overpaid for the acquired commodities (Capen, Clapp, and Campbell 1971; Cassing and Douglas 1980; Kagel and Levin 1986; Roll 1986). This occurs because the highest bid is likely to be from an individual with one of the more optimistic estimates of the commodity's value. If this adverse selection problem is not accounted for by the bidders, winning bids will frequently result in negative returns. Bazerman and Samuelson (1983) and Kagel and Levin (1986) have shown that this adverse selection process increases with the number of bidders and the uncertainty of the value of the commodity. However, bidder judgment fails to incorporate the relevance of adverse selection or the mediating influences of the number of bidders and commodity uncertainty.

While some argue (e.g., Smith 1982) that observed failures of rational models are attributable to the cost of thinking and will thus be eliminated by proper incentives, Tversky and Kahneman (1986) document many failures of incentives to correct systematic deviations from rationality. Indeed, research has shown that individuals fail to consider the cognitions of others even when they were paid for good performance, when their intellectual reputations were at stake, when they were given hints, and when unusually analytical subjects were used (Samuelson and Bazerman 1985; Carroll, Bazerman, and Maury 1988; Ball, Bazerman, and Carroll 1991).

Overconfidence in Judgment

Why can a war be waged that will leave *both* sides worse off than they would have been had no war occurred? Why can a strike go on for an extended period of time that works to neither side's advantage? One reason is that competitive actors have a tendency to be overconfident in their fallible judgments (Einhorn and Hogarth 1978; Fischhoff 1981). Neale and Bazerman

(1985a) discuss this problem in terms of the following negotiations example: each side in a labor dispute is inappropriately optimistic that a neutral third party would agree with its perspective. Assume that the union is demanding $8.75/hour, management is offering $8.25/hour, and the "appropriate" wage is $8.50/hour. Labor will typically expect a third party (an arbitrator) to adjudicate at a wage rate somewhat over $8.50, while management will expect a wage rate somewhat under $8.50. Typically, neither side will be willing to accept an $8.50 agreement. Both sides will frequently incur the costs of an impasse (e.g., the commitment of time and money to select an arbitrator and have him or her adjudicate the case, the loss of control over the selection of the outcome, the long-term implications of having an outsider make an important decision) and often do no better (in the aggregate) through the use of an arbitrator. The key point is that competitive actors are likely to be overconfident and can anticipate similar overconfidence in the behavior of opponents.

Why does overconfidence exist? It results from competitive actors not considering the perspective of opponents. If the competitive actor considered the actions of others, he or she would see the limitations of his or her own analysis. Instead, the competitive actor often hears only his or her own arguments, which will have a biased slant. The statements that a competitor may use to gain team spirit, for example, "we're going to run them out of the industry," is likely to be far too overconfident to be useful in developing a rational competitive action plan. The press releases made to give the public confidence in a military action are likely to be too overconfident to provide a realistic depiction of the actual situation.

Nonrational Escalation of Commitment

The most frequent pattern of deteriorating competitive relationships consists of a small dispute that each side continually escalates to the next level. Decision makers tend to make decisions to justify their earlier charted directions (Staw 1976; Bazerman, Giuliano, and Appleman 1984), and competitive situations simply aggravate this tendency (Rubin 1980; Bazerman 1986). An interesting aspect of escalatory traps is that it is very difficult to disengage. Once caught up in a trap, the course of action required to extricate oneself is not at all obvious. The more useful advice is to avoid getting involved in situations that can be expected to escalate commitment and create such escalatory traps. Yet, decision makers often fail to follow this advice.

The essence of the escalation phenomenon has been captured in the dollar auction game developed by Shubik (1971) and used extensively in social psychological research (cf. Brockner and Rubin 1985). In this game, the auctioneer announces that he or she is going to auction off $1 to the highest bidder, with bidding entered in five-cent increments. The winning bidder gets the dollar for the amount that he or she bid; however, the second highest bidder must also give the auctioneer his or her last bid and get nothing in return. The result of these auctions is that the bidding starts out with lots of bidders, with all but two dropping out as the bid approaches $1. Then, the two remaining bidders realize that they are trapped, and neither can quit without suffering a sure loss. The bidding continues, with each bidder escalating in order to justify being in the auction and trying to "beat" the other party. A dollar bill typically sells in the $3 to $7 range. In addition, the game works with equal success if one auctions a $20 bill at $1 increments. Thoughtful examination of the problem suggests that bidders create real difficulties for themselves. It is true that one more bid may lead the other party to quit. However, if both parties think this way, the result can be catastrophic for the trapped participants (see O'Neill in this volume).

The logic behind dollar auction behavior has been used to analyze a variety of failures of negotiation, including the Vietnam War (Staw 1976; Teger 1980) and the Falklands crisis (Bazerman and Neale 1983). A central reason competitive decision makers get trapped in an escalatory pattern is that they fail to consider the cognitions of the other side before engaging in competitive behaviors. If we put ourselves into the perspective of the other side, we could see the likely pattern of escalation, anticipate the escalatory response of the other, and devise a more appropriate competitive response (which is, in some cases, not to become involved). In practice, however, most negotiators fail to think about the other side in competitive situations. This may be caused by the competitive spirit that is emphasized in our society, where striving to achieve one's own goals tends to dominate the perceived need to understand what other competitors are doing.

The Mythical Fixed-Pie of Negotiations

Helping negotiators find Pareto-efficient agreements is a central concern of negotiation analysis (Kochan and Bazerman 1986). A key element in this training is the recognition that individuals enter into negotiations assuming that they are in direct competition with the opponent negotiator. This frequently false assumption, the mythical fixed-pie of negotiations, is the result of the negotiator using an inappropriate simplification strategy of a complex cognitive task (Bazerman and Carroll 1987). In addition, folklore and past experiences may convince us that we are in competition with the other negotiator and direct us to attend to the distributive or competitive aspects of negotiation.

The tendency of negotiators to approach bargaining with a fixed-pie perception has been documented by Bazerman, Magliozzi, and Neale (1985).

In their study, individuals act as buyers and sellers to complete multiple transactions on a three-issue, integrative bargaining problem. The goal was to complete as many transactions with as many opponents as possible in a fixed amount of time, while maximizing total individual profit. The profit available to sellers and buyers for various levels of the three issues on a per transaction basis is shown in the net profit columns of table 1. Note that buyers achieve their highest profit levels and sellers their lowest profits at the *A* level of delivery, discount, and financing; whereas sellers achieve their highest profits and buyers their lowest profits at the *I* levels. A negotiated transaction consisted of the two parties agreeing to one of the nine levels for each of the three issues. As can be observed, a simple compromise solution of *E-E-E* results in a \$4,000 profit to each side. However, if the parties are able to reach the fully integrative solution of *A-E-I* (by trading issues), then each receives a profit of \$5,200.

The fixed-pie bias argues that negotiators will approach this competitive context with a fixed-pie assumption and only relax this assumption when provided with evidence to the contrary. As illustrated graphically in figure 1, Bazerman, Magliozzi, and Neale (1985) found that subjects initially focused on the competitive aspect of the negotiation, reaching Pareto-inefficient agreements. Early in the negotiation simulation, participants accepted agreements that were predicated on the fixed-pie bias and the resulting strategy of splitting the difference between the parties' initial positions. This behavior results in agreements that are worth approximately \$4,000 to each negotiator, a figure significantly lower than the \$5,200 value to each negotiator of the symmetrical, fully integrative agreement. This result is consistent with findings in social/cognitive psychological studies of negotiation (Pruitt 1981 and 1983; Neale and Bazerman 1985a; McAlister, Bazerman, and Fader 1986). While it is reasonable to assume that experts are better at finding Pareto-efficient agreements in their own area of expertise, Neale and Northcraft (1990b) provide evidence that experienced negotiators have limited ability to find integrative agreements when faced with novel negotiation problems.

The fixed-pie assumption has been used to explain a variety of economic and political conflicts. Bazerman (1983) argued that the fixed-pie assumption contributed to the decline of the housing market in 1979 and 1980. When interest rates rose to over 12 percent in 1979, activity in the housing market almost ceased. Sellers continued to expect the value of their property to increase. Buyers, however, could not afford the monthly payments on houses they aspired to own—primarily because of the drastically higher interest payments. Viewing this problem as a distributive one, buyers could not afford the prices the sellers were demanding. Existing financing arrangements were simply not able to cope with buyer and seller needs in an environment of rapidly increasing interest rates. Once the industry began viewing the real

TABLE 1. Buyer and Seller Schedules for Positively and Negatively Framed Negotiations

| | Seller | | | | | | Buyer | | | | | |
| | Net Profit | | | Expense[a] | | | Net Profit | | | Expense[a] | | |
Terms of Trade	Delivery Time	Discount Terms	Finance Terms	Delivery Time	Discount Terms	Finance Terms	Delivery Time	Discount Terms	Finance Terms	Delivery Time	Discount Terms	Finance Terms
A	$ 000	$ 000	$ 000	$−1,600	$−2,400	$−4,000	$4,000	$2,400	$1,600	$ 000	$ 000	$ 000
B	200	300	500	−1,400	−2,100	−3,500	3,500	2,100	1,400	−500	−300	−200
C	400	600	1,000	−1,200	−1,800	−3,000	3,000	1,800	1,200	−1,000	−600	−400
D	600	900	1,500	−1,000	−1,500	−2,500	2,500	1,500	1,000	−1,500	−900	−600
E	800	1,200	2,000	−800	−1,200	−2,000	2,000	1,200	800	−2,000	−1,200	−800
F	1,000	1,500	2,500	−600	−900	−1,500	1,500	900	600	−2,500	−1,500	−1,000
G	1,200	1,800	3,000	−400	−600	−1,000	1,000	600	400	−3,000	−1,800	−1,200
H	1,400	2,100	3,500	−200	−300	−500	500	300	200	−3,500	−2,100	−1,400
I	1,600	2,400	4,000	000	000	000	000	000	000	−4,000	−2,400	−1,600

Source: Bazerman, Magliozzi, and Neale 1985.
[a]Gross profit = $8,000.

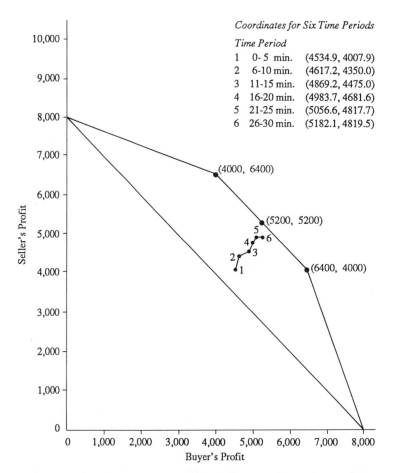

Fig. 1. Average profit for buyers and sellers of transactions completed in each five-minute segment of the market (aggregated across markets). (From Bazerman, Magliozzi, and Neale 1985.)

estate transaction as a potentially integrative process, the market began to move again. Specifically, sellers typically cared a great deal about price—partially to justify their past investment. Buyers, alternatively, cared about finding some way to afford the monthly payments on homes they aspired to own, perhaps even their first home. The answers to this bind were the wide variety of creative (integrative) financing arrangements that have become part of standard practice in the 1980s and 1990s (e.g., variable rate mortgages and seller financing). Creative financing integrated the interests of buyers and sellers, a process allowing sellers an artificially high price for their homes in exchange for favorable financing assistance for the buyer.

The Mythical Perception of Monolithic Action

Negotiators are typically nonmonolithic, with different stakeholders having very different priorities. Each party may be comprised of people who are on the same side but whose values may differ sharply.

While the evaluation of the level of monolithic action of the other side is important, we typically simplify our attribution processes and place credit or blame for all actions with the leaders (Northcraft and Neale 1990a). We not only place responsibility with them for the actions of their followers, but also we assume that they had a direct hand in any action. This is true in the case of the Korean airliner going down from Soviet fire, where the U.S. government and press presented the situation as if the USSR was a monolithic actor. This was also true when the United States failed miserably in its foreign policy in Iran in the late 1970s because it did not understand the complexities of the Iranian government (Sick 1985; Bazerman and Sondak 1988). Finally, many Iranians acted as if the United States were a monolithic actor in 1988 in the Iranian response to the airbus disaster.

We not only make monolithic assumptions about the other side, but we also often fail to consider the activities of our own side. We tend to view our behavior as a monolithic enterprise. However, we often later find out that our head does not know what the body parts are doing. The recent Irangate fiasco has elements of this problem. This is simply a natural problem of negotiating in any complex, bureaucratic environment. However, ignoring this as a problem is the result of cognitive limitations in the decision-making process.

Why do we make these mistakes? Because it is very difficult to think through the multitude of possibilities that are developing within the other side or within your own side. It is cognitively easier to view them in a monolithic manner. We do not fully consider the complex patterns of cognitions in the development of a nation's policies. Rather, we make a simplified assumption that aids our ability to grasp the situation. Unfortunately, such assumptions can be very costly as a negotiation strategy.

Limited Perspective and Frame to the Problem

Creativity in competitive situations requires looking at the problem from new and different perspectives (Winklegren 1974). Based on Tversky and Kahneman's (1981) work on framing, Neale and Bazerman (1985) and Bazerman, Magliozzi, and Neale (1985a) found that the frame in which negotiators viewed a negotiation could have a dramatic effect on their negotiation behavior. Bazerman, Magliozzi, and Neale (1985) instructed positively framed negotiators to maximize net profit (listed in the net profit columns of table 1) and negatively framed negotiators to minimize expenses (listed in the expense columns of table 1). In the latter case, expenses were subtracted from gross profit, making the two frames equivalent. While both frames provided the same information, positively (gain) framed negotiators experienced the risk aversion necessary to have an incentive to compromise. This incentive to compromise led negotiators with a positive frame to (1) complete a larger number of transactions, and (2) obtain greater overall profitability than negotiators with a negative frame. However, negatively framed negotiators reached agreements of higher individual profit than positively framed negotiators, although they completed fewer transactions (Neale, Huber, and Northcraft 1987). Our general conclusion, consistent with that of Tversky and Kahneman (1981), is that a decision maker's cognitive frame can have an important impact on the decisions that he or she makes, and that this effect extends to environmentally rich domains such as negotiation.

The implications of the framing effect can be critically important in affecting the likelihood of a negotiated resolution. Both sides may talk in terms of the *loss* that they would suffer if they concede more. What happens if both parties begin to think in terms of the way that they argue their case to the opponent? The negotiators adopt a negative frame, become relatively more risk seeking, and are less likely to reach a negotiated agreement than if they had positive frames. Ideally, one would like to maintain a negative frame (to increase the value of one's own outcome if an agreement is reached) and negotiate with a positively framed opponent (to increase the probability of an agreement being reached).

The framing effect also suggests that *how* a negotiator frames information to an opponent can be critical to the decisions that the opponent makes in an uncertain environment. Framing is also important beyond the limited focus of Tversky and Kahneman's positive/negative frame distinction. There are a wide variety of frames that we create in negotiation. For example, we often limit our focus in negotiation, as a result of our need to simplify problems cognitively, and miss important elements that surround the negotiation. Thus, we are likely to ignore the importance of linkage effects. This can be seen in the following example: Our boss does not give us a raise, despite our threat to leave. We are convinced that the organization needs us more than it needs to save the salary differential. However, the real reason for the boss's intransigence may be that, to grant our request, the organization will be subject to a wide range of salary requests, destroying the internal equity that currently exists. Without understanding this explanation, we may be very frustrated and leave the organization—an action that may not be in our own best interest.

This psychological tendency to ignore linkage effects is in direct contrast to Raiffa's advice: "One must be aware of the intricacies caused by linkages and, to put it more positively, one must use linkage possibilities to break impasses in negotiation. This is not done creatively enough in most disputes"

(1982, 13). We agree with Raiffa's advice and his awareness of the fact that most parties do not give sufficient attention to linkage effects. We offer the psychological aspects of framing as a viable cognitive description of why negotiators fall into this irrational course of action. The relevance of linkage effects is developed in more detail in the chapter by Lax and Sebenius in this volume.

Overall, this section has described a variety of biases that create important limitations in creating an accurate descriptive model. In the next section, we explicitly address the implications of prescriptive models for developing better descriptions and explore the relevance of these descriptions for developing better prescriptions.

How Do Prescriptive Models Help Us Describe Negotiation Behavior?

Description for the sake of description is a worthy scientific objective. However, well-executed descriptive research does not necessarily produce a *useful* scientific contribution. While not all research need be immediately useful, we believe that applicability is a valued attribute of an optimal descriptive model of negotiation research. This implies that the description should lead to obvious directions for negotiator improvement. We argued earlier that much of the descriptive research in negotiation prior to 1980 lacked this quality. While earlier descriptive research attempted to provide insight to negotiators, it did so in a vacuum. That is, the descriptions lacked any clear direction for self-improvement. The negotiator did not know whether changing a particular tactic would lead to an improvement in current or future negotiated outcomes.

The primary contribution that prescriptive models make is to provide a goal and benchmark to evaluate the importance of related descriptive research. Within the context of negotiation, Raiffa's prescriptive model identifies an important dyadic-level outcome—a Pareto-efficient solution of the dispute. Such an outcome is based upon the rational behavior of the disputants. That is, they make a decision or set of decisions that maximizes their individual expected utilities. By having such an a priori target, the task of identifying behaviors that are inconsistent with this goal (such as ignoring the cognitions of others) and developing prescriptions to counter these dysfunctional cognitive tendencies (negotiators should change their decision making to fully consider the cognitions of the opponent) is made more concrete.

The importance of coupling prescriptive and descriptive research for the practitioner becomes more salient when examining the application of descriptive research alone. Consider the options open to a negotiator upon learning that he or she scores highly on an internal (or external) locus of control scale. Such information suggests little in the way of specific behavioral intervention.

In contrast, both having the goal of reaching a Pareto-optimal agreement that is favorable on the distributive dimension and using this goal as a benchmark to evaluate the effectiveness of behavioral strategies augment the attractiveness of the research for researchers and practitioners alike. The goal of a favorable Pareto-optimal agreement has had a unique impact on the growth and expansion of the behavioral decision area (Kahneman, Slovic, and Tversky 1982). This literature has focused on how decisions deviate from rationality, identifying the specific changes that would improve an individual's decisions. Such benefits are only beginning to accrue to descriptive models of negotiation.

The benchmark of rationality in prescriptive models can be the basis for evaluating whether or not negotiators improve over time and learn from experience. A fundamental debate existed in the decision research community over whether deviations from rationality exist as minor quirks that disappear in real markets or whether they represent lasting limitations to rational decision making. This debate also exists in the competitive context. For example, Kagel and Levin (1986), in their analysis of the winner's curse in an auction context, argued:

> Given sufficient experience and feedback regarding the outcomes of their decisions, we have no doubt that our experimental subjects, as well as bidders in "real world" settings, would eventually learn to avoid the winner's curse in any particular set of circumstances. The winner's curse is a disequilibrium phenomenon that will correct itself given sufficient time and the right kind of information feedback. (917)

Consistent with this argument, Kagel and Levin (1986) show a reduction in the winner's curse in the auction context as "the market" learns over time. Some of this learning occurs through the disappearance of the most aggressive bidders from the market. Additional learning occurs through the observation of consistent losses suffered by the "winners" in the auctions.

Undoubtedly, people learn many things through their experiences in life. However, the case regarding judgmental distortions is less clear. Tversky and Kahneman (1986) have argued that biases are unlikely to be corrected in the real world because learning requires accurate and immediate feedback that is rarely available because:

> . . . (i) outcomes are commonly delayed and not easily attributable to a particular action; (ii) variability in the environment degrades the reliability of feedback . . . ; (iii) there is often no information about what the outcome would have been if another decision had been taken; and (iv) most important decisions are unique and therefore provide little oppor-

tunity for learning . . . any claim that a particular error will be eliminated by experience must be supported by demonstrating that the conditions for effective learning are satisfied. (274–75)

In an examination of learning to avoid the winner's curse in the Acquiring a Company problem, Ball, Bazerman, and Carroll (1991) used a repeated trial version of the game. Subjects were playing for real money, they played twenty times, full feedback was provided immediately after each trial (based on a random determination of the value of the firm), and subjects could observe changes in their asset balance (which virtually always decreased over time). Thus, the ideal conditions existed for learning according to the suggestions of Tversky and Kahneman (1986). Only 5 of 72 subjects from a leading MBA program learned. Our general conclusion is that a variety of the biases that affect negotiators are not fully eliminated by experience or feedback. This conclusion is supported across a variety of biases and in empirical work across a number of contexts in the research of Neale and Northcraft (1990b).

It is easy to see that this debate about the *description* of how competitive actors actually behave could not exist without prescriptive models for defining rationality as the goal that all negotiators should be striving toward. More generally, we argue that the most powerful and useful descriptions need a prescriptive anchor to provide clear specifications of the actual decisions and behaviors of negotiators.

A common claim from the economic side of the negotiation literature is that the use of rational models is the best existing complete theory of decision making, and that we should not throw out rational models as descriptive models until we have a replacement. In a Kuhnian (1970) sense, this argument suggests that we are in the middle of a paradigmatic revolution, and the rational model stays in power until a legitimate successor is provided. We do not accept this argument. First, we do not expect a full replacement theory to develop that includes corrections for all of the systematic deficiencies that have been identified in the rational model. To the extent that one can be developed, it will end up being less specific in making clear predictions (e.g., March and Simon's [1958] concept of bounded rationality). Rather, what is offered from behavioral decision theory is a set of adjustments that must be made to rational models to improve their predictive power. A model that adjusts the basic rational model and incorporates known systematic biases offers a better description of actual behavior than the rational model operating alone. This follows in March and Simon's (1958) tradition of realizing that while decision makers try to be rational, they are limited by a variety of cognitive constraints. Behavioral research is only beginning to identify these constraints.

How Do Descriptive Models Improve
Our Prescriptions?

We have often been asked what we try to teach students in our MBA elective course on negotiation—sometimes by the students in the class. Our answer is that we have three goals. First, we want the students to learn to think about the negotiation problem prescriptively with respect to their own behavior, and descriptively with respect to the other's behavior. Second, we hope they develop psychological skills in assessing the likely behavior of the opponent. Third, we want them to identify and counteract the forces that keep negotiators from acting rationally. As a result, we spend most of our time focusing on ways to improve the students' psychological assessment of an opponent and to identify and overcome barriers (biases) that might prevent them from following prescriptive advice.

Raiffa suggests that we must consider the actual decisions of the other side. But precisely what should we expect from the other side? Ideally, a theory that predicts the opponent's behavior, with the necessary specification of the risk surrounding this assessment, would be very attractive. However, as we have argued above, such a theory does not exist and is unlikely to exist in the foreseeable future. Rather, we can identify what we do know about the information that we have about the other, and start by addressing what a rational model would suggest about his or her future behaviors. In addition, we can do a "judgmental limitation audit." Our overview of biased negotiator information processing begins to specify a variety of deviations from rationality that can be anticipated in the opponent's decision making. As descriptive research completes this list, prescribers of good advice must evaluate the degree to which each of these biases can be expected in the decisions of the other party. A laundry list approach to considering how the other side might deviate from rationality offers an improvement over the rationality assumption that governs many existing prescriptive models.

The other contribution of descriptive research to a prescriptive approach is that it provides necessary information on impediments to an individual's attempt to follow a rational course of action. An important element of the biased decision processes discussed earlier is that each follows a degree of "naive" rationality; that is, they follow a train of thought that many people would see as rational (e.g., consider the naive logic to the Acquiring a Company example). Thus, giving recommendations based on the assumption that a negotiator will follow rational advice may assume a variety of naturally occurring rational processes. A parallel example of this problem occurs in accounting, where instructors tell students that ignoring sunk cost is a rational manner to analyze problems. This advice lasts until the next exam. However, when the student is confronted with an escalation problem that involves sunk costs in a future course, the accounting professor's message is often long forgotten or not generalized to a nonaccounting situation.

A fundamental description of actual negotiator behavior is that individuals have a variety of natural ways of doing things, and that prescriptive advice must overcome these "hardwired" cognitive biases. Research suggests that debiasing is very difficult (Fischhoff 1982; Carroll et al. 1989). However, many years ago, Lewin (1947) gave us some very good advice on changing behavior. He suggested that telling people the changes that must be made is not sufficient to create change in most contexts because the status quo behaviors have become too well ingrained in the target's behavioral repertoire. Rather, added steps are needed. Specifically, Lewin's "unfreezing-change-refreezing" model suggests that targets must first be unfrozen from their past behavior—they must see something wrong with their current thought processes and resulting outcomes. Only then can one successfully impose the prescriptive model. Finally, the new behaviors must become practiced and reinforced. The important aspect of this model is that the results of behavioral research are critical in convincing students of their current limitations, before we can expect them to adopt more rational models. Thus, a healthy dose of descriptive decision theory and demonstrating to students that they are affected by these biases may be the beginning necessary to inculcate the prescriptive approaches to negotiation.

REFERENCES

Applebaum, A. 1987. "Knowledge and Negotiation: Learning under Conflict, Bargaining under Uncertainty." Ph.D. diss. Harvard University.
Ball, S. B., M. H. Bazerman, and J. S. Carroll. 1991. "An Evaluation of Learning in the Bilateral Winner's Curse Game." *Organizational Behavior and Human Decision Processes* 48:1–22.
Bazerman, M. H. 1983. "Negotiator Judgment: A Critical Look at the Rationality Assumption." *American Behavioral Scientists* 27:618–34.
Bazerman, M. H. 1986. *Judgment in Managerial Decision Making*. New York: Wiley.
Bazerman, M. H., and J. S. Carroll. 1987. "Negotiator Cognition." In *Research in Organizational Behavior*. Vol. 9, ed. B. M. Staw and L. L. Cummings. Greenwich, Conn.: JAI Press.
Bazerman, M. H., T. Giuliano, and A. Appleman. 1984. "Escalation in Individual and Group Decision Making." *Organizational Behavior and Human Performance* 33:141–52.
Bazerman, M. H., T. Magliozzi, and M. A. Neale. 1985. "Integrative Bargaining in a Competitive Market." *Organizational Behavior and Human Performance* 34:294–313.

Bazerman, M. H., and M. A. Neale. 1983. "Heuristics in Negotiation: Limitations to Dispute Resolution Effectiveness." In *Negotiation in Organizations,* ed. M. H. Bazerman and R. J. Lewicki. Beverly Hills: Sage.

Bazerman, M. H., and W. F. Samuelson. 1983. "I Won the Auction but Don't Want the Prize." *Journal of Conflict Resolution* 27:618–34.

Bazerman, M. H., and H. Sondak. 1988. "Judgmental Limitations in Diplomatic Negotiations." *Negotiation Journal* 4:303–17.

Brockner, J., and J. Z. Rubin. 1985. *Entrapment in Escalating Conflicts.* New York: Springer-Verlag.

Capen, E. C., R. V. Clapp, and W. M. Campbell. 1971. "Competitive Bidding in High Risk Situations." *Journal of Petroleum Technology* 23:641–53.

Carroll, J. S., M. H. Bazerman, and R. Maury. 1988. "Negotiator Cognitions: A Descriptive Approach to Negotiators' Understanding of Their Opponents." *Organizational Behavior and Human Decision Processes* 41:352–70.

Carroll, J. S., P. Delquie, J. Halpern, and M. H. Bazerman. 1989. "Improving Negotiators' Cognitive Processes." MIT. Working paper. Typescript.

Cassing, J., and R. W. Douglas. 1980. "Implications of the Auction Mechanism in Baseball's Free Agent Draft." *Southern Economic Journal* 47:110–21.

Cross, J. 1969. *The Economics of Bargaining.* New York: Basic Books.

Dawes, R. M. 1988. *Rational Choice in an Uncertain World.* New York: Harcourt Brace Jovanovich.

Einhorn, H., and R. M. Hogarth. 1978. "Confidence in Judgment: Persistence of the Illusion of Validity." *Psychological Review* 85:395–416.

Farber, H. S. 1981. "Splitting the Difference in Interest Arbitration." *Industrial and Labor Relations Review* 35:70–77.

Fischhoff, B. 1981. "Debiasing." In *Judgment under Uncertainty: Heuristics and Biases,* ed. D. Kahneman, P. Slovic, and A. Tversky. New York: Cambridge University Press.

Fischhoff, B. 1982. "Latitudes and Platitudes: How Much Credit Do People Deserve?" In *New Directions in Decision Making,* ed. G. Ungson and D. Braunstein. New York: Kent.

Kagel, J. H., and D. Levin. 1986. "The Winner's Curse and Public Information in Common Value Auctions." *American Economics Review* 76:894–920.

Kahneman, D., P. Slovic, and A. Tversky, eds. 1982. *Judgment under Uncertainty: Heuristics and Biases.* Cambridge: Cambridge University Press.

Kochan, T. A. 1980. "Collective Bargaining and Organizational Behavior Research." In *Research in Organizational Behavior.* Vol. 2, ed. B. M. Staw and L. L. Cummings. Greenwich, Conn.: JAI Press.

Kochan, T. A., and M. H. Bazerman. 1986. "Macro Determinants of the Future of the Study of Negotiations in Organizations." In *Research in Negotiation in Organizations.* Vol. 1, ed. R. J. Lewicki, B. Sheppard, and M. H. Bazerman. Greenwich, Conn.: JAI Press.

Kuhn, T. S. 1970. *The Structure of Scientific Revolutions.* 2d rev. ed. Chicago: University of Chicago Press.

Lax, D. A., and J. K. Sebenius. 1986. *The Manager as Negotiator: Bargaining for Cooperation and Competitive Gain.* New York: Free Press.

Lewin, K. 1947. "Group Decision and Social Change." In *Readings in Social Psychology,* ed. T. M. Newcomb and E. L. Hartley. New York: Holt, Rinehart, and Winston.

McAlister, L., M. H. Bazerman, and P. Fader. 1986. "Power and Goal Setting in Channel Negotiations." *Journal of Marketing Research* 23:228–36.

March, J. G., and H. A. Simon. 1958. *Organizations.* New York: Wiley.

Myerson, R. B., and M. A. Satterthwaite. 1983. "Efficient Mechanisms for Bilateral Trading." *Journal of Economic Theory* 29:265–81.

Nash, J. 1950. "The Bargaining Problem." *Econometrica* 18:128–40.

Neale, M. A., and M. H. Bazerman. 1985a. "The Effect of Framing and Negotiator Overconfidence on Bargainer Behavior." *Academy of Management Journal* 28:34–49.

Neale, M. A., and M. H. Bazerman. 1985b. "When Will Externally Set Aspiration Levels Improve Negotiator Performance? A Look at Integrative Behavior in a Competitive Market." *Journal of Occupational Behavior* 6:19–32.

Neale, M. A., and M. H. Bazerman. 1991. *Cognition and Rationality in Negotiation.* New York: Free Press.

Neale, M. A., V. L. Huber, and G. B. Northcraft. 1987. "The Framing of Negotiation: Context versus Task Frames." *OBHDP* 39:228–41.

Neale, M. A., and G. B. Northcraft. 1990a. "Behavioral Negotiation Theory: A Framework for Conceptualizing Dyadic Negotiation." In *Research in Organizational Behavior,* ed. L. L. Cummings and B. M. Staw. Greenwich, Conn.: JAI Press. Forthcoming.

Neale, M. A., and G. B. Northcraft. 1990b. "Experience, Expertise, and Decision Bias in Negotiation: The Role of Strategic Conceptualization." In *Research on Negotiating in Organizations,* ed. B. Sheppard, M. H. Bazerman, and R. J. Lewicki. Greenwich, Conn.: JAI Press.

Nisbett, R. E., and L. Ross. 1982. *Human Inference: Strategies and Shortcomings of Social Judgment.* Englewood Cliffs, N.J.: Prentice-Hall.

Northcraft, G. B., and M. A. Neale. 1990. *Organizational Behavior: A Managerial Challenge.* Hinsdale, Ill.: Dryden Press.

Pruitt, D. G. 1981. *Negotiation Behavior.* New York: Academic Press.

Pruitt, D. G., and J. Z. Rubin. 1986. *Social Conflict: Escalation, Impasse, and Resolution.* Reading, Mass.: Addison-Wesley.

Raiffa, H. R. 1982. *The Art and Science of Negotiation.* Cambridge, Mass.: Belknap Press.

Roll, R. 1986. "The Hubris Hypothesis of Corporate Takeovers." *Journal of Business* 59:197–216.

Rubin, J. Z. 1980. "Experimental Research on Third-Party Intervention in Conflict: Toward Some Generalization." *Psychological Bulletin* 87:379–91.

Rubin, J. Z., and B. R. Brown. 1975. *The Social Psychology of Bargaining and Negotiation.* New York: Academic Press.

Samuelson, W. F., and M. H. Bazerman. 1985. "Negotiating under the Winner's Curse." In *Research in Experimental Economics.* Vol. 3, ed. V. Smith. Greenwich, Conn.: JAI Press.

Shubik, M. 1971. "The Dollar Auction Game: A Paradox in Noncooperative Behavior and Escalation." *Journal of Conflict Resolution* 15:109–11.

Sick, G. 1985. *All Fall Down.* New York: Penguin Books.

Smith, V. 1982. "Microeconomic Systems as an Experimental Science." *American Economic Review* 72:923–55.

Staw, B. M. 1976. "Knee Deep in the Big Muddy: A Study of Escalating Commitment to a Chosen Course of Action." *Organizational Behavior and Human Performance* 16:27–44.

Teger, A. I. 1980. *Too Much Invested to Quit.* New York: Pergamon Press.

Tversky, A., and D. Kahneman. 1981. "The Framing of Decisions and the Psychology of Choice." *Science* 211:453–58.

Tversky, A., and D. Kahneman. 1986. "Rational Choice and the Framing of Decisions." *Journal of Business* 59:251–84.

Winklegren, W. A. 1974. *How to Solve Problems.* San Francisco: Free Press.

Zeuthen, F. 1930. *Problems of Monopoly and Economic Welfare.* London: George Routledge and Sons.

CHAPTER 7

Structuring and Analyzing Values for Multiple-Issue Negotiations

Ralph L. Keeney and Howard Raiffa

In complex negotiations with multiple issues, each party is faced with vexing value trade-offs: how much to give up in terms of one issue in order to obtain a specified gain in another issue. We will demonstrate how analysis can provide insights to negotiators in such situations, addressing both the qualitative and quantitative aspects of such analyses and focusing on what should be done, how to do it, and what should be learned in the effort.

We begin by examining a problem that has already been prestructured as follows: (*a*) the parties have jointly agreed upon the issues to be negotiated and on the possible resolution levels for each issue; (*b*) each side is given a confidential additive scoring system over these issues; and (*c*) each side has already scored its best alternative to a negotiated agreement (BATNA). The parties are then asked to negotiate a compromise agreement that is mutually acceptable. Using this format, it is pedagogically convenient to investigate negotiation tactics, the sharing and withholding (and perhaps distorting) of information, and efficiency and equity concerns.

We next examine when it is appropriate to use additive scoring systems, how to cope with nonadditivity, how to identify and score a BATNA, and how computer aids can be used to mediate or arbitrate such disputes and to jointly improve a nonefficient negotiated outcome.

We then back up to consider how the issues to be negotiated are chosen. These issues are of relevance because they are related to the underlying fundamental interests of the parties. The theory of multiattribute value and utility can help structure these underlying fundamental interests and this structure has three purposes: (1) to help the parties select the issues to be negotiated, (2) to help a party to better quantify his or her preferences over the resolutions of the issues, and (3) to provide guidance for negotiator decisions that must be made about the process and substance of the negotiation.

Work on this chapter was supported, in part, by National Science Foundation Grant No. SES-8809129.

131

In the closing section, we provide some guidance for the role and style of analysis that we believe is useful in negotiations. It concludes that systematic qualitative structuring of values can have huge payoffs and that a bit of quantitative thinking about value trade-offs can sharpen these qualitative insights.

Basic Analysis for Multiple-Issue Negotiations

Let us identify with party A, who is in a dispute with party B. There could be additional parties, but we prefer to keep it simple, though complicated enough to clarify some complexities. Also suppose (naively and, admittedly, counter to common practice) that A and B, in a prenegotiation session, have brainstormed without commitment, have shared their interests with each other, and have identified ten (any other specific number will do) issues $(I_1, I_2, \ldots, I_{10})$ that need to be resolved. Furthermore, assume that, for each issue, A and B have unambiguously stipulated a set of possible resolution levels. Ultimately, in a later negotiation session, the task will be for the two of them to select a particular resolution level for each of the ten issues under consideration. Hence, we can identify a final compromise agreement with the joint selection of a given level on each issue. At this stage, we explicitly assume that all inventing and *creating of issues*[1] and options have occurred. The task is purposefully restricted.

Preparation for Negotiation

What should A do in preparation for later negotiation? When he[2] starts negotiating, he might want to have a wish list or an aspiration list ready for the joint resolution of issues, but his counterpart might force him to make some tough value trade-offs. During the negotiations, she might say something like: "I'll move from level d on issue 5 to level c as you want, if you'll go from b to c on issue 4 and g to h on issue 7."

So in preparing for negotiations, A had better *sort out* his *preferences*. We choose notation that, for each issue, orders the resolution levels alphabetically and in decreasing preference for A. Thus, on an issue with four levels, A prefers a to b to c to d. The number of possible ways of choosing one resolution for each of the issues is the product of the number of levels for each of the ten issues. With our convention, A would most prefer level a on

---

1. Italics in the text of this section indicate a topic related to the assumptions in the basic analysis that is examined in the next section.

2. Let party A be male and party B be female; a negotiation session will be between "him" and "her." With this convention, we can use the personal pronouns to identify the parties.

each of the ten issues. But, of course, B will deem this outcome totally unacceptable; otherwise there would be little need for a negotiation.

What else? The recommendation is often proffered that not only should A rank the prespecified levels for each issue, but he should order the issues themselves by importance. In a labor negotiation, is salary more important than number of vacation days? Operationally, many individuals feel comfortable *ranking the issues* to be resolved according to their importance. But often when this is done, a common mistake is made. If we are talking about a range of possible salaries that is very small and a range of vacation days that is very large, then the issue of vacation days may be more important than the issue of salary. The decision whether one issue, X, should get more weight than another issue, Y, in an overall scoring system should not be divorced from the ranges in the levels of resolution for the two issues. Adding a more diverse and extensive list of possible levels on issue X should raise the importance of X in comparison to the other issues.

As a consultant to party A, we now have ranked the possible prespecified levels of resolution for each issue and, keeping in mind the ranges on each issue, we have ranked the importance of each issue. Now what else? During the course of negotiations, A might be asked to give up something on issue X for something on Y. In preparation for negotiation, he needs to be clear about such trade-offs. Let us draw an analogy to a teacher who has to grade an exam involving ten questions on the basis of 100 points. The teacher may choose to sprinkle these 100 points among the ten questions, giving one question a potential total of 20 points and another only 5 points because of the relative importance of the two questions. Then the teacher might assign partial scores depending on the answer to each question. Finally, the grader will add up the scores over all ten questions to determine an overall grade. We could help A do an analogous additive scoring that will, among other things, help him to be precise about value trade-offs across issues. It is additive because we add up the scores over the issues.

Best Alternative to a Negotiated Agreement

Keeping with our analogy, the teacher might have to decide whether or not to pass or fail the student. On the basis of a number of considerations, the teacher might establish a cutoff grade: below the cutoff means failure; above means pass. Just so with negotiator A. He might establish a cutoff score for acceptance of an agreement: below the cutoff means no agreement; above the cutoff means an acceptable agreement. Our client A not only wants to jump over his cutoff hurdle, but to soar over it and he may not want to disclose just how high this hurdle actually is to B. The determination of this cutoff requires a major piece of preparation for A because it involves reflecting deeply about the *best alternative to a negotiated agreement*—the so-called BATNA—and *scoring that BATNA* on the 100 point additive scale evaluating the ten issues.

Let us suppose the BATNA is scored at 60 points. A lot of deep analysis might have gone into that evaluation. The best alternative to an agreement might involve many issues not considered in the negotiation and myriad uncertainties over time because outcomes may not be fully under A's control. In reality, a BATNA will not be given to A on a silver platter; before entering into negotiations with B, he will have to work hard to identify his BATNA and he may have to be creative and entrepreneurial in searching for ways to improve his BATNA—for example, by creating new alternatives. The methodology of decision analysis can be helpful in identifying and evaluating a BATNA (see, for example, Raiffa 1982). The better his BATNA, the more demanding he can be with B. By improving his BATNA, he will improve his power in negotiation by having less to lose if no agreement is reached.

Before exploring some reasonable complications to this simplified model (e.g., what if an additive scoring is not appropriate, or what if A is not monolithic and A cannot make up its collective mind, or what if the resolution levels on a given issue involve exogenous uncertainties), let us proceed with this comparatively simple story.

Consideration of the Other Side's Interests

Before going into negotiations, A should also do some homework about his perceptions of B's preferences, value trade-offs, and BATNA. He should *structure the other side's values* and opportunities, which should affect his strategy for negotiation. But A's perceptions about B's values and opportunities should not be hard and fast, they should include any uncertainties in A's judgments about B's circumstances and adaptively change as the real negotiation proceeds.

Courses in negotiation often feature role playing in negotiation exercises. Many of these exercises involve so-called scorable games, as in this typical example. Alba and Belga are two nations with a territorial dispute. In prenegotiations, technical teams have structured a template that identifies a specific set of issues to be resolved (say ten) and, under each issue, a specific set of possible resolution levels. Each side is given the description of this template. Then, each side is given its own confidential additive scoring system, a confidential cutoff score corresponding to its BATNA, and some vague information about the interests and possible BATNA alternatives of the other side. Suppose Alba and Belga, after a lot of give-and-take, settle for an agreement that yields a score of 70 for Alba and 58 for Belga. Since the negotiation is now over and an agreement is reached, an obvious question to many is: Who won the negotiation? There are several ways to address this; let us consider two.

First, both Alba and Belga won. They jointly reached an agreement that presumably is better than each negotiator's BATNA. Hence, they are both better off than would be the case if no agreement were reached. But there is a tendency to say that Alba won the negotiation since its score was 70 while Belga scored only 58. This somewhat intuitively appealing conclusion is, simply, wrong. Suppose the extreme case where Alba's BATNA was 60 and Belga's BATNA was 10. The relative power (in terms of BATNAs) apparently rested with Alba and yet Alba only exceeded its BATNA by 10 points, whereas Belga exceeded its BATNA by 48 points. With this information, it appears as if Belga won.

Consider the same situation, but now assume that the BATNAs for both Alba and Belga have been independently evaluated to be 50. Now it seems as if Alba has "won" on two counts: (1) its score is higher than Belga's (70 to 58), and (2) Alba's 20 point excess over its BATNA is higher than Belga's 8 point excess over its BATNA. The issue is, in part, whether these 20 points to Alba are more important than the 8 points to Belga. This brings up the notion of interpersonal comparison of preferences that has intrigued economists for quite some time (see, for example, Luce and Raiffa 1957). We will not resolve this general problem here, but just suppose that the best agreement for Belga, scoring 100 on its scale, was practically nirvana. And suppose 100 on Alba's scale was just "reasonably better" than its BATNA of 50. Again, the jump from Belga's BATNA of 50 to 58 may be more significant than Alba's jump from 50 to 70, so you may conclude that Belga "won."

Two comments emerge from this discussion. First, unlike games of chance and athletic events, the notion of a winner and a loser in a negotiation does not correspond to the true negotiation situation. Second, because one rarely would have crucial information about BATNA's and scoring systems of all parties in real negotiations, after-the-fact appraisal of the negotiators' performances is very difficult. Still, some insights can be gained about this topic.

Suppose, in a class of 100 students, that 50 negotiating pairs are assigned the case of Alba and Belga. Suppose that each Alba-Belga pair starts off with identical confidential instructions on additive scoring rules and BATNA values. And further suppose that pair 1 comes to an agreement that yields Alba a score of 70 and Belga a score of 58. But there are 49 other pairs and if most of the other role-playing Albas did better than 70, then we could conclude that, relative to other negotiators, Alba in pair 1 did not do well. It is instructive in the debriefing of such a class exercise to realize that, although Alba and Belga came to an acceptable agreement (such as point *P* in fig. 1),

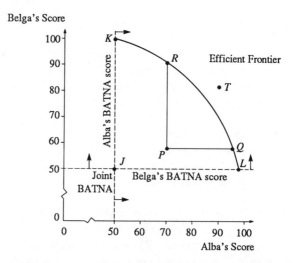

Fig. 1. Joint evaluations of negotiated outcomes. The point _J_ represents the BATNA scores of Alba and Belga. In this example, they are each 50, but, in general, the BATNA scores may be different. Point _P_ represents the outcome of one pair of negotiators where Alba scores 70 and Belga scores 58. Points to the northeast of the Efficient Frontier (along _L, Q, R, K_) are not achievable. A point such as _R_ on the frontier is efficient in the sense that either party can improve only at the expense of the other party.

they left possible joint gains on the table. Indeed, Alba could have moved from _P_ to _Q_ without hurting Belga, and Belga could have moved from _P_ to _R_ without hurting Alba. Of course, the negotiators for each side, each being given only one set of confidential instructions, cannot compute the *efficient frontier* by themselves.[3] The teacher or the designer of the simulated exercise, knowing both sets of confidential instructions, can find the efficient frontier. There are computer aids to help with this task. The negotiators could also collectively pool their information and jointly compute the frontier. But should they? Should they also disclose their BATNA values? Alternatively, they could disclose some or all of their confidential material to a third party or an analytically inclined mediator who could perform the calculations. But once again, should they? And if they do, how truthful should they be? There are no hard and fast answers to these questions. It depends on context, on future relationships, on postnegotiation leaks and verification, on the dynamics of the prenegotiations, and on earlier negotiations.

---

3. The efficient frontier is the set of pairs of scores for Alba and Belga such that neither score can be improved without lowering the other score.

Postsettlement Joint Improvements

In a paper on postsettlement settlements, Raiffa (1985) points out that parties might choose not to disclose their full confidential information until after they have come to an agreement. Only after that, might they be willing to employ a third party (a contract embellisher) who would investigate the potential for additional joint gains. Alternatively, we could dispense with this embellisher and ask the parties to enter their confidential scoring systems and existing agreement point directly into a specially designed computer software package that will process the information and report to them.

Yes, you both achieved more than your BATNA scores, but joint gains are still possible. I (i.e., the computer) could do the following for you:

(*a*) I could suggest a set of issues that you should resolve differently in order for both of you to improve your scores. (Option *a* can be iterated.)

(*b*) I could compute the part of the efficient boundary that jointly dominates your agreement contract and disclose it to you.

(*c*) I, acting as an arbitrator, could suggest a joint (arbitrated) contract on the efficient boundary that jointly dominates your agreement contract.

(*d*) I could ask you for logical guidelines to be followed in selecting a new contract that would jointly dominate your agreement contract.

The parties, of course, could employ the postsettlement computer program by jointly entering the joint BATNA point—point J in figure 1—instead of an actual agreement, P. For option c, the parties could voluntarily decide to bind themselves to accept the proposed arbitrated contract, or they might wish to view the computer's proposal as merely a suggestion.

For the computer to choose an arbitrated point on the efficient segment from R to Q in figure 1 (assuming P is the agreement point to be jointly dominated), the computer must invoke some fairness principle. Two prominent contenders are the Nash point or the Raiffa (Kalai-Smordinsky) point (see Raiffa 1982, chap. 16). If we want to gild the lily, the parties might wish to specify one particular fairness principle rather than leaving it to a default option in the computer.

When scorable games are used for instructional purposes, it is customary to prespecify the negotiation templates (i.e., the set of issues and the possible levels of resolution for each issue) as well as the confidential scoring rules for each role player. But after the appropriate lessons are learned, it is now possible to back up: give the players a negotiation template but not the additive scoring rules, and let them develop their own additive scoring rules. Each negotiator will enter his or her confidential set of scores into the computer. For each pair of negotiators, the computer will then compute the efficient frontier that dominates their joint agreement point and be prepared to give the feedback shown in options *a* to *d*.

We can back up even further and let the role players develop their own negotiation template based on some qualitative, unstructured information given to the players. They now decide the issues and the possible resolutions on each issue. Before backing up even one step earlier, we will pause to comment on the appropriateness or inappropriateness of the additive scoring system.

Appropriateness of the Additive Scoring System

Once again, let us return to the case where we sprinkle 100 points of total value over ten issues and add up the partial scores for each player as a function of the agreement that is jointly chosen. *When is the additive scoring system legitimate?* It certainly would not be legitimate if the value we want to associate with a given resolution on one issue depends on the particular resolution of another issue, or if the relative importance of two issues depends on the levels chosen for still other issues. In these interdependent cases, an additive scoring system would not be appropriate. Keeney and Raiffa (1976), among others, have shown that an additive scoring system is appropriate if and only if the value trade-offs between any two issues do not depend on the levels chosen on the remaining issues. The appropriateness of the additive scoring system is also discussed in Raiffa (1982). But suffice it to say that there will be many cases where strict additivity does not apply. Our purpose now is twofold: (1) to talk about the case of almost-additivity, and (2) to point out that not all is lost if we have to resort to nonadditive scaling. In fact, in the more complex world where additivity does not seem appropriate, a little thoughtful analysis can often provide more useful insights than in the simpler additive case.

Let's imagine that value trade-offs between issues 1 and 2 depend on the level of resolution on issue 3, but that the value trade-offs among issues 1, 2, and 3 do not depend on issues 4 to 10. In technical parlance, we would say that the set of issues $\{1,2,3\}$ is preferentially independent of issues $\{4, \ldots, 10\}$. Because of this preferential dependence within the set of issues $\{1,2,3\}$, however, we will not be able to achieve an additive scoring system over the set $\{1,2,3,4, \ldots, 10\}$. But we may be able to define a new composite issue X that comprises issues $\{1,2,3\}$ and achieve additivity across the redefined set of issues $\{X,4,5, \ldots, 10\}$. It is like the teacher who refuses to score test questions 1, 2, and 3 separately but gives a "gestalt grade" to those questions collectively, and then proceeds as before to add this collective score to the scores on questions 4 through 10. We can think of this as an additive scoring procedure on eight independent questions.

The point of all this is that additivity makes life especially simple and, if violated, it can sometimes be artificially reinstated. The method we have demonstrated shows how we can accommodate some simple dependencies. There are other ways to *convert nonadditivity to additivity,* like redefining the set of issues. For example, if one issue is compensation to beginning workers and another issue is compensation to senior workers, and if there is a concern for balance and equity between the resolutions on these two issues, we might redefine the issues by considering (1) average compensation and (2) the spread of compensation between beginning and older workers. With this redefinition of issues, it might be more plausible to justify the additivity assumption.

But now let us suppose life is just more complicated and, no matter how hard we try, we cannot justify an additive scoring system. Nevertheless, we can associate a total score to each possible contract that specifies how each of the ten issues is to be resolved. The recipe or function is no longer additive with simple pluses and minuses, but it includes multiplicative aspects (doing well on issue 2 is extra important if we do poorly on issue 1), minimum and maximum requirements on issues, and if-statements sprinkled all over. The analyst must now give more intricate instructions to the computer in order for the computer to find the efficient frontier that jointly dominates some specified point like *P* in figure 1. Still, it can be done when the efficiency of the computer is coupled with sophisticated numerical analysis. Conceptually, the results of analysis without additivity are little different from the results of analysis with the additivity assumption that is glibly assumed in simple text-book examples.

There is one violation of additivity that deserves special attention because it arises so often in practice. This complication involves the specification of minimum levels of achievement on separate issues as well as on the composite agreement. Suppose, for example, that you are the agent of A and you are told, not only do you need 60 points overall (your BATNA value), but you cannot accept any resolution below level *c* on issue 2 or below *d* on issue 7. In other words, you are instructed to impose a reservation cutoff level of *c* on issue 2 and *d* on issue 7. With the levels on issue 2 restricted to *a, b,* and *c,* and on issue 7 to *a, b, c,* and *d,* then once again you might look for an additive scale on the restricted domain. It is not additive over the full domain because you are effectively scoring level *d* on issue 2, or *e* on issue 7, with a minus infinity value. But still, the problem is analytically tractable.

Internal Equity and Hierarchical Negotiations

Should reservation levels be imposed on individual issues as well as on the overall composite score? It is not hard to imagine how, in practice, such reservation levels on individual issues might arise. Imagine that player A is not monolithic, but comprises a group of subplayers A_1, A_2, and A_3, and A_2 is guardian of the interests revolving around issue 2. Individual A_2 absolutely insists that no contract with B be agreed upon that will result in a resolution level below c on issue 2, or else . . . Or else A_2 will quit the team and try to sabotage the deal. Actually, A_2 could live with level d on issue 2, but he might exaggerate his claim by opting for a cutoff of c rather than d. And so it goes with other advocates of special interests within the A team. The rub is that when these restrictions are pooled, there may be little room for external negotiator A to maneuver, and potential joint gains may not be realizable. A little analysis may again help in this situation. By showing subplayers what they potentially lose by demanding reservation levels on individual issues, the subplayers may conclude either that the loss is not worth the potential gain, or they may negotiate an internal procedure for dividing joint gains that might include compensation to the internal losers.

Let us stay with the case where team A has three coprincipals A_1, A_2, and A_3. This situation can once again lead to a set of scoring instructions to the external negotiator that is nonadditive. Each of the subplayers, A_1, A_2, and A_3, might have his own private scoring system. When they collectively instruct A how to negotiate with B, they consciously try to balance the desires of A_1, A_2, and A_3. In doing so, they hobble external negotiator A by restricting him to negotiate with B in a manner that tries to keep an equitable balance among the internal preferences of A_1, A_2, and A_3. In this case, the scoring instructions to A will likely not be additive over issues. But once again, with the help of a computer aid, we could take the complex scoring instructions from A (that is not additive) and from B, and compute the efficient frontier. Fritz Mayer (1988) examines the problem of synchronizing internal and external negotiations and shows that the subplayers of A, instead of individually demanding cutoffs on specific issues and collectively demanding an equity balance, may be better advised to link the present negotiation with other internal negotiations in a manner that will enable the internal winners of A (in the negotiation with B) to creatively compensate the internal losers of A. When linkage and compensation are included in A's superproblem, then it might be the case that some semblance of additivity across issues is once again obtained.

Structuring Fundamental Interests

We will return to the beginning, where we assumed that, in prenegotiation, the set of issues to be resolved was already determined. We talked about the desirability that A and B be jointly creative in devising a set of issues without prematurely becoming embroiled in the divisive claiming activity that occurs when the negotiators try to choose a resolution level on each issue. But even before getting involved in jointly creating an agenda of issues, it would be advisable if each party would separately and then collectively probe its real fundamental interests such as economic well-being, stability and security, protection of cultural values, and so on. At the most fundamental level, there may be only a handful of such basic interests, whereas, in the negotiation itself, there may be tens or hundreds of issues that need to be jointly resolved between A and B. A specific issue to be negotiated may tap into several of the fundamental interests and each fundamental interest may be influenced by numerous issues.

An important question to address is why bother with *identifying fundamental interests* when it will be the issues and not the interests that will be negotiated. The answer is simple. The fundamental interests provide the foundation for all that you should care about in the negotiation. Without fundamental interests, you would not care at all about the outcome of the negotiation or whether, indeed, an agreement was reached. The issues are important because they are the means that influence ultimate satisfaction with respect to the fundamental interests (Keeney 1992).

To render these notions more concrete, consider the perspective of labor negotiating with management over a work contract. Labor may have fundamental interests concerning the economic well-being of its members, the stability of their lives, and the safety of the workplace. Issues may include the term of the contract, the beginning salary for new workers, the base pay of journeymen, the pay increases over the lifetime of the contract, the health benefits package, time off for maternity leave, upgrading the safety of some equipment, and so forth. Clearly, many of the issues affect each of the three fundamental interests. The reason to care about the issue of the health-care package is that a better package: (1) covers more medical expenses and, therefore, improves economic well-being, (2) covers higher costs and, therefore, a significant illness or injury is less likely to bankrupt a family and produce instability, and (3) allows more time to recover from injuries and, thus, reduces the likelihood of recurring injury upon return to work.

The assignment of relative weights (degrees of importance) to issues and the scoring of different resolution levels of the issues should be determined by the relative values of the fundamental interests. In other words, the values for issues and levels of issues are derived values in principle. They are derived from consideration of the values concerning the different fundamental interests and the relationships of the issues to those interests.

There are several advantages to allocating some of the time in preparing for negotiations to identifying and structuring fundamental interests. The most obvious advantage has already been mentioned but is worth repeating. The fundamental interests are the reason for being concerned with a negotiation.

Because of the relationship of issues to fundamental interests, one can use the values about fundamental interests to promote logical, consistent evaluation of separate issues in a negotiation. Furthermore, fundamental interests do not change as rapidly as issues do over time. Nor do values related to fundamental interests change as much or as often as the relative values attached to issues. Thus, a focus on fundamental interests can be useful for guiding consistent action by a negotiator across a set of negotiations over time. A thorough understanding of your fundamental interests is extremely useful in guiding all your actions in a negotiation context, from defining the issues to designing negotiation strategy to evaluating the possible agreements. This understanding increases your power in the negotiation process.

Preparing for the Negotiation

To conduct useful analyses to assist negotiators, a good deal of preparation is necessary. This preparation mainly involves activities aimed at providing qualitative information though sometimes complemented with some numbers. (In the previous section, a number of critical components of the preparation process were identified by italic type for consideration in this section.) Here, we will address some of the art and science of structuring a negotiation with regard to each component and point out the important insights that can be gathered from the structuring process itself.

Creating Issues

Creating issues and identifying fundamental interests (discussed later in this section) have a natural relationship. Agreement on the issues is the means by which a particular negotiation affects the degree to which fundamental interests are met. Hence, one useful way to probe for issues relevant to a negotiation is to begin with the fundamental interests and ask "How might the upcoming negotiation contribute toward these interests?" The responses should suggest specific issues.

In an analogous manner, one should try to specify the fundamental interests of the other side in a negotiation. Indeed, there will likely be less uncertainty about the other side's fundamental interests than about its issues, because the fundamental interests do not change rapidly over time and because there is more similarity of interests of opponents than similarity of issues. Given a perception of the other side's interests, one can make inferences about which potential issues should be important to it in the negotiation.

Even if you do not care directly about the resolution of an issue that concerns your opponent, you should care indirectly. If an issue matters to your opponent, you stand to gain something with respect to another issue that you do care about when you yield on the first issue in question. In short, an issue of relevance to your opponent should also be an issue of relevance to you.

Issues that pertain to style may be as important as those that deal with substance. Being gracious on issues of style may, in fact, yield significant benefits on issues of substance. For example, a fundamental interest of many negotiators might be to be treated decently and with respect. You may give up little to conform to this interest and, as a quid pro quo, gain on the substantive issues. But, in addition, treating someone with decency and respect may be one of your fundamental interests.

Sorting Out Preferences

The field of decision analysis has developed a sound methodology and numerous procedures to quantify preferences in situations involving multiple issues. As discussed in detail in Keeney and Raiffa 1976 and von Winterfeldt and Edwards 1986, the quantification can be characterized by five activities. The first two are qualitative and consist of identifying a complete set of issues and specifying possible agreement levels (this may be a continuum) on each issue. The third activity is to determine a reasonable value model, like the additive scoring system, for combining the multiple issues. The set of issues that have been identified has a significant influence on the form of the overall value model. The fourth and fifth activities are quantitative in nature. The fourth is to assign relative values (or utilities in situations involving uncertainty) to the respective levels of each of the different issues. The fifth activity is to address the value trade-offs and state exactly how much achievement on issue 1 that one will just give up to increase achievement by a specific amount on issue 2.

There are some important insights that usually follow from the quantification of preferences over issues. In many cases, the maximum scores possible on the different issues varies significantly. For example, if there are 10 issues, 75 of the possible 100 points may be assigned to just 3 of the issues. This suggests not only which alternative agreements are preferable and why, but it helps focus your efforts in a negotiation.

It is just as important to try to construct your opponent's preferences as it is to speculate about those issues that are important to him or her. Knowledge of the preferences is extremely useful. Especially when you think he or she will score the issues differently than you do, the opportunity to create jointly outstanding agreements (i.e., "win big–win big" agreements) will become apparent from careful review of the two sets of preferences.

Ranking Issues

It is usually not too difficult to rank issues. However, in any such ranking, the individual doing the ranking must consider two things: the substance of the issue and the range of possible resolutions of the issue. The problem with many rankings is that the range of possible resolutions is not considered. Suppose, in a labor dispute, that salary is ranked higher than work hours. Does this mean that a 40-hour week for $26,000 annually is preferred to a 35-hour week for $25,500? Probably not, but then what does it mean that salary is ranked higher than work hours if an option with higher salary (i.e., $26,000) is not preferred to an option with fewer work hours (i.e., 35 hours)?

When issues are inappropriately ranked without consideration of their ranges, several other difficulties occur. For instance, two individuals with different rankings of issues can appear to be in disagreement but can, in reality, be in complete agreement. One individual may rank salary over work hours, and mean $30,000 for 40 hours per week is preferable to $25,000 for 38 hours per week. A second individual may rank work hours over salary and mean $30,000 for 40 hours per week is less preferable than $29,000 for 35 hours per week. Misinterpretations occur because the ranges of salary and work time are never explicitly articulated in conjunction with the ranking of issues. By making the ranges explicit, the quality of the value judgments improves along with the clarity of their meaning.

In an analogous manner, two individuals can apparently have similar values because of their rankings of issues and yet, in actuality, be in complete disagreement. It follows that providing only a ranking of issues to a party that is representing you in a negotiation provides little substantive guidance. The ranges over issues will be crucial in the negotiation, and the ranking of issues will not address this.

What, then, can one constructively do to avoid these difficulties? The solution is simple: rank outcomes rather than issues. This means that the whole range of possible outcomes needs to be clearly laid out. This is the first step in the assessment of the value trade-offs between issues that is a part of the quantification of preferences.

Scoring the Best Alternative to a Negotiated Agreement

Scoring the BATNA is usually not as easy as scoring the different possible resolutions of a negotiation. The complexity occurs because the set of issues relevant to identifying and scoring the BATNA could be completely different from those in the negotiation itself. Hence, the BATNA cannot be separately scored on a set of issues whose scores can then somehow be combined (e.g., added) to provide an overall evaluation.

Some of the different issues involved in the consideration of the BATNA may relate to the same fundamental interests that underlie the issues in the negotiation. But often the implementation of the BATNA may affect some fundamental interests that are not even relevant in the ongoing negotiation. For example, consider a U.S. manufacturer negotiating with a domestic parts supplier about a contract. To keep things simple, suppose that the fundamental interests of the manufacturer concern profits, providing quality products, providing quality service, and making a contribution to U.S. society. In the negotiation with the domestic supplier, the issues might be price, quality, and length of contract, which relates to the profit and quality product interests. The manufacturer's BATNA, however, may involve a supplier from a developing nation. In addition to the issues involving a domestic supplier, another issue affecting profitability might be the handling of foreign exchange fluctuations. There may also be an issue about the dependability of deliveries that would affect quality of service. Such an issue might legitimately be taken up in the negotiation with the developing country supplier. The interest of contributing to U.S. society would be influenced by the loss of domestic jobs by switching to a foreign supplier. This may lower the BATNA value, but there is no corresponding issue to negotiate. If the developing nation supplier is chosen, domestic jobs will be lost.

To score the BATNA requires identifying a potential agreement that one feels is equivalent in value to the BATNA. A partial BATNA score might be determined by scoring the BATNA on issues common to those in the negotiation—on price, quality, and length of contract in this illustration. To this, adjustments must be made for other issues and considerations (e.g., loss of domestic jobs) relevant to the BATNA. These adjustments might be made sequentially, either by adjusting the level of one of the issues and calculating the implied change in score, or by changing the score directly. As an example of the former, potential losses due to foreign exchange dealings may raise a potential $70 million annual cost of purchased items to an $80 million cost. In other words, the foreign exchange risk would be worth $10 million to eliminate.

If, with all issues considered with the BATNA, the current tallied score was 70 of 100, the remaining task would be to assess the impact due to lost domestic jobs. One could consider any actual or hypothetical agreement that scored 70 except that it also caused the loss of a specified number of American jobs and search for some actual or hypothetical agreement that one felt had equal value. If an agreement that scored 55 was determined to be equivalent (in value) to the 70 combined with the lost jobs, then the lost jobs score a −15 and the BATNA score is 55.

Structuring the Other Side's Values

By knowing your negotiating partner's values and value trade-offs better, you may be better able to move northeasterly toward the efficient frontier shown in figure 1. Remember that it is not mathematically possible to achieve an outcome such as point T in figure 1, given the configuration of issues being negotiated. But it may be possible to extend the frontier outward by creatively adding new issues to the negotiation or by linking two separate negotiations. In order to devise such creative opportunities, it is crucial to understand your own and the other side's underlying fundamental interests as well as how these interests relate to the new issues to be introduced.

It is customary to focus on the issues that divide the contending parties in negotiations. But an agreement on those issues might open up a new round of negotiation on a myriad of new issues that can yield joint gains for both. For example, if Greek and Turkish Cypriots can settle their differences about territorial sovereignty, they may open up all sorts of opportunities for long-range joint development in medical services, in development of natural resources, in higher education, and so on. It may be desirable to combine some of these long-range development issues with the original set of contentious issues in order to stretch the efficient frontier.

It sort of sounds like getting something for nothing. It is not. It is getting something for something. By thinking deeply about your own and your opponent's underlying fundamental interests, you may be able to devise win-win opportunities. Since these interests are much broader than the set of issues in a negotiation, they suggest how the issues may be expanded to both parties' advantage (some notions on this process are found in Keeney 1992).

Characterizing the Efficient Frontier

If you do not have unambiguous scoring systems for both partners in a negotiation, you cannot precisely construct the efficient frontier. But you can often do almost as much, even if your opponent does not wish to disclose his or her scoring system. You can estimate the other side's scoring system with uncertainties in your estimates specified. You then can calculate the efficient frontier for each combination of his or her possible scoring system and your known scoring system. This will provide a set of possible efficient frontiers, which must divide the set of possible agreements into those that may be on the efficient frontier (i.e., they are on one or more of the possible efficient frontiers) and those that are definitely not on the efficient frontier (i.e., they are inferior regardless of which possible frontier actually holds). Calculating the "envelope of the set of possible efficient frontiers" is not an overwhelming task given the efficiency of computers. All of the ideas for using the efficient frontier to improve agreements can be used equally well with an envelope as with a single efficient frontier. In simple terms, the principle is: analysis can be just as useful for eliminating bad agreements as it is for identifying good ones.

Appraising an Additive Scoring System

We have said that an additive scoring system is appropriate if and only if the value trade-offs between any two issues do not depend on the levels chosen on the remaining issues. But if the value trade-offs between two issues do depend on levels of other issues, we learn much more than that additivity is inappropriate. An important reason for such a dependency is that some issues that are relevant to the negotiation have not been explicitly articulated. Trying to understand why the value dependency occurs is the key to redefining the issues in a clearer manner.

As an example, suppose a management-labor negotiation had, among other issues, the following three: salary raises for type 1 workers, salary raises for type 2 workers, and vacation time for both types. Value trade-offs between salary raises of type 1 workers and vacation time may strongly depend on the level of salary raises of type 2 workers. Pursuing the reason for this dependency, a negotiator may state that more vacation time should be given up to raise salaries for type 1 workers when salary raises for type 2 workers are high than when they are low. This would suggest that the equity of the salary raises for the two types of workers was a hidden issue that is worthwhile bringing into the open.

Converting Nonadditive to Additive Scoring

The specification of the set of issues to be negotiated is itself a product of negotiations or prenegotiations. For the moment, let us ignore the question of rivalry or dissent and examine the choice of issues to be examined in a noncontroversial setting. Suppose you have to make up your own mind when confronted with complex, multiple, competing objectives, and suppose that you specify a set of issues in a negotiation context. Ideally, you would want the set of issues to address your "real" concerns and to be complete. When this is not the case, as with the situation where equity between salary raises for two types of workers was not included as an issue, the investigation of the independence assumptions often indicates that additivity cannot be justified. What should be done in such a situation?

When assessments lead to nonadditive scoring, the usual corrective action is to examine the reasons why. If it is lack of completeness, the addition of an issue is appropriate. If the original issues were not the real issues,

change them. The back-and-forth interplay between the qualitative definition
of issues and the quantitative assessment necessary to provide the scoring
system should lead one to situations where additivity is at least a pretty good
approximation (several examples involving the conversion of nonadditive to
additive evaluations are given in Keeney 1981).

Now let us return to the case where issues have to be jointly specified by
the disputants in a negotiation context, and suppose that they do not justify an
additive scoring system. You purposefully may choose not to include the real
issues or not to add missing issues. In the Camp David negotiations, Begin
and Sadat may have been wise not to include in their deliberations the issue of
Jerusalem. In negotiations between the Canadian government and the
Mohawk Tribe on fishing rights, it may be desirable not to include the basic
issue of Indian sovereignty in the negotiation agenda. The inclusion of this
issue may not be resolvable and may have to be finessed. What is excluded
may be very delicate and outweigh the desire for additivity. The reality is that
in negotiations, we may sometimes know how to achieve additivity across
issues, but we may purposefully choose not to do so. The upshot of all this is
that, in formal analyses of issues in a negotiation setting, you may have to
deal with nonadditive structures.

Identifying Fundamental Interests

Identifying your fundamental interests is an exercise in creativity typically
played out between an analyst-facilitator and a negotiator or negotiation team.
There is no set of rules that will result in a well-structured list of fundamental
interests, but a few guidelines will help.

First, simply ask the negotiator to write down his or her fundamental
interests. After the list is completed, challenge him or her in different ways to
search further; for example, going back and forth between issues and interests
might stimulate thinking. In a negotiation between a county and a company
regarding a proposed toxic waste facility, a partial list of issues relevant to the
county may include economic impacts, socioeconomic impacts, environmental effects, public health and safety, inconvenience, and public image of the
county. County negotiators may be asked to think of fundamental interests in
each area.

Once the initial lists of interests are established, it will likely include
many items that are derivative and not really fundamental. Items that are not
fundamental interests may still be useful, later, for identifying actual issues.
To identify fundamental interests, the "why test" is indispensable. Taking one
item at a time from the initial list of interests, ask: Why is that item important?
There are generally two types of responses: (a) the item is important for some
reason, or (b) the item *is* important. The latter response indicates that you

have probably identified a fundamental interest. The former essentially provides a new item to which the why test can be applied. After a chain of why tests, you should eventually arrive at a fundamental interest.

As one simple example, consider a negotiation context between the EPA and the owners of an industrial facility. On its initial list of potential interests, the EPA may have included the quality of fuel burned by the facility. So why is the quality of fuel burned important? The response could quite conceivably be that, with higher quality fuel, less pollution would be emitted from the facility. So a new item of potential fundamental interest is the pollution emitted from the facility. Again the why test is employed. Now we find that pollution is important because it affects visibility. Then we ask why is visibility important. Here we may get a response that visibility simply *is* important or maybe that it is important because it directly impacts quality-of-life. Either response indicates that visibility is one of the fundamental interests for the problem. How far you probe backward toward your basic needs and wants depends in part on the use you might make of the set of interests in devising a set of issues to be negotiated.

Conclusions

We have presented various insights that we feel are useful for the analysis of negotiations. Here, we will synthesize these insights into a collection of principles that both guide the analysis of a negotiation and place it in proper perspective.

Principle 1: Systematic qualitative structuring of values can yield a big payoff. Qualitative inputs include defining the issues, specifying levels of issues for possible agreements, identifying fundamental interests, and deciding what quantitative analysis to conduct. A great deal of useful systematic thinking can occur both in the structuring process, itself, as well as in the process of examining the implications of that structure for the negotiation.

Principle 2: A little quantitative analysis of values can yield a high benefit-to-effort ratio. Once the qualitative structuring is done, quantifying scoring functions and analyzing possible agreements is relatively straightforward, although it does require significant skill and judgment. If the positions of both parties to the negotiation are quantified, the efficient frontier can be determined and possible joint gains identified. Sensitivity analyses can easily be conducted answering numerous "what if" questions. Considering all the effort and cost that goes into an important negotiation that often yields an inferior agreement, the relatively little additional effort and cost needed for analysis to move the agreement to the efficient frontier is often well worth it.

Principle 3: Quantitative analysis is a complement to qualitative thinking. Analyses with models do not make decisions, negotiators make decisions. Thus, the insights from quantitative analyses based on qualitative structuring are again turned back to the qualitative world. Negotiators must use these insights to improve their intuition and enhance their judgment in the negotiations.

Principle 4: Qualitative types have a lot to contribute to and gain from quantitative structuring of values. This principle essentially follows from principles 1 and 3. No quantitative analysis can proceed without qualitative structuring, and analysis without insights for the negotiator is useless. Insights from a quantitative analysis, even a very sophisticated mathematical analysis, can be communicated effectively to nonquantitative types. The burden for ensuring that this communication occurs must rest with the analysts.

Principle 5: Structuring and quantifying your opponent's values can be invaluable. Analysis is time consuming and costly. How much qualitative and quantitative structuring you should do of the other side's fundamental underlying interests and value trade-offs across issues depends on a host of considerations. But suffice it to say that, in our opinion, not enough is usually done. In devising a set of issues to be jointly resolved, you might want to assign someone from your negotiating team to reflect on the other party's fundamental interests. In the give-and-take of quid pro quo trade-offs during negotiations—I'll give up this if you give up that—it is often helpful not only to quantify your own value trade-offs but to speculate about their value trade-offs. Open discussion of these trade-offs can help both of you seek a joint solution to your joint problem.

Principle 6: Value analysis can be used to squeeze out joint gains. Simply stated, analysis provides insights and understanding and, as such, can certainly sharpen a negotiator's mind for the negotiation. When there is a team of negotiators on one side, analysis can also greatly facilitate communication. Several team members can try to structure the negotiation and quantify scoring functions for both sides independently. Invariably some apparently significant differences will occur. Identifying these should help lead to a standard position prior to negotiating with the opponent. With subplayers who may each want reservation levels on separate issues, analysis may sensitize them to the overall cost our side will pay for this "narrow-minded" attitude. Relaxing these reservation levels on separate issues may lead to much greater collective gains for one side that should then be able to be distributed to all subplayers' benefit. A negotiator must often play the role of mediator, and a mediator must often play the role of teacher. Good analysis may help you to teach your "adversary" how to be a better joint problem solver.

Principle 7: Value analysis should be iterative. There should be a flow from qualitative analysis to quantitative analysis—back and forth. During prenegotiations and negotiations, you may learn some things about your adversary's fundamental interests and value trade-offs across issues that can help you to modify your own tactics and aspirations. But sometimes learning can even be deeper: you might learn more about your own fundamental interests as you try to clarify these interests to the other side and hear what they have to say about them.

REFERENCES

Keeney, Ralph L. 1981. "Analysis of Preference Dependencies among Objectives." *Operations Research* 29:1105–20.
Keeney, Ralph L. 1992. *Value-Focused Thinking*. Cambridge, Mass.: Harvard University Press.
Keeney, Ralph L., and Howard Raiffa. 1976. *Decisions with Multiple Objectives*. New York: Wiley.
Luce, R. Duncan, and Howard Raiffa. 1957. *Games and Decisions*. New York: Wiley.
Mayer, Fritz. 1988. "Bargains within Bargains: Domestic Politics and International Negotiation." Ph.D. diss. John F. Kennedy School of Government, Harvard University.
Raiffa, Howard. 1982. *The Art and Science of Negotiations*. Cambridge, Mass.: Harvard University Press.
Raiffa, Howard. 1985. "Post-Settlement Settlements." *Negotiation Journal* 2 (1): 9–12.
von Winterfeldt, Detlof, and Ward Edwards. 1986. *Decision Analysis and Behavioral Research*. New York: Cambridge University Press.

CHAPTER 8

Thinking Coalitionally: Party Arithmetic, Process Opportunism, and Strategic Sequencing

David A. Lax and James K. Sebenius

In recent years, many analysts have improved our knowledge of negotiation, yet it is probably fair to say that the clearest and most powerful advances in the theory have been within or mainly inspired by the bilateral or two-party case.[1] While multilateral bargaining has been the subject of considerable investigation, the additional complexities posed by coalitional possibilities render the analytic task much more formidable. As Howard Raiffa observed, "There is a vast difference between conflicts involving two disputants and those involving more than two disputants. Once three or more conflicting parties are involved, coalitions of disputants may form and may act in concert against the other disputants" (1982, 11).

Much work has been done on coalition formation in legislative and voting situations (see, e.g., Brams 1975). The realist school of international relations and, more particularly, theories of the balance of power have coalitional dynamics at their core.[2] Closely related is the study of alliances (Rothstein 1968; Walt 1987 and 1988), which may result, of course, from balance of power considerations as well as factors accounted for by the theories of collective action (Olson and Zeckhauser 1968). Within alliances, joint decisions to take particular actions (i.e., alliance politics) have been the object of study (see, e.g., Neustadt 1970). The bureaucratic politics school focuses attention on the actors as being composed of many parties and factions (Allison 1971). Finally, in the international arena, are the studies of conference diplomacy such as the various North-South and East-West gatherings on topics ranging from the law of the sea to trade to the environment (Rothstein 1979; Sebenius 1984).

We would like to thank Arthur Applebaum, Max Bazerman, H. Peyton Young, Saadia Touval, Howard Raiffa, Gilbert Winham, William Zartman, and referees for useful comments on earlier versions of this chapter.

1. See, e.g., Schelling 1960 and 1966; Iklé 1964; Walton and McKensie 1965; Rubin and Brown 1975; Raiffa 1982; Zartman and Berman 1982.
2. See Morganthau and Thompson 1985 for an updated version of the classic treatise.

Less obviously, many seemingly bilateral negotiations involve multiparty negotiations because each "side" contains several different parties with different interests. These "two-level" games, involving "internal" as well as "external" bargaining, have been the object of considerable study.[3] As former Secretary of Labor John Dunlop once said, "Every negotiation involves at least three negotiations—one across the table and one on each side" (Raiffa 1982, 166). When one includes two-level games, it is likely that multiparty negotiation is the predominant mode of negotiation.

With such interactions in mind, we use the terms *multiparty* or *multilateral* to refer to negotiations involving more than two monolithic parties or factions, which may be countries, distinct regions, or organizations, as well as groups or even individuals within larger entities. Coalitional interactions among such factions or parties in dealings ranging from two-level games to conference diplomacy, as well as to organizational bargains and bureaucratic politics, fall within the scope of this essay.

Despite an impressive body of work on multiparty bargains, however, an explicit focus on characteristic dynamics in multilateral settings, along with their effects on negotiated outcomes, remains generally lacking. It is this gap that our analysis in this chapter addresses. To sharpen our focus, we need to be more precise about the most salient, inherent differences between bilateral and multilateral negotiations that give rise to a rich array of dynamics and tactics. Apart from various group dynamics that have no bilateral counterparts, many elements of multiparty situations simply cannot occur in negotiations between two monolithic parties. We will analyze a number of such possibilities, including *coalitional alignments and realignments,* the potential for de facto alliances, "natural" coalitions, and blocking coalitions. Our analysis may lead to a blurring of the concept of *side* in negotiation—where more than one entity nominally comprises a side, but *internal* divisions and coalitions cutting across the different sides may act in concert. The bulk of our analysis, however, will deal with three overlapping classes of tactics distinctive to multiparty situations: (1) *party arithmetic,* or actions to affect which entities are and or are not actively involved in a given negotiation, that is, "adding" and "subtracting" parties; (2) *process opportunism,* or tactics that depend on more complex structural or process restrictions such as who can directly talk with whom, how information is transmitted, who may speak for whom, and which parties must approve the actions of others; and (3) *strategic sequencing,* or tactics that depend on the order and sequencing of how the different entities are approached and/or informed of the actions of other players. This may lead to agreements among subsets of the involved parties,

---

3. See Lax and Sebenius 1986; Lax and Mayer 1988; Putnam 1988.

not necessarily coalitionally aligned, that may or may not pyramid to encompass a larger group.

It is toward developing an understanding of the purposes and effects of these multilateral possibilities that our analysis is aimed. In our exploration, we place special focus on the dynamics of these interactions. The predominant emphasis of coalition theories developed thus far, however, has been on the *outcomes* of coalitional actions rather than on the *processes* of arriving at those outcomes. In the words of Anatol Rapoport, when reviewing the contributions of *N*-person game theory,

> If the behavioral scientist thinks about decision making in conflict systems in the mode suggested by *N*-Person Game Theory, he will focus on two fundamental questions: 1. Which coalitions are likely to form? 2. How will the members of a coalition apportion their joint payoff? (1970, 286)

Rapoport goes on to note that game theory "lacks almost entirely the dynamic component, i.e., a model of the conflict *process*." Similarly, Steven Brams, in his extensive review of game theory and politics, noted

> Studies of coalition behavior have focused more on *static outcomes* than on the dynamic processes that produced them prior to the point at which one coalition has gone on to win. Even in the relatively well-structured context of voting bodies . . . the development of dynamic models has only recently been initiated. (1975, 232)

While there are important exceptions to these generalizations, several of which we discuss below, we respond to these gaps in the literature by focusing on (1) the *processes* as well as *outcomes* associated with (2) *tactics* and *dynamics* arising in *multilateral,* rather than *bilateral,* settings. Before exploring possibly less familiar coalitional tactics, we first review what might be called canonical coalition dynamics.

Canonical Coalition Dynamics

"Classical" Coalition Dynamics

Although most existing theories do not explicitly address process questions, they often strongly point to or imply classes of coalitional dynamics. Certain dynamics—such as the efforts of two competing groups to recruit an as yet uncommitted third party into their coalition, and the efforts of one party to play other, typically larger, powers against each other—have been extensively studied. For example, in 1902, given the Anglo-Japanese alliance, Japan's threat to settle a Manchurian dispute with Russia was an effective threat to obtain better terms in the alliance with the British (Snyder and Diesing 1977, 436). Similarly, shortly before World War II, the Soviets bargained openly with the British and French for a mutual assistance pact against German aggression while they secretly negotiated a nonaggression treaty with the Germans. The open Anglo-French discussions significantly enhanced the Soviet position in the latter talks (Ikle 1964, 55). Further, if a so-called debtors' cartel, greatly feared by large U.S. banks, could form and commit itself to a far lesser stream of payments, the banks would find this action much more difficult to deal with than such an action by an individual debtor. Hence, standard "divide and conquer" responses. For example, the international commercial banking community has, at times, sought to reward "good" behavior from debtor countries such as Mexico and to punish "bad" behavior in debtor countries such as Argentina to discourage a cartel from forming (see Cohen 1986, 221–22).

In the postwar period, relations among the United States, the USSR, and the People's Republic of China offer a virtual textbook case of coalitional dynamics in a balance of power context. First, China was seemingly strongly aligned with the Soviet Union. Then, following the Sino-Soviet split, was a period of nonalignment, finally leading to a tilt toward the United States. This balance of power competition for third parties has been well studied.[4] Indeed, a recent article by Stephen Walt serves as the latest addition to a debate between adherents of the view that states align with each other in order to *balance* larger powers versus the view that states more frequently engage in *bandwagoning,* that is, aligning themselves with what seems to be the dominant power either for appeasement or to share in the spoils (Walt 1988).

Steven Brams and a number of his colleagues have written several papers that explicitly address the problem of two "protocoalitions" vying for the membership of an uncommitted party.[5] They derive conditions for the optimal timing for the uncommitted party to join either rival group. These conditions are expressed in terms of a relationship between the probabilities that each protocoalition will become a winning coalition. This formalized version of the bandwagon effect has been generalized to the case of many parties by Philip Straffin (1977).

Early game theories (such as those promulgated by von Neumann and Morgenstern) included conditions for "solutions" to coalition games, such as the requirement that a party be able to do better in an ultimate coalition than

---

4. See, for example, Gulick 1955 for a very nice synthesis.
5. See Brams 1972; Brams and Heilman 1974; Brams and Garrigo-Pico 1975.

that party could do alone.[6] That gives rise to simple dynamics of comparison of one outcome relative to another for each party. Aumann and Maschler (1964) later assumed this kind of individual rationality, but based their approach to bargaining in coalitions on the concepts of *objections* and *counterobjections*. In dealing with a tentatively formed coalition, another group— which might include members of the tentatively formed coalition—could object by offering a better deal to some of the members of the tentative coalition. Unless a valid counterobjection could be raised, the tentative coalition might become the ultimate coalition. Our point is not the mathematics nor the ultimate conclusions of these investigations, but rather the hint they give of possible coalitional dynamics arising from objections and counterobjections in tempting one group away from another.[7]

An alternative dynamic was suggested by McKelvey, Ordeshook, and Winer (1978). They envisioned a coalition not as a single entity but, instead, as a collection of individual parties, each of whom is playing two roles simultaneously. First, each member is seeking to attract and retain potentially pivotal members of its coalition; second, each member is offering itself as a potentially pivotal member to other potential coalitions. Though this is a very complex process, both conceptually and mathematically, it yields quite specific, testable predictions of outcomes (called the *competitive solution*). For our purposes, however, the process it isolates is the interplay between efforts to lure others and offers to join them.

Driving these game-theoretically highlighted dynamics—objection, counterobjection, offer, enticement, threat, and promise—are calculations by all parties of the value that a potential member or members of an as-yet-unformed coalition might add by joining and the alternative value that those members might obtain by other coalitional courses of action.[8] (Related dynamics have been suggested and investigated in the work of social psychologists and political scientists.)[9]

---

6. For general discussions of the game-theoretic contributions, see von Neumann and Morgenstern 1944; Luce and Raiffa 1957; Murnighan 1978; Straffin and Grofman 1984.

7. An insightful exposition of these dynamics is given in chapter 17 of Raiffa 1982.

8. A very insightful exposition of these dynamics is given in Raiffa 1982, 257–74.

9. From the social psychological and sociological perspectives, a number of models have been proposed that are driven by or give rise to characteristic coalitional dynamics. Good reviews of this literature appear in Rubin and Brown 1975 and Murnighan 1978. Caplow (1959 and 1968) proposed a model in which the players sought to control as many other players as possible; thus, resources such as votes or productive capacity became the focal point. Gamson (1961 and 1964) suggested that those players possessing the minimum necessary resources to prevail would, in fact, form a coalition and, in effect, that the payoffs to those individual members would be proportional to the resources they brought. Other social psychologists proposed that combinations of the resources brought to the encounter, notions of equity, and alternative coalitional possibilities available to the players as the game unfolds are critical elements in coalition formation

Natural and de Facto Coalitions

When two independent actors negotiate with each other, the concept of a negotiating *side* (i.e., each actor) is obvious. Yet in multiparty dealings, what may be called sides may not indicate whose interests are actually aligned with whose. *Natural coalitions* can consist of parties—regardless of nominal side—who have powerful shared interests, who are able to make highly valuable trades, or who, as a unit, can extract significant value from others without much risk of being split. It is often worth asking which entities in a multilateral encounter could form a natural coalition.

National Football League Labor Negotiations
For example, the National Football League (NFL) and its Players' Association (the NFLPA) negotiated over a contract in 1981. The NFLPA was a coalition made up of a few "stars" and numerous "journeymen" players whose interests differed, as well as of young and old players whose interests also differed. While all players benefited, to some extent, by a union that could create a unified front with respect to the league, different contracts could confer relative advantage to stars or journeymen or to young or old players. The stars' performance is most directly related to team revenue; that is, the bigger and better performing a star, the more revenue "his" team would generate. Thus, if stars were paid according to performance, there would be a de facto natural coalition between the stars and the league. In contrast, the stars would be hurt by a salary schedule that depended solely on position and seniority.

Thus, by initial bargaining proposals in 1981 that set salary schedules as a function of position and seniority, the NFL strongly favored the journeymen,

---

and payoff allocation (see Komorita and Chertkoff 1973; Komorita 1974). Again, the implied dynamics involve normative discussions of comparative resources furnished and alternative coalitional partners.

Within the realm of political science, Riker (1962) offered the first formal model of coalitional behavior. He proposed the *size principle,* which, in a zero-sum context, essentially predicts two dynamics. First, his model points to a process in which those parties necessary to form a minimal winning coalition aggregate; second, when coalitions are larger than minimal winning, Riker's model posits a process of disintegration until the coalition has declined to that minimal size. His model has been subjected to intense efforts at scrutiny and elaboration, the most significant of which for our purposes involve models in which "ideological proximity" (as measured on a unidimensional scale) plays an additional role in the choice of coalitional partners. For good surveys of such evaluations, see Brams 1975 or Murnighan 1978. Axelrod (1970), Leiserson (1970), Rosenthal (1970), and DeSwann (1970 and 1973) have all offered variants based on this idea, which seems intuitively plausible and has some empirical support. Each of the forces driving these models isolates a class of coalitional tactics and dynamics—scaling up or down to minimum size, seeking to coalesce with the smallest amount of resources, or striving for the least postcoalitional policy distance.

especially older ones, who formed the largest and most supportive block of the union. In contrast, any proposal that allowed teams to bid for free agents in a limited way or that pushed away from a fixed salary schedule would have been in the stars' interests. Thus, when the NFL's original proposals failed and a strike began, it floated an offer for limited free agency. This had the effect of splitting the stars from the union. When some of the stars began crossing the picket line, the union's resolve appeared to weaken. The important point in this situation is realizing that de facto coalitions supported different kinds of contracts; to analyze this situation as if it were two monolithic parties ("the player's union" versus "the NFL") would overlook crucial coalitional dynamics.

Chrysler and the U.K. Government
Consider a de facto natural coalition in negotiations between Chrysler and the British government over the sale of the money-losing and inefficient Chrysler-U.K. operations (see Lax and Sebenius 1986). Given Chrysler-U.K.'s shutdown costs and likely future losses, liquidating the U.K. operations would have been costly; thus Chrysler should have been willing to pay any lesser amount to avoid these costs.[10] The British government in power at the time was relatively fragile. Its existence depended on the support of Scottish labor. Chrysler's Scottish workers feared unemployment. Indeed, given the costs of unemployment and welfare, as well as other political considerations, the Labour government should have been willing to pay a great deal to keep the Chrysler operations going. Hence, the potential bargaining range between the company and the government was quite large.

Tony Benn, the British government negotiator, pushed for a fairly low price. Chrysler, reacting to Benn's offer and mounting losses, threatened to liquidate its plants one-by-one, starting with a Scottish plant in a key electoral district. Intense union pressure from this district on key cabinet ministers forced Benn's hand, and he ended up paying Chrysler a handsome price for the inefficient operations.

Ironically, there was a latent natural coalition between the workers and the British government behind a low purchase price. The money saved by paying a low purchase price could have been used to the workers' benefit—for retraining, for investing in more modern equipment, and so forth. Further, a low price could have resulted in lower costs for the subsequent operation, thus making employment more stable.

Yet, partly because the workers and their union leaders were outside the deliberations, they did not see how Benn's tough tactics (a very low offer)

---

10. Therefore, its reservation value in the sale of the operations should have been negative.

could, in fact, further their interests. Their pressure on the key ministers played right into the company's hands. If Benn had brought union leaders into the negotiations early on and created a plan that shared the benefits of a low purchase price with the workers, persuading them to build support for their common interests in a low price purchase, British taxpayers might have paid considerably less. Chrysler managed to prevent this adverse coalition from forming by its strategically chosen plant closings before Benn had taken any steps to forge the alliance.

In short, where a natural coalition has the potential to form and commit to a position that would be disadvantageous to another party (here, Chrysler), there is sometimes the possibility of actions to prevent the adverse coalition from forming and making the undesirable commitment.

The 1975 U.S.-USSR Grain Agreement

Negotiators can sometimes—and quite unhappily—be struck by the belated recognition that apparently opposing groups indeed share a powerful interest, can consummate a valuable trade, and/or can extract value from other parties. A common result is the explicit emergence, or attempts at such emergence, of what has been a latent natural coalition. The force behind this dynamic is the joint gain that can result from forging separate pieces of the potential coalition together.

The 1975 grain deal between the United States and the Soviet Union, as described by Roger Porter, provides an instructive example (see Porter 1980). In that year, an extremely poor grain harvest was forecast for the Soviets, while a very good one was forecast for U.S. farmers. The question thus arose in high Ford administration councils of how this "agripower" might be used to offset OPEC's oil power. Other issues beyond agricultural ones were quickly linked to the prospect of causing the Soviets economic hardship by withholding additional grain. Some of these other issues included the extent to which Soviet seaborne commerce would be carried on U.S. ships; apparently Soviet treaty commitments were unfulfilled on this score. A second issue involved Soviet conduct in the Middle East. A third set of issues, stimulated by the AFL-CIO and the International Longshoreman's Association led to their refusal to load ships bound to or from the Soviet Union without assurances that any grain sales would not lead to inflationary consequences. Memories were very close of the "great grain robbery" of a few years before, when Soviet grain purchases caused the U.S. bread price to skyrocket.

The major problem for the administration involved Gerald Ford's earlier campaign promise to U.S. farmers not to embargo agricultural products to the Soviet Union. As the administration began to play its embargo card with the Soviets again, the Farm Belt erupted in protest. In important part, this was the result of the *process* of negotiation whereby State Department officials such as Henry Kissinger and Labor Department officials such as John Dunlop were seen to be in control of agricultural policy. (Earl Butz, the then secretary of agriculture, seemed to be irrelevant in public eyes; in fact, he was a participant.) Nevertheless, with the impending farm state primaries and farm pressure mounting, the administration found it necessary to drop its major demands of the Soviets and settle on a long-term agreement that involved no apparent concessions by the Soviets on oil prices or conduct in the Middle East.

Intriguingly, many participants and other observers saw these negotiations as a *U.S.-USSR grain deal*. That it surely was in terms of explicit agreements sought and sovereign entities involved. Yet the familiar characterization of these two opposing sides obscured what was a powerful de facto coalition between U.S. farmers and the Soviet Union. These two parties very much wanted to consummate a grain deal. Analytically, if one ceases to view the negotiation in terms defined by nationalities, one could understand it as a negotiation between a tacit coalition of the farmers plus the Soviet Union versus all the other participants who were either trying to frustrate or capitalize on that deal.

Incidentally, in the U.S.-USSR grain negotiation, a number of White House tactics might have prevented the farm belt debacle. First, simply *recognizing* the congruence of interest between the farmers and the Soviets would have increased attention to that possible alignment as a source of real negotiating difficulty. Sending the correct signals about process—by, for example, giving Agriculture Department players far more visible roles in the deliberations, public announcements, and negotiations—would have taken away the trigger that enraged the farmers. Moreover, the tacit coalition between the farmers and the Soviets, while sharing an interest in sales, had conflicting interests over price and terms. Those who wished to prevent this alliance from emerging or split it once it had emerged might have exploited those potential divisions. Further, it would have been possible for elements of the administration to mount appeals to superordinate interests of the farmers such as patriotism early on. And finally, despite the apparent congruence of interest in a grain sale the following year, the administration might have sought to be persuasive that the long-run real interest of the farmers lay in a coalition with the U.S. government sufficient to obtain a long-term agreement from the Soviets on guaranteed levels of grain purchase. Such classes of maneuvers, from enforcing alliance cohesion toward splitting potential adverse coalitions, characterize many international interactions.

As these examples—in football negotiations, U.K.-Chrysler, and the U.S.-USSR grain deal—indicate, the apparent coalition structure and the obvious "sides" in multilateral dealings may require deeper consideration. Analysis of the patterns among subsets of the involved parties of shared interest, of potentially valuable trades, and of the possibility of extracting value from other parties can reveal de facto natural coalitions that may play key roles in the negotiating dynamics.

An Approach for Interpreting Coalitional Dynamics

Despite the array of dynamics suggested by the literature cited here, the observed complexity of coalitional interactions is scarcely fully captured.[11] As we said in the introduction, certain *inherent* differences between bilateral and multilateral situations give rise to a widely varied set of tactical possibilities that have not been systematically analyzed. In particular, these include the possibility of *party arithmetic,* or actions to affect which entities are involved in a given negotiation, that is, "adding" and "subtracting" parties; *process opportunism,* or tactics that depend on more complex structural or process restrictions such as who can directly talk with whom, how information is transmitted, who may speak for whom, and which parties must approve the actions of others; and *strategic sequencing,* or tactics that depend on the order and sequencing of how the different entities are approached and/or informed of the actions of other players. This may lead to agreements among subsets of the involved parties, not necessarily coalitionally aligned, that may or may not *pyramid* to encompass a larger group.

We will investigate, through a variety of examples, a range of coalitional interactions and their intended effects on negotiated outcomes. In particular, we propose viewing the classes of coalitional dynamics as efforts to improve negotiated outcomes for the coalition members by favorably affecting the *zone of possible agreement* among the players. By the zone of possible agreement (or *bargaining set*), we mean the set of possible agreements that are better for each potential coalition than the noncooperative alternatives to such agreement (see Lax and Sebenius 1986). By *better,* we mean more satisfactory in terms of the perceived interests of the coalition members. In particular, we mean that the expected value of agreement (meaning its subjective probability times its value) is enhanced in the view of the entity taking the action under consideration. We will focus on three classes of favorable effects of coalitional action on the zone of possible agreements: (1) coalitional action to improve one's alternative to negotiated agreement or worsen that of other coalitions; (2) coalitional action to realize joint gains; and (3) coalitional action to credi-

---

11. As examples of such complexity, see Putnam and Baynes's (1987) accounts of economic summitry, Winham's (1986) work on the Tokyo round of GATT negotiations, Talbott's (1984 and 1988) detailed reporting of the bureaucratic coalitional machinations in arms control talks, Sebenius's (1984) analysis of the Law of the Sea talks, or Rothstein's (1979) discussion of UNCTAD deliberations.

bly commit to positions within the perceived zone of possible agreements.

We stress the fact that it is each party's perception of the zone of possible agreement that informs its actions. While perceptions may be influenced by "objective" interests, especially in the longer run, perceived interests in the short run are necessarily subjective. Naturally, there may be differences of interest within nominal coalitions, such as the Group of 77 or the EC. If such differences are significant enough to motivate internal factions to act independently, then, for purposes of our analysis, we would treat the factions as separate coalitional actors. In the extreme, factions may consist of individual actors. In analyzing various dynamics, we shall assume that the relevant coalitional entities act purposively to further their interests, whether straightforward or complex and conflicting. (Note that purposive action need not meet strict [e.g., game-theoretic] criteria of rationality.)

In the next sections, we shall illustrate and elaborate these three broad classes of coalitional action, namely, party addition, process opportunism, and strategic sequencing. Within them, we will examine the processes of *coalition building* and *coalition breaking*. Under the rubric of coalition building, we include decisions taken by coalitions to act collectively as well as efforts to maintain coalitional solidarity. Within each category, we shall consider *overt, covert,* and, sometimes, *tacit* actions. Our broader purpose is to provide a framework within which to interpret the myriad tactics and dynamics that appear in multilateral (but not bilateral) contexts. We begin the discussion with the phenomenon we call party arithmetic and offer some relatively simple examples. As we move to process opportunism and strategic sequencing it will be obvious from the increasingly complex examples that these are not pure versions of each class of tactic; indeed, elements of each become closely intermingled.

Party Arithmetic

Existing theory, by and large, proceeds from the assumption of a well-specified and fixed situation within which coalitional actions are taken and outcomes determined. In other words, the issues, parties, and set of possible actions are taken as the starting point for analysis. In effect, the analysis posits a mapping between the structure of the situation and the ultimate outcome. Yet purposive action on behalf of the parties can change the structure of the situation itself and, hence, the outcomes. Often actions can be understood as a contest for what the game itself will be (Sebenius 1983 and 1984; Lax and Sebenius 1986).

For example, one party will sometimes try to act as if a particular item is on the negotiating agenda; other parties may strenuously resist including it. Such situations can result in tacit or explicit negotiation over the game itself.

To proceed further down this line of analysis, we need to ask precisely what determines the configuration of the game. The answer, to us, seems simple, yet it has deep implications for the analysis and practice of negotiation, especially in coalitional situations. The game is that which the parties act as if it is. There is no a priori reason why this or that issue should be included or why this party or that interest should be excluded. If the parties deal with a particular set of issues, alternatives to agreement, and possible agreements, then, those elements, in fact, make up part of that game.

In particular, analytically interesting coalition dynamics often arise in such situations where the game cannot be considered well-specified in terms of the parties involved. (In the example of the U.S.-USSR grain deal, what initially appeared to be an agricultural issue rapidly expanded to include broader foreign policy actors, as well as the maritime industry and unions, the longshoremen and the AFL-CIO.) Yet actions to add parties can be purposive. For example, a country may wish to enlist the aid or assistance of others in achieving a particular objective. The process of choosing, then approaching and persuading, others to go along may best be studied without the common assumption that the game is fully specified at the outset of analysis.[12] Among the most interesting examples of this phenomenon, which we call party arithmetic, are cases in which the coalitions are tacitly or covertly built.

Kennecott in Chile

In the early 1960s, the Chilean appropriation of Kennecott Copper's El Teniente mine seemed increasingly likely (Smith and Wells 1975). In preparing to negotiate the terms of expropriation, such as the timing, compensation, and any continued management involvement with the mine, Kennecott sought (early on) to involve a variety of other parties to change the nature of Chile's alternatives to agreement on Kennecott's preferred terms. Somewhat surprisingly, the company offered to sell a majority interest in the mine to Chile. Kennecott planned to use the proceeds of this sale of equity along with a loan from the U.S. Export-Import Bank to finance the expansion of the mine. The Chilean government guaranteed this loan and made it subject to New York law. The company then insured as much as possible of its assets under a U.S. guarantee against expropriation. The mine's output was to be sold under long-term contracts with Asian and European customers and the collection rights for these contracts were sold to a consortium of European banks and Japanese institutions.

---

12. Conceptually, of course, one could argue that if the "supergame" of all possible issues and parties were specified at the outset, the phenomenon on which we focus would not exist. But this would be to define a very real set of dynamics out of bounds. See Oye 1979 or Sebenius 1983.

The result of this elaborate maneuvering was that customers, governments, and creditors shared Kennecott's concerns about future changes in Chile. A potent coalition to worsen Chile's alternatives to agreement had been tacitly built. Moreover, the guarantees and insurance improved Kennecott's alternative if no deal could be worked out with the host country. When no agreement could be reached and Chile acted to expropriate the operation, Kennecott was able to call this host of parties in on its side. In effect, Kennecott engaged in a tacit process of coalition formation by adding parties to worsen the other side's alternatives. Though the mine was ultimately nationalized, Chile's worsened unilateral alternative to Kennecott's preferred outcome seemed to give the firm a better position in the dealings than those of similar companies, such as Anaconda, that did not take such actions.

Maltese Base Negotiations

The 1971 Maltese-U.K. negotiations over renewed naval base rights provide a different, instructive example that included tacit coalition building by adding parties (Wriggins 1976). For a number of years, Britain had enjoyed the use of a Maltese naval base and had extended its use to other NATO countries. Nevertheless, changes in ship design, surveillance technologies, and warfare methods had rendered the Maltese bases of considerably less importance than they were, say, during World War II, when Malta had played a crucial role for the allies.

To obtain much improved base rental terms, however, the Maltese made highly visible overtures to the Soviet Union about possible base rights. They also approached Libya and other Arab states for large assistance payments in return for Malta's neutrality. At a simple level, these actions to add other parties to the potential bargain increased the attractiveness of Malta's alternatives to a negotiated agreement with the British. Yet the same moves made Britain's alternatives to agreement with Malta considerably worse. As the *Times* of London noted: "What is important . . . is not that the (the facilities) are badly needed in an age of nuclear war but that they should not, on the other hand, be possessed by Russia (Wriggins 1976, 219).

Not only did these actions put pressure directly on Britain, but NATO anxiety, which the Maltese carefully cultivated, served to indirectly increase the pressure on Britain. As the United States, Italy, and other members of NATO pressured the British to offer more money for base rights in Malta, the British sought to explain the relative unimportance of these bases and the lack of credibility of the Maltese alternatives—loudly touted—of Libya and the Soviet Union. Nevertheless, Malta had, in effect, tacitly aligned itself with the United States, Italy, and other NATO countries against the British in seeking additional money. British efforts to increase the coherence of the NATO parties, while to be expected, were largely too late. Beyond *quadrupling* their base rental payments from the British, other NATO members ultimately agreed to provide supplemental aid to Malta.

Without passing judgment on the tactics employed, it is worth highlighting the fact that the Maltese actions to add other parties to a de facto coalition against Britain in order to improve Malta's own no-agreement alternative and worsen those of others did appear to shift both sides' perceptions of the bargaining range in a way that favored Malta. This appeared to result in a substantially better agreement from Malta's perspective.

In the cases of both Kennecott and Malta, this class of tactics might be referred to as tacit coalition building by party addition. While the specific methods are particular to a given context, the intention is clear: affecting the bargaining range in a favorable manner by adding parties to the interaction that desirably affect no-agreement alternatives. As we shall see in later cases, however, parties may be added in order to generate joint gains or to extract value from others. Parties can also be "subtracted"—meaning separated, ejected, or excluded—from larger potential coalitions. For example, the Soviets were excluded from an active Middle East negotiating role in the process leading up to the Camp David accords that involved only Israel, Egypt, and the United States. Similarly, the Eighteen Nation Disarmament Conference in the early 1960s proved unwieldy and gave way to largely bilateral U.S.-Soviet talks over a nuclear test ban.[13] Whether adding or subtracting players, however, this class of coalitional tactics can have potent effects on negotiated outcomes.

Process Opportunism

When more than two parties are involved in a negotiation, complex rules or norms often govern the interactions and open the door to a class of tactics that we call *process opportunism*. It may be difficult for one party to communicate directly with another; one party may have or assume the right to speak for another in a forum to which the first party has no access; certain parties may fail to ratify or may even veto tentative agreements among other parties. In such situations, entrepreneurial negotiators may exploit the lack of full information to affect coalitional actions. They may also seek to alter the process itself to affect possible agreements. We shall consider four very different examples of this class of tactics that begin to illustrate the range of such possibilities.

---

13. For a number of other examples, see Sebenius 1983 as well as subsequent sections of this chapter.

Internal-External Dynamics and Coalitional Commitments: The INF Talks

As the complexity of the "internal" negotiations grow, the interactive dynamics associated with making commitments in the "external" negotiation can become correspondingly complex. For example, in U.S.-USSR talks over intermediate range nuclear weapons, consider an incident springing from initial U.S. pressure on West German Chancellor Kohl to support a "zero option." As time passed with no progress in the talks,

> Kohl himself held to an unequivocal endorsement [of the zero option] . . . mainly because he knew it to be Reagan administration policy and he did not want to appear to be wavering. He would have been glad, however, had the U.S. . . . adopted a more flexible approach. . . . But in Washington, [Kohl's] support for the zero proposal was used to justify the administration's own adherence to it. (Talbot 1984, 171)

The intended effect was very clear: a set of internal coalitional dynamics was used to reinforce Soviet perceptions of a firm Western commitment to the "zero option." A process in which representatives from Washington and Bonn were effectively separated—and in which Washington spoke on behalf of the NATO alliance—opened the possibility for self-reinforcing perceptions to interact and generate a firm alliance commitment vis-à-vis the Soviet Union.

The 1978 Bonn Summit

By virtue of the number of parties involved, economic summits can generate interesting coalitional dynamics among the leaders actually attending the summit meetings. Robert Putnam's (1988) insightful analysis of the 1978 Bonn economic summit among the major Western powers illustrates how joint gains can be realized by coalitional action. In his words:

> At the Bonn summit, however, a comprehensive package deal was approved, the clearest case yet of a summit that left all participants happier than when they arrived. [West German Chancellor] Helmut Schmidt agreed to additional fiscal stimulus, amounting to 1 percent of GNP, [U.S. President] Jimmy Carter committed himself to decontrol domestic oil prices by the end of 1980, and [Japanese Prime Minister] Takeo Fukuda pledged new efforts to reach a 7 percent growth rate. Secondary elements in the Bonn accord included French and British acquiescence in the Tokyo Round trade negotiations; Japanese undertakings to foster import growth and restrain exports; and a generic American promise to fight inflation. (1988, 428)

Yet Putnam's analysis offers more than a classic example of how different interests of several parties at a summit can be dovetailed into mutual gains; it illustrates an important kind of process opportunism commonly present in two-level games that involve internal and external bargaining. The heads of state in Bonn were maneuvering not only to fashion an accord among themselves, but also using the prospect of a valuable larger package deal and pressures from other governments as excuses to adopt policies opposed by important domestic factions. In particular, Carter's advisors and broader U.S. public opinion were divided on oil decontrol and Fukuda's government was split (the reluctant Ministry of Finance vs. MITI, some business interests, and others) about higher growth targets. Most interesting was the case of Helmut Schmidt, who had privately grown increasingly persuaded of the substantive and domestic political value of some economic stimulus, but who (*a*) faced powerful traditional German opposition in many quarters to calling for it, and (*b*) could extract concessions from other summiteers by acting reluctant and having to be induced to endorse stimulative measures by concessions from the others.

As with other two-level games, the number of involved factions was far greater than the heads of state gathered in Bonn; thus, the coalitional interaction was more complex. In each country there were supportive and opposing groups, who could communicate with their respective head of state, and sometimes among each other, but did not take part directly in the Bonn proceedings. Their interactions displayed a characteristic dynamic of mutual influence between the summit and the domestic political environment. Supporters of a proposed policy in one country could influence "their" head of state to induce the other heads of state to "put intense pressure" on him into endorsing the policy. This real and contrived international pressure, plus the lure of a desirable package deal, could then tip the domestic balance in favor of the policy preferred by domestic supporters. This common dynamic springs from the fact that only a subset (the heads of state) of the full set of interested factions carried out the direct negotiations. These led to joint gains among both the principals and the domestic supporters of the policies endorsed by the principals at the summit.

Financial Arrangements in the Law of the Sea Negotiations

One key aspect of the Law of the Sea (LOS) Treaty negotiations was potentially the largest mining contract ever negotiated internationally.[14] Here, a very different set of coalitional dynamics that led to considerable joint gain

---

14. Some of this material is taken from Lax and Sebenius 1986 (102–5). See also Sebenius 1984.

was induced by the efforts of Singapore's U.N. Ambassador, Tommy T. B. Koh, who acted almost as a mediator and exercised a strong and influential hand over the process. In particular, part of the overall sea law negotiations came to concern a system of fees, royalties, and profit shares to be paid by future seabed miners to an international entity for the right to mine the deep seabeds. This negotiation was often viewed as inherently conflictual—its subject was frequently described as "how to divide the economic pie" expected to flow from seabed mining.

Instead, the results of intense coalitional bargaining that was widely predicted to be intractable proved to be an arrangement that effectively exploited differences among the participants of probability assessments, of risk aversion, and of time preference in order to create a remarkable degree of joint gain. We will consider each difference in turn before analyzing Koh's approach.

First, a great deal of technical and economic uncertainty surrounded the prospects for deep ocean mining. Even after lengthy negotiations and the introduction of much common information, a strong divergence of opinion persisted between developed and developing countries about its likely economic profile. Developed countries saw mining providing a new, low-cost source of minerals. They argued that this industry would most likely show attractive, if modest, economic returns. Many negotiators from developing countries felt, however, that profitability prospects were very good indeed. In short, expectations diverged.

Second, any eventual revenues from seabed exploitation would be divided among all treaty signatories, and would not represent a major share of any country's national income. Thus, countries signing the treaty could be thought of as a large syndicate that should try to maximize expected income rather than trying to assure itself a smaller, but steadier stream. For corporations, in contrast, investments in seabed mining operations could represent significant portions of their assets. In particular, managers of the ocean mining division of these companies were concerned about the potential impact of relatively fixed charges such as fees and royalties on the economic success of troubled projects. They seemed willing to share profits at high rates for successful projects in return for "low end" protection of economically marginal ventures. Attitudes toward risk thus differed.

Finally, there was the question of timing. The companies' private, after-tax discount rates appeared to be higher than those implicitly used by the negotiators from many developing countries, who saw themselves as setting up an enduring system. The welfare of future generations figured heavily in their negotiating statements and in their evaluations of proposals. The two sides' attitudes toward time seemed to differ, with developed countries acting relatively less patiently than the developing countries.

An agreement was reached only after two years of difficult bargaining.

The outcome dovetails these differences in probability assessments, risk aversion, and time preference. Two sharing schedules were agreed on, one with a low royalty and a low profit share, the other with much higher payment rates in each category. The low schedule is in effect until the overall cash flow of the operation, accumulated forward at an appropriate real interest rate, suffices to recover the preproduction investment costs (also accumulated forward with interest). Higher royalty and profit-sharing rates then take effect.

The negotiation of a single set of rates had proved extremely difficult, with any proposal either being opposed by the developed countries as too high or being opposed by the developing countries as too low. The two negotiated schedules, however, used the differences in profitability estimates by giving each side an advantageous tax schedule for the economic outcome it portrayed as likely. Given the developing countries' expectations of high profits, the negotiation of low rates from modestly successful projects was no great concession. Similarly, accepting high rates for bonanza projects was tenable for potential mining companies, given their lower profit forecasts. It was critical, however, that the low rates were neither so low, nor the high rates so elevated, that the ultimate result would be politically or economically unsustainable. The parties knew that they would have to live with and defend the outcome, however, the profit uncertainties resolved themselves.

The agreement protects troubled and marginal projects against overly high fixed charges. In return for such lower rates, however, the miners face higher rates for successful projects than would likely have otherwise been negotiable. The signal for switching to the higher rates is based on the "accumulated" present value of a project's cash flows, that is, inflows and outflows accumulated forward with interest. Therefore, the higher rates apply only to projects whose risk—that the investment and opportunity costs would go unrecovered—had substantially diminished. Differences in risk attitudes are dovetailed: the international community has a higher expected take, while companies enjoy "low-end" protection. In effect, contingent high-end premiums are paid for contingent low-end insurance.

Finally, since the economic success of the project can normally be expected to increase over time, the stream of international payments should be low at first, then much higher later; the firms' share should start high and then decline. This matches the expressed attitude toward the passage of time of the parties during the negotiation.

While it is not likely that any one of these differences, by itself, would have been sufficient to lead to a negotiated settlement of this set of issues, in combination they reinforce each other in pointing toward a solution. It is remarkable that this negotiation produced a new form of mineral taxation agreement designed to use differences among the participants to fashion joint gains. This novel outcome helped to avert the negotiating impasse on financial issues in the treaty that was widely predicted. Though seabed mining has largely remained an uneconomic proposition, the coalitional dynamics leading to what was taken to be joint gain merit discussion.

It is first worth noting that well over 140 countries actively participated in the LOS talks and that a large fraction of these actively participated in the discussions and negotiations over the financial terms of seabed mining. The reader will notice that we have described the joint gains achieved as between two large coalitions of parties in these financial talks: potential seabed mining countries and the coalition of developing countries. Though there were many other divisions and crosscutting coalitions in the talks, these two groups rapidly coalesced in the financial discussions and largely determined their course.

In charge of these talks was Singapore's ambassador, Tommy T. B. Koh. As chair of this particular set of the sessions, he was very innovative with respect to the process he set in motion to explore and build agreement around the set of mutually advantageous terms described here. Koh's method was analogous to a three-ring circus. First, a small group under his direction was constantly utilized to invent new ideas and suggest means for negotiating impasses. Second, important delegates were invited into an enlarged version of this group to test their reactions to the working ideas. Based on these reactions, the smaller group's proposals would be modified and ultimately gain a degree of acceptance or would be rejected by some of the key delegates. Finally, Koh would have promising ideas introduced into larger plenary sessions. He would often ask a prominent member attending the session to raise the idea. In discussion of the idea's merits, Koh's summaries would creatively interpret comments in an effort to build momentum toward agreement.

Successful proposals typically followed a path of increasing familiarity to the delegates, followed by incorporation into a sense of conventional wisdom, to gaining a degree of legitimacy, and finally inclusion in the draft treaty text. Of course, inclusion did not guarantee a permanent place; a dynamic process of textual change continued throughout the conference.

Thus far we have described a process of the diffusion of knowledge over time about the issues under negotiation. This was not, however, a pure learning process but, instead, involved considerable conflict of interest. Thus, the final structure of the financial arrangement as well as the rates and magnitudes involved were differentially advantageous to the various conference participants. Thus, when final arrangements had to be agreed, Chairman Koh devised a process far more conducive to distributional negotiations than were the large plenary sessions—in which concessions by one party could be rapidly accepted without reciprocity. After two years of negotiation over this set of issues, Koh had been able to discern what might be called *patterns of deference* among the delegates. Within each of the broad geographic blocs, certain delegates had come to be seen as especially knowledgeable about the issues and as sufficiently committed to their respective groups' interests that Koh felt a small-scale negotiation among this group of such trusted delegates could bear fruit. Koh chose the delegates informally, and secretly closeted them for several days. Carrying out these final negotiations were diplomats from Argentina, Pakistan, the United States, Mauritius, and, of course, the chairman from Singapore. The trade-offs that were made in that five-party negotiation were never explicitly revealed; instead, the results were put forward by the Chairman as his best attempt at consensus, with the hope and expectation that those delegates who had participated in the small discussion would "deliver" their geographic groupings.

Koh's process opportunism was responsible for the result in no small measure. The consensus so achieved was not an endorsement of the financial terms but a tacit agreement not to attack them. They survived into the final text and were generally acclaimed by the conference—which subsequently elected Koh president of the overall negotiations.[15] (Indeed, although the United States had a long list of objections to the seabed mining provisions of the treaty, the financial provisions largely went uncriticized.) Yet the "pyramiding" and maturation of smaller agreements into near-consensus is a common feature of international negotiations.[16]

In sum, two-level games offer fertile ground—not present in bilateral dealings—for process opportunism in seeking to affect coalitional dynamics. In the first example we presented, the lack of full information about the U.S. position in the INF talks led Chancellor Kohl to take what he felt to be a supportive position—while a powerful argument for *maintaining* that same U.S. position was taken to be Kohl's stance. These mutually supporting perceptions were thus welded into a firm commitment vis-à-vis the Soviets. Similarly, the fact that the domestic opponents of the policies being adopted at the 1978 Bonn summit did not have access to the direct negotiations among the heads of state made it possible for the summit to contrive added international "pressure" for such policies—as well as to use the lure of an international package involving a broader set of issues—to influence adoption of the policies.

Ambassador Koh's careful design of a sequence of procedures intended to lead to consensus in the LOS talks represents a different class of process tactics. With the leeway as chairman to influence who dealt with whom, in

15. A number of other factors, of course, contributed to this successful resolution of the financial terms. These are discussed in Sebenius 1984.

16. Winham (1986) coined the term *pyramiding* in negotiation. An additional example involving the chairman's actions at the Uraguay round of GATT, with strong parallels to the LOS experience, can be found in Winham 1989.

which forum, and over which issues, Koh was able to stimulate the effective diffusion of knowledge about the issues. Small, private groups generated ideas that were successively considered and, if promising, modified by larger groups of delegates. Further, by discerning emerging patterns of deference among the delegates, Koh was later able to constitute a very small negotiation, whose agreement could be pyramided into a larger accord. Rather than process opportunism, which suggests tactics that take existing processes for granted, this episode really represents what more accurately might be called process entrepreneurialism.

Across these examples, the observed tactical complexities derive from three factors that are inherently absent from bilateral dealing. First, obviously, there are many parties. Second, the patterns of interaction among these parties are not merely free-form interactions among the full group; instead, there are actual or de facto restrictions on communication and the order and conditions of negotiating. Thus, third, in the absence of full information by all parties, the process can be shaped or exploited for the ends of one or more of the participants. Coalition building and breaking can take place by stages, in separate places, and among carefully chosen subsets of the participants.

This section has by no means systematically analyzed the role of process-related tactics in multilateral bargaining. For example, it has not dealt with multilevel hierarchies or ratification requirements by players that may be separated in time or place from the "primary" negotiators. In special settings such as legislatures, procedural complexity breeds enormous sophistication in coalitional action.[17] Nevertheless, this section highlights and begins to illustrate a broad class of process-driven coalitional tactics that deserve extensive investigation.

Strategic Sequencing

When numerous players are actually or potentially involved in a negotiation, the sequence of approach can play a significant role in influencing negotiated outcomes. A party involved in such a situation may seek to assess who should be approached first and on what basis. Depending on the results of this interaction, who next? And so on.[18] The reasoning behind the answers to these questions is the subject of this part of our discussion. This is not, however, a separable subject from the tactics considered in our discussions of party arithmetic and process opportunism. In particular, elements of the formal or informal process may significantly influence sequencing choices; in-

---

17. For a sophisticated tactical elaboration in a U.S. context, see Heymann 1987.

18. Insightful discussions of bilateral interactions pyramiding into agreements involving many parties can be found in Aumann and Myerson 1986 and Murnighan and Brass 1989.

deed, some process-inspired tactics might more felicitously be considered as examples of strategic sequencing. Moreover, it may become important to assess whether new players should be brought in, or existing ones "cut out," and, if so, how. As such, party arithmetic also influences sequencing choices.

Coalitional Commitments in Arms Control

An intriguing coalition-building episode involving elements of the Reagan administration as well as the Soviets nicely illustrates the way that commitments can be attempted by careful consideration of the sequence of negotiations. Within the U.S. government, Secretary of State Shultz and National Security Advisor McFarlane conceived an approach to achieve a "grand compromise" whereby restrictions on the Strategic Defense Initiative would be traded for significant reductions in heavy offensive Soviet missiles. In Strobe Talbott's 1988 account, Schultz and McFarlane developed

> . . . the idea of getting [President] Reagan to approve, in its vaguest terms, a secret negotiation: The administration would open a back channel to the Soviets in a way that at least initially excluded the Pentagon civilians; McFarlane would quietly enlist the support of the uniformed military. With luck and skill, the negotiation might produce an agreement that could be presented to the President as virtually a done deal. Nitze would be both the chief designer and the chief negotiator [with the Soviets] of the American position.
>
> Nitze knew that as soon as [Defense Secretary] Weinberger learned what had happened, he would "fight like hell," but by then, he and McFarlane hoped, it would be too late. The alliance between the State Department and the Joint Chiefs of Staff on behalf of a deal that the Soviets had already accepted would be unbeatable. With the grand compromise a fait accompli, and with his own soldiers and diplomats as well as the Soviets lined up to support it, Reagan would impose it on Weinberger. (1988, 264)

Talbott reports that the idea was never implemented, largely due to Soviet reluctance. Even so, the intended complex series of intra–U.S. government maneuvers as well as dealings with the Soviets illustrates coalitional tactics designed to commit to an advantageous position within the relevant bargaining range (here, conceived as between Weinberger and everyone else—U.S. and Soviet). The intended sequence of dealings envisioned by Schultz—Reagan, the U.S. military, the USSR, and, only then, the Pentagon civilians—was intended to get allies on board first, generate momentum, and then, with public disclosure of the deal, overwhelm potential arms control opponents. To see the importance of this sequence, imagine an initial approach to Weinberger and the Pentagon civilians; the process would have had a far smaller chance of success.

The 1985 Plaza Accord on the Dollar

When James Baker became Secretary of the Treasury in 1985, the strong dollar was taking a severe toll on U.S. industry and generating powerful protectionist reactions. The United States, under former Secretary Donald Regan, then chief of staff at the White House, had spurned international economic cooperation to bring the dollar down for some time. Baker's complex efforts to build a domestic and international coalition committed to a coordinated effort to bring the dollar down merits review. To go forward with the strategy domestically, Baker relied on secrecy from most of the Reagan administration as well as the general public. Among the necessary players in the administration, deft tactics were used.

> Reagan knew of the [Plaza Hotel] meeting in advance, of course, but was apprised of the full scope of Baker's plan only two days beforehand. Devaluation "was sold to the President as necessary to stem the protectionist tide in Congress," says a Baker intimate. "It was sold to Don Regan as being consistent with an earlier call he had made for an international conference to discuss exchange rates. To this day, I don't think Don understood what we were about to do. [Then Federal Reserve Chairman Paul] Volcker was managed because we had carefully split his board. Paul had no alternative but to go along." (Kramer 1989, 32)[19]

Armed with this domestic "mandate," Baker used the Plaza meeting to build the necessary international coalition both to act and to make it very difficult for his domestic rivals to later reverse the resulting policy course.

> "At first," says one of [the Finance Ministers at the Plaza negotiations], he split us just like he split the Fed. He began by using the U.S. and Japan against West Germany. Then he combined those three to bring along the whole Group of Five [including Britain and France]. He bluffed us constantly and regularly threatened to go home. . . . [Yet] it all seemed so mellow." (Kramer 1989, 32)

Again careful sequencing to break and build coalitions is evident as Baker achieved an effective commitment of the finance ministers to his pre-

---

19. For considerably more detail, see Funabashi 1988.

ferred agreement—which was, indeed, implemented. Here, the zone of possible agreements must be understood as encompassing both domestic and international players. Secrecy and ambiguity, divide-and-conquer tactics, along with a tight deadline were used domestically to gain Baker the right to move into the actual Plaza process. There, with the initial concurrence of the Japanese—whose position on the dollar was firmly allied with that of the United States—it was possible to get German agreement. Then, this powerful three-way coalition could press the others into the final agreement. (To see the potential importance of sequencing here, imagine that the Germans, *in advance,* had been able to forge an ironclad coalition with the British, French, and others against the likely American proposal.) As before, the coalitional machinations are complex, but they are members of a broad class of such sequencing actions intended to create an irreversible commitment to a preferred agreement.

The Bureau of Security and Consular Affairs

A more involved example from the realm of bureaucratic politics illustrates a characteristic form of strategic sequencing. The acting Administrator of the State Department's Bureau of Security and Consular Affairs (the Visa Bureau) in 1966, Phillip Heymann, sought to permit non–U.S. citizens to obtain lifetime visas rather than visas of a single year's duration (see Heymann 1987). Heymann's bureau had been at the center of an enormous public (liberal vs. conservative) controversy the previous year that involved allegations of FBI investigations of U.S. citizens abroad (notably anti–Vietnam War intellectuals). Though this controversy had finally passed, the bruising public battle had left a strong preference for peace and quiet from Heymann's bureau at high levels of the State Department.

A revocable lifetime visa could, in fact, be terminated at any time should unfavorable information be uncovered on a foreign citizen; hence, there was no substantive security threat posed by Heymann's proposed policy change. Nonetheless, this issue could be seen as an explosive one that might again pit conservative guardians of national security against liberal proponents of a more open society. It was likely to reopen old wounds and flare up into the same kind of controversy as had occurred in the previous year around the bureau's alleged complicity in the FBI's requests for questionable surveillance abroad. Quite likely, the simple announcement that this policy had been adopted administratively—a move that was entirely within Heymann's formal authority—would antagonize relevant congressional subcommittees and committee chairmen as well as the FBI and other national security–conscious parties.

Beyond Heymann, there was, however, no real support for the idea of a lifetime visa. Only a very few potentially involved parties would be even weakly positive toward this proposal if it were unexpectedly presented to them for support. Given the possible political risks, premature appeal by Heymann to Secretary of State Dean Rusk for support of this visa proposal—although Rusk was broadly sympathetic with the notion of an open society—would have almost certainly produced a negative response. To the secretary, the risks of generating bureaucratic opposition and a public flare-up would have been too great for the general benefits of the idea.

Thus, before presenting the idea to the secretary of state, it was necessary for Heymann to build a coalition of support for it by adding a series of parties whose assent would signal a less risky, and hence more desirable, measure. The dynamics of this process were very similar to those one encounters in international conferences and legislative bodies and among countries seeking support for various other initiatives. To accomplish this goal, Heymann paid careful attention to the sequence for approaching the various parties and to the nature of his proposed appeal to each one of them. Who should be approached first and on what basis? Then who? And how should the subsequent order of approach be determined?

Let us briefly review the set of potentially involved parties who need to be consulted for any initiative to succeed.

A Key Subordinate. Heymann had a key subordinate who was extremely familiar with the operational side of the Visa Office. He had briefly been an FBI agent and was sympathetic to the security concerns that might be raised by Heymann's visa proposal. Nonetheless, he would fully understand the lack of any real security threat posed by Heymann's idea. This subordinate had close links to the relevant congressional subcommittees as well as to the Immigration and Naturalization Service (INS) at the Justice Department with whom the Bureau of Security and Consular Affairs closely worked. This subordinate had felt sufficiently close to Heymann at one time to ask him to propose the subordinate for an ambassadorship, a post not normally given to those who had followed his career path.

A Key Congressman. This midwestern representative, a Democrat, chaired the House subcommittee that oversaw Heymann's bureau's operations. He was strongly security-conscious and would likely be suspicious of any proposed change of the sort suggested by Heymann. Despite his subcommittee's formal oversight role, however, he and Heymann had not met in the year since Heymann became acting Administrator of the Bureau of Security and Consular Affairs.

Dean Rusk, Secretary of State. As indicated, Rusk was sympathetic to Heymann's goal for a more open society in the United States, certainly one that was more open to foreign visitors. Yet Rusk's preoccupation with the diplomatic difficulties involved with the Vietnam War and his extremely unhappy experience with the previous year's blowup emanating from Heymann's bureau's activities would lead him to be very skeptical of any proposal with political risks.

A Key Senator. This southern senator chaired the Senate committee in whose charge fell the activities of the Visa Bureau. He was strongly security-minded, but had so many issues before his committee that he tended to defer to those in the House of similar mind and who could focus more on particular issues.

The Director of the Immigration and Naturalization Service (INS). This man's office closely coordinated with the Visa Office and exchanged many favors back and forth. In particular, this man and Heymann's key subordinate were good working colleagues. The INS director was concerned with security but very knowledgeable about the actual effects of any changes in procedure.

J. Edgar Hoover, Head of the FBI. Hoover, whose agency had been entangled with the previous year's imbroglio, was actively security-minded and could be expected to oppose actions brought to him for approval.

The U.S. Attorney General. The attorney general, within whose department both the INS and the FBI were located, was concerned about security issues with substantive merit. He had, however, worked closely with Heymann before, and had both trust and respect for him. Nevertheless, he could be expected to be skeptical of the proposal unless it was fine on the merits.

The Secretary of Commerce. The commerce secretary chaired a recently convened committee on emergency measures to address the growing balance of payments deficit due to the Vietnam War. President Johnson had urgently requested a list of measures intended to address the payments problem, but under the constraint that little new expense for implementing the suggested measures would be available.

The Department of State's European Bureau. This bureau had long chafed under the asymmetry between European countries, which allowed free travel for U.S. citizens without visas, and the United States, which required visas of foreigners. This bureaucratic entity would likely find Heymann's proposal attractive.

Having thought through this likely set of potentially involved players and how they might see his proposal—on balance, quite negatively—Heymann needed to think through a strategy for building his supportive coalition for bringing in Rusk. Without going into great detail about the building of his coalition, it is worth tracing the sequence of steps he took, recounting some of his reasoning, and, then, extracting analytical lessons.

From the time he became interested in the visa proposal, Heymann waited almost a year until the balance of payments crisis arose. As noted, President Johnson was politically desperate for a series of measures that could be publicly presented as at least conceivably improving the payment balance. A lifetime visa would arguably make it easier for foreigners to visit the United States and, hence, increase tourism and boost the balance of payments. At worst, it would make no difference. Thus, Heymann responded to the call of the Secretary of Commerce for members of the administration to suggest proposals intended to improve the balance of payments. His visa proposal had been a "solution awaiting a problem." Of course, Heymann could only present this as a tentative personal idea, without formal State Department support.

Once the Commerce Secretary's grateful assent had been given, Heymann then returned to the State Department and approached the European Bureau with his "personal suggestion." The European Bureau was delighted with the idea, which Heymann again stressed did not yet have any official standing.

It was then desirable and possible to approach Heymann's key subordinate. Heymann did so, taking care to stress that his discussions of the idea to date were only exploratory. He then solicited his subordinate's informed professional view of the merits of this issue as a security matter. Of course, the merits were not in question and, after adopting a few modifications suggested by the subordinate, Heymann convened a meeting of the European Bureau and his subordinate to discuss the issue. This was a chance for his subordinate to act "statesmanlike" in front of a group of people who would be his peers should an ambassadorship become available.

By this approach, in particular, sticking to the strict merits of the proposal, Heymann won over his powerful subordinate who controlled the implementation of the process and to whom many relevant legislative staff members as well as key legislators looked for guidance on the security dimensions of such issues.

The next step was also clear. With his subordinate on board it was relatively easy to earn the endorsement of the Immigration and Naturalization Service, given their close working relationship. Yet how should Heymann's coalition-building efforts continue? Rather than reasoning "forward" (asking who next?) as he had done thus far, Heymann asked a hypothetical question, reasoning "*backward*" from Secretary of State Dean Rusk. Whose approval would Heymann ideally gain in order to maximize the probability that Rusk would acquiesce to Heymann's proposal? Heymann's answer: if Heymann could tell Rusk that the Secretary of Commerce, the Attorney General, the key congressman, and the key senator were all on board, then it would be relatively easier for Rusk to say yes to Heymann's proposal—since the political risks would largely have been neutralized, given that constellation of support.

But continue this process of reasoning "backward." If Heymann were to approach the key senator with his proposal, whose prior approval would maximize the chances of the senator's acquiescing? Heymann's answer to this question seemed to be the combined support of the most knowledgeable House player and the Attorney General.

Continuing this reasoning, who would the representative want to see on board to maximally increase the chances of approval? To Heymann, the answer to this question seemed clear. If both Heymann's key subordinate and the INS director—who represented the operational side of this issue and whom the representative knew to share his security concerns—were on board, some of his concern would be assuaged. Moreover, if the nation's senior law enforcement officer, the Attorney General, were behind the issue, and if the Secretary of Commerce and, arguably, the President wanted the proposal, there would be still greater allure. Since Heymann already had his subordinate's support, plus the INS director's and the direct support of the Commerce Secretary, his next target—the Attorney General—became clear.

Given Heymann's personal relationship with the Attorney General, the Commerce Secretary's support, and the acquiescence of the INS (the Justice Department's responsible agency), the Attorney General gave his blessing. Then the representative could be approached with the full set of desirable supporters in tow. The senator's acquiescence would be relatively easy. Then the approach to Secretary of State Rusk could be made in the most persuasive manner.

This exercise illustrates a more complex version of strategic sequencing as a central dynamic of coalition building. A few observations are in order. First, the *prior commitments* of other parties may be used as resources in obtaining the acquiescence of other subsequent parties. Second, the sequence of approaches depends on what we called patterns of deference in the Law of the Sea case, that is to say, who defers to whom on the basis of perceived expertise, status and reputation, or obligations of reciprocity and friendship. By choosing early parties to whom later ones will defer, it is possible to build a coalition by this method. (Similarly, *patterns of antagonism* would likely preclude the United States seeking Iranian or Libyan support early on in any international initiatives taken in the 1970s or 1980s.)

The method illustrated by Heymann's actions might be called *backward mapping,* an approach closely related to the mathematical technique of dynamic programming.[20] Starting with the party whose agreement is ultimately needed—in this case, Secretary of State Dean Rusk—one then works backward, asking whose prior assent would maximize the probability of agreement from the parties ultimately needed. Then, from that prior group of parties, ask who is most likely to agree and whose assent prior to approaching this group would be most helpful. By this logic, one can work backward from an ultimate target to a present situation. In alliances, both formal and informal, in

---

20. See Bellman 1957 or Dreyfus 1965.

international conferences, as well as in legislative bodies, this kind of backward mapping—albeit on an intuitive basis—is a common feature. Critical to the process, the sequence of parties approached can significantly affect the probability of success; that is, there is *path dependence.*

It is worth noting in this example that the tacit alliance formed by Heymann not only furthered his interest but also decreased the perceived political risk of the initiative from Rusk's perspective. Hence, as between the Secretary of State and the acting administrator, at least, a mutual gain was attained as a result of elaborate coalitional tactics.

Effects of Coalitional Action on the Perceived Bargaining Set

In our analysis thus far, we have examined tactics and dynamics associated with the two basic multiparty processes: *building and breaking coalitions.* Beyond reviewing canonical coalition dynamics and analyzing sometimes unexpected, de facto coalitions, we have focused on three classes of tactics that we have called *party arithmetic, process opportunism,* and *strategic sequencing.* The tactical actions themselves as well as the intent behind them and their effects can be covert, tacit, or explicit.

It now remains to relate tactical action to its intended effect on negotiated outcomes. We will argue that the tactics are intended to favorably affect the zone of possible agreement in three distinct ways: (1) improving one's alternative to negotiated agreement or worsening that of other coalitions; (2) realizing joint gains; and (3) credibly committing to advantageous positions within the perceived zone of possible agreements. We consider each class of favorable effect on the zone of possible agreement in turn.

Tactics that Favorably Change Alternatives to Negotiated Agreement

The negotiation process, including that involving many parties, typically consists of each party trying to reach an agreement that advances its interests as much as possible, subject to exceeding (in value terms) its best alternative to negotiated agreement. Such alternatives to agreement may include legal action, forming a coalition with another party, imposing military or economic sanctions, withdrawal from the negotiation, or other unilateral actions. Each side's perceptions of the alternatives to negotiated agreement are of central tactical importance in negotiated interactions. Indeed, a necessary condition for agreement is that each side see cooperative action as advancing its interests more than would be the case in the event of no agreement. (In coalitional cases, the value of a party's no-agreement alternative is its assessment of the possible agreements that might be reached among the other parties.) If the no-agreement alternatives of one coalition improve, the zone of possible agreement—which is defined as those potential agreements that are better for each side than its alternatives to agreement—correspondingly shrinks. In general, the more attractive one's alternatives to agreement with other coalitions (or, for that matter, within one's own coalition), the more favorable agreement is likely to be. A significant amount of analytical and experimental evidence supports this general proposition.[21] By contrast, worsening the no-agreement alternatives for others can improve the likely attractiveness of an agreement for one's own side.

A variety of the cases we have discussed illustrate this class of effects. In particular, Chrysler U.K. acted to worsen the Labour government's alternatives in order to prevent the formation of an adverse union-government coalition. Similarly, the tacit coalition building by Kennecott and Malta improved their own no-agreement alternatives while worsening those of Chile and Great Britain, respectively.

Coalitional Actions That Realize Joint Gains for the Parties

The second potential favorable effect of coalitional action on the zone of possible agreement involves moves to realize additional joint gains for the parties relative to those presently perceived as available. By *joint gains* we mean improvements in the outcomes of all parties to potential agreement—improvements that do not come at the expense of any party. At a fundamental level, all joint gains arise from three sources (Lax and Sebenius 1986, chap. 5). First, the parties may have identical or shared interests in the outcome; that is, they want the agreement to contain the same elements. Second, there may be differences in interests or perceptions that may be dovetailed. For example, if different interests are accorded different levels of importance by the various sides, mutually beneficial trades or exchanges may be fashioned. (Certain linkage and logrolling strategies fall within this category; see, e.g., Tollison and Willett 1979 or Sebenius 1983.) If the various sides have different forecasts of the likelihood of future events, different attitudes toward risk, or different discount rates, for example, contingent agreements or agreements that vary over time may yield joint gains for the parties. Finally, agreements may yield joint gains to the parties where there exist economies of scale or number, as in the case of alliances or jointly undertaken ventures.

When coalitional action increases the possibility or salience of joint

---

21. See, e.g., Lax and Sebenius 1985 and 1986 or Neale and Northcroft forthcoming for recent experimental evidence.

gains, it reduces the perception of a conflict of interest among the parties.[22] Intuition suggests that negotiations are likely to be more successful when they offer greater joint gains or, equivalently, have less conflict of interest. Indeed, in a series of carefully controlled experiments, Malouf and Roth (1981) found that agreements took longer to achieve as the conflict of interest among the parties increased. Axelrod (1970) found a strong positive relationship between conflict of interest in Prisoner's Dilemma games and the probability of defection (rather than mutually beneficial cooperation). Reviews of the social-psychological literature lend support to the propositions that lower conflicts of interest (1) lead to speedier settlements, (2) have higher agreement probabilities, (3) reduce the danger that one or more parties will repudiate the agreement, (4) tend to strengthen relationships among the parties, thus facilitating later agreements, and (5) contribute to organizational effectiveness where subunits (individuals, subunits, departments) with distinct needs and values engage in intraorganizational bargaining.[23]

Coalitional actions to realize joint gains from different interests and capabilities were taken in the case of the Bonn summit, and, to a lesser extent, at the Plaza in 1985. Tommy Koh's carefully orchestrated process entrepreneurialism in the Law of the Sea talks was aimed at generating joint gains (that derived from differences in forecast, risk aversion, and time preference). Phillip Heymann's covert coalition building led to joint gains in his tacit agreement with the Secretary of State. Perhaps less obvious was the lure of joint gains from a grain deal that drove the emergence of the de facto farm community–Soviet alliance in 1975.

Coalitional Actions That Commit to Advantageous Points within the Zone of Possible Agreement

Coalitions may form or take actions to commit to points within the perceived bargaining range. In line with Schelling's pioneering work in this area, a visible, binding, irrevocable, and credible commitment within the zone of possible agreement effectively presents others with the equivalent of a take-it-or-leave-it offer (see Schelling 1960 and 1966). If the process has been such that the commitment does not generate hostility or spite, or engender a conflict spiral, the other sides will have to choose between the agreement to which the first coalition has committed and less attractive alternatives to agreement.

A great deal of analytical and experimental evidence considers the condi-

22. For a precise discussion of the concept of *conflict of interest,* see Axelrod 1970. An elaboration of the effects of changes in perceptions of joint gains can be found in Sebenius 1984 (114–16).

23. Some of this paragraph is paraphrased from Sebenius 1984. In particular, see Pruitt 1982.

tions under which commitments are effective (Bachrach and Lawler 1981; Lax and Sebenius 1986), but for present purposes, it is worth specifying the mechanism by which a commitment functions. In effect, a commitment incurs significant costs for the committed party in the event that the party violates its commitment. Other points, formerly within the (precommitment) bargaining range, are thus rendered unacceptable—given the conditional costs incurred for violating the commitment. Thus, a successful commitment reshapes the bargaining range in a favorable way for the committed party. Notice that, while the members of a coalition may create joint gains among themselves by coalescing, they may also extract value from nonmembers by committing to advantageous demands vis-à-vis the outsiders. Either way, by creating value internally or extracting it from others by credible commitment, the coalitional members are better off.

Thus, the third class of coalitional action for advantageously influencing the outcome of negotiations involves building support among a group to credibly stake out an advantageous position. For example, agreement among the heads of state at the Bonn summit effectively committed their governments to actions that might otherwise have been blocked by domestic, opposing coalitions. The MacFarlane-Shultz plan to covertly build a coalition inside the U.S. government, with the Soviets, was intended to lead to an agreement that would neutralize the Pentagon civilians. James Baker's coalitional actions vis-à-vis the Plaza Accords led to a commitment by the industrial countries to a policy devaluing the dollar; that commitment also neutralized his domestic opponents.

Accounting for the Effects of Coalitional Actions on the Perceived Bargaining Set

Thus far, we have related classes of coalitional tactics to intended negotiated outcomes through changes in perceptions of the bargaining set. Of course, such effects are necessarily subjective and only change the perceived probabilistic distribution of possible ultimate agreements. At least one important analytic task remains, namely, accounting for the means by which each class of tactics achieves its effects on the perceived zone of possible agreements. We shall consider each class of coalitional action in turn.

Accounting for the Effects of Party Arithmetic on the Perceived Bargaining Set

In general, tactics to add or subtract parties from coalitional interactions function by observing and exploiting actual or potential linkages between the targets of the tactics and the other involved parties. These linkages may involve interests, alternatives to agreement, or other existing or potential interdependencies.

Consider first the tactics to add parties. In the Kennecott case, a variety of potential but nonobvious financial links were forged by the company to build an advantageous coalition vis-à-vis the Chilean government. Similarly, Maltese Prime Minister Dom Mintoff exploited NATO alliance relationships with Britain as well as longstanding usage patterns of Maltese facilities by NATO members to expand the scope of what could otherwise have been a simple U.K.-Malta negotiation over base rental terms.

When seeking to "subtract" the assuredly hostile FBI director from his bureaucratic coalition-building efforts, Phillip Heymann relied on the hierarchical linkage between the FBI and the attorney general—with whom Heymann had a good relationship and could make an argument on the merits—to speak for and prevent FBI involvement. (Notice how this tactic relied opportunistically on the formal process that determined who could speak for whom in the Justice Department.)

Accounting for the Effects of Process Opportunism on the Perceived Bargaining Set

Recall that, by the term *process,* we encompass the formal and informal factors that influence or determine who can speak on whose behalf (and in what order), who can and cannot communicate with whom, who can commit whom to an agreement (even if provisionally), who must ratify or can overturn whose previous actions, as well as the nature of the decision rules (e.g., voting, unanimity, nonobjection, etc.). Normally, laws, formal rules, protocol, or informal patterns embody these elements of process, but physical, temporal, and spatial considerations often exercise significant process influence.

Obviously, an infinitude of possible processes exist and we could not possibly investigate all the classes of coalitional tactics to which they give rise. Yet we have examined a number of characteristic processes: intra-alliance consultation (Kohl and the "zero option"), "internal" bureaucratic politics (the Bureau of Security and Consular Affairs), two-level games and their first cousins, internal-external bargaining (the 1978 Bonn summit; the 1985 Plaza accord; the Shultz-MacFarlane arms control plan); as well as international conference diplomacy (Koh and the Law of the Sea).

Notice that process opportunism, as we have used the term, can mean tactical choices that take advantage of a given process (e.g., the Bonn summit) as well as entrepreneurial efforts to put in place or alter a process (e.g.,

Koh and the Law of the Sea). We should also stress that opportunistic action can be intended to advance individual policy choices (e.g., Heymann) or facilitate a collectively beneficial agreement (e.g., Koh).

That the involved parties were often not all present at the same time in the same place was among the factors across these varied situations that permitted tactical action to change perceptions of the zone of possible agreement. With physical and temporal separation, there was typically less than full, ongoing communication. With secrecy, partial communication, and/or imperfect information, one player could act treacherously (as in the Hitler-Stalin nonaggression pact), or "merely" opportunistically shape the perceptions of others in ways that made that player's preferred agreement seem more valuable. Potential allies could be enlisted early and potential opponents separated to prevent their forming an opposing coalition.

To the extent that partial or full commitment to an emerging interpretation or agreement resulted from such subgroup interactions, it could become harder subsequently to dislodge for at least four reasons. First, commitments (even provisional commitments) carry costs to reversing. Second, the agreement could become something of a focal point and gain psychological prominence and attractiveness (Schelling 1960). Third, renegotiation can become increasingly costly and uncertain. Fourth, potential opponents may become isolated, thwarted from forming effective opposing coalitions, or coopted. As increasing numbers of involved parties become committed to an emerging agreement, we might describe the process as one of *pyramiding* toward ultimate agreement; this can be as simple as adding needed allies or changing the expectations of a large number of parties about the likely ultimate outcome and thereby generating bandwagon effects.

Accounting for the Effects of Strategic Sequencing Actions on the Perceived Bargaining Set

As we have noted at several points in the course of the analysis, the classes of coalitional action under consideration are not at all mutually exclusive. Indeed, our presentation took advantage of the fact that certain cases involving process opportunism also involved party arithmetic and that strategic sequencing actions sometimes depended on process elements as well as the possibility of adding or subtracting parties. In seeking to give an account of the effects of process opportunism, we described a dynamic that is very common in coalitional interactions, namely, that bilateral agreements (or agreements among subgroups) often expand to become agreements of the whole. This pyramiding phenomenon necessarily implies some order of actions that can be chosen with the goal of affecting perceptions of the target zone of possible agreement.

The choice of sequence can be made by a reasoning process that we have called backward mapping that works from the desired end back through the sequence of possible choices until it reaches the starting point. The path so chosen should involve actions—approaches, appeals, proposals, and other tactics—that pyramid to offer the highest subjective probability of reaching the ultimately desired agreement.[24] The choice of path matters, of course, because the effectiveness of subsequent actions depends—sometimes heavily, sometimes lightly—on the path of previous actions and their results; in short, the unfolding outcomes of coalitional actions are path-dependent. To give a satisfactory account of the functioning of strategic sequencing, then, we must ascertain the conditions that give rise to this path dependence and efforts to pyramid coalitional actions into desired agreements. Three factors stand out.

First, as we argued in the case of process opportunism, prior commitments to emerging agreements necessarily entail a cost to change. For example, as the Plaza and Bonn summit agreements took shape and drew adherents, they became progressively harder for potential opponents to dislodge. Hence the commitment possibilities that inhere in a situation can affect the chosen path.[25]

A second factor involves the possibility that prior actions can build credibility and reputation that favorably shape expectations of players at subsequent stages of the process. James Baker, by early successes, was able to do this effectively, persuading those with whom the government would later negotiate that the alternatives to agreement on the proposed terms were bad and that opposition would likely be costly. As a result, something of a bandwagon might gain momentum.

Third, if patterns of deference exist (as in the Bureau of Security and Consular Affairs) or can be discerned over time (as with Koh in the Law of the Sea), the strategic sequence may be affected. If such patterns of deference exist, the prior agreement of those to whom others defer can serve as a resource in later encounters. Parties approached later in the sequence, having been made aware of the prior acquiescence of others, may take the others' action as a substantive signal: "If X or if X and Y agreed, it must be a good idea; I'll go along." Those approached later may also be more willing to go along if others have already agreed, since the risk of being wrong is spread over more parties. Further, it may be that some relationship of rec-

---

24. Another objective may be appropriate, such as maximizing the expected value or utility of the outcome, perhaps subject to a constraint of not exceeding a certain risk level.

25. See Schelling 1966 in particular for an elaboration of the conditions under which various commitments can be made and undone.

iprocity exists, that if an earlier party agreed, a later party may be returning a favor (or "banking" one) by joining the group.

In short, the presence and extent of commitment possibilities, opportunities to build a reputation and shape expectations, as well as patterns of deference (as substantive signals, for risk spreading, or as a result of reciprocity) comprise conditions that permit path-dependent pyramiding, in which the effectiveness of subsequent actions depends on the path of actions previously taken. These are the factors behind strategic sequencing calculations.

Conclusions

We have used the term *multilateral* to refer to negotiations involving more than two monolithic parties or factions, which may be countries, distinct regions, or organizations, as well as groups or even individuals within larger entities. Coalitional interactions among such factions or parties ranging from two-level games to conference diplomacy, to alliance dealings and bureaucratic politics, have fallen within the scope of this chapter. As we noted in the introduction, and which for convenience we revisit here, much is possible in multiparty situations that simply cannot occur in strictly bilateral settings, including coalitional alignments and realignments, the possibilities of de facto alliances, "natural" coalitions, and blocking coalitions. In particular, this can lead to blurring the concept of side in negotiation—where more than one entity nominally comprises a side, but "internal" divisions and coalitions cutting across the different sides may act in concert. In particular, we have investigated three classes of tactics and dynamics that can only occur in a multiparty context: (1) party arithmetic, or actions to affect which entities are and/or are not actively involved in a given negotiation, that is, "adding" and "subtracting" parties; (2) process opportunism, or tactics that depend on more complex structural or process restrictions such as who can directly talk with whom, how information is transmitted, who may speak for whom, and which parties must approve the actions of others; and (3) strategic sequencing, or tactics that depend on the order and sequencing of how the different entities are approached and/or informed of the actions of other players. This may lead to agreements among subsets of the involved parties, not necessarily coalitionally aligned, that may or may not pyramid to encompass a larger group.

An almost bewildering variety of coalitional tactics and dynamics flow from the inherent differences between bilateral and multilateral settings. The detailed examples we have discussed should amply bear out this claim. Despite the literature that we reviewed on multiparty bargains from several fields, however, we found that a thorough and explicit focus on process, on characteristic tactics and dynamics in multilateral settings, along with their effects on negotiated outcomes, was generally lacking in key respects. While some elements of process and certain coalitional dynamics in relation to negotiated outcomes have been investigated, the set of observed behaviors—even those illustrated by the various examples presented in this chapter—was far wider than that which appeared to be accounted for by the literature.

In response, we offered a relatively simple framework to interpret such extremely varied coalitional actions in terms of their intended effects on the zone of possible agreement among a relevant set of parties. This framework, which has significant negotiation analytic and empirical support, interpreted coalitional actions as shaping the zone of possible agreement in desirable ways by (1) favorably influencing alternatives to negotiated agreement, (2) realizing joint gains, and/or (3) committing to favorable points within the zone. For each broad class of coalitional action—party arithmetic, process opportunism, and strategic sequencing—we offered an account of the conditions that permitted it to affect perceptions of the bargaining set. We used this framework to account for a number of observed behaviors, including both coalition building and breaking, covert and tacit as well as explicit. To us, a virtue of this framework lies in its capacity to make ready sense out of apparently highly diverse phenomena observed in multiparty settings.

Of course, there are many other rationales for coalitional action. For example, group action may seek to establish or reinforce important norms, either among the members or with respect to dealings with another coalition. Further, beyond what a coalition can do collectively may be values intrinsic to its formation and continuation, the benefits of simply being together affirming common values or, as James Q. Wilson (1975) referred to it, the "solidary" rather than the individual incentives for action as a group. Yes, as illustrated by our examples, the three basic purposes described here account for significant classes of observed behavior.

Valuable next steps would include a more systematic characterization of the dynamics we have identified, a careful investigation of specific kinds of tactics, along with a specification of the conditions under which particular classes of such dynamics arise. Although we have moved among numerous substantive areas, certain dynamics may frequently be associated with particular types of multilateral negotiation, such as bargaining within alliances as opposed to with adversaries, or those with economic as opposed to military focus, or others taking place within an ongoing forum (such as a United Nations conference), or in an ad hoc setting.

It is probably fair to assert that the predominant mode of bargaining is multilateral, especially where one considers the possibilities of different factions within each "side." Yet theoretical attention has largely been focused, for understandable and justifiable reasons, on the bilateral case. We hope our exploration of tactics and dynamics in multiparty situations has helped redress the balance.

BIBLIOGRAPHY

Allison, Graham T. 1971. *Essence of Decision: Explaining the Cuban Missile Crisis.* Boston: Little, Brown.

Aumann, Robert, and Michael Maschler. 1964. "The Bargaining Set for Cooperative Games." In *Advances in Game Theory,* ed. M. Dresher, L. S. Shapley and A. Tucker. Princeton: Princeton University Press.

Aumann, Robert, and Roger B. Meyerson. 1986. "Endogenous Formation of Links between Players and of Coalitions: An Application of the Shapley Value." In *The Shapley Value: Essays in Honor of Lloyd S. Shapley,* ed. Alvin Roth. Cambridge: Cambridge University Press.

Axelrod, Robert. 1970. *Conflict of Interest.* Chicago: Markham.

Bachrach, Samuel B., and E. J. Lawler. 1981. *Bargaining.* San Francisco: Jossey-Bass.

Bellman, R. 1957. *Dynamic Programming.* Princeton: Princeton University Press.

Brams, Steven J. 1972. "A Cost/Benefit Analysis of Coalition Formation in Voting Bodies." In *Probability Models of Collective Decision Making,* ed. R. G. Niemi and H. F. Weisberg. Columbus, Ohio: Merrill.

Brams, Steven J. 1975. *Game Theory and Politics.* New York: Free Press.

Brams, Steven J., and J. E. Garrigo-Pico. 1975. "Deadlocks and Bandwagons in Coalition Formation: The 1/2 and 2/3 Rules." *American Behavioral Scientist* 18:34–58.

Brams, Steven J., and J. C. Heilman. 1974. "When to Join a Coalition and with How Many Others Depends on What You Expect." *Public Choice* 17:11–25.

Caplow, Theodore. 1959. "Further Development of a Theory of Coalitions in the Triad." *American Journal of Sociology* 64:488–93.

Caplow, Theodore. 1968. *Two against One: Coalitions in Triads.* Englewood Cliffs, N.J.: Prentice-Hall.

Cohen, Benjamin J. 1986. *In Whose Interest?* New Haven: Yale University Press.

Davis, Lynn E. 1988. "Lessons of the INF Treaty." *Foreign Affairs* 66:720–34.

DeSwaan, A. 1970. "An Empirical Model of Coalition Formation as an *N*-Person Game of Policy Distance." In *The Study of Coalition Behavior,* ed. S. Groennings and E. W. Kelley. New York: Holt, Reinhart and Winston.

DeSwaan, A. 1973. *Coalition Theories and Cabinet Formations.* San Francisco: Jossey-Bass.

Dreyfus, S. E. 1965. *Dynamic Programming and the Calculus of Variations.* New York: Academic Press.

Funabashi, Yoichi. 1988. *Managing the Dollar: From the Plaza to the Louvre.* Washington, D.C.: Institute for International Economics.

Gamson, W. A. 1961. "A Theory of Coalition Formation." *American Sociological Review* 26:373–82.

Gamson, W. A. 1964. "Experimental Studies of Coalition Formation." In *Advances in Experimental Social Psychology,* ed. L. Berkowitz. New York: Academic Press.

Gulick, Edward Vose. 1955. *Europe's Classical Balance of Power.* New York: Norton.

Heymann, Philip. 1987. *The Politics of Public Management.* New Haven: Yale University Press.

Iklé, Fred C. 1964. *How Nations Negotiate.* New York: Harper and Row.

Komorita, S. S. 1974. "A Weighted Probability Model of Coalition Formation." *Psychological Review* 81:242–56.

Komorita, S. S., and J. M. Chertkoff. 1973. "A Bargaining Theory of Coalition Formation." *Psychological Review* 80:149–62.

Kramer, Michael. "Playing the Edge." *Time,* February 13.

Lax, David A., and Frederick W. Mayer. 1988. "The Logic of Linked Bargains." Harvard Business School Working Paper no. 89-012.

Lax, David A., and James K. Sebenius. 1985. "The Power of Alternatives and the Limits of Negotiation." *Negotiation Journal* 1:163–79.

Lax, David A., and James K. Sebenius. 1986. *The Manager As Negotiator.* New York: Free Press.

Leiserson, M. 1970. "Power and Ideology in Coalition Behavior." In *The Study of Coalition Behavior,* ed. S. Groennings and E. W. Kelley. New York: Holt, Rinehart and Winston.

Luce, R. D., and Howard Raiffa. 1957. *Games and Decisions.* New York: Wiley.

McKelvey, R., P. Ordeshook, and M. Winer. 1978. "The Competitive Solution for *N*-Person Games without Transferable Utility, and an Application to Committee Games." *American Political Science Review* 72:599–615.

Malouf, Michael K., and A. E. Roth. 1981. "Disagreement in Bargaining: An Experimental Approach." *Journal of Conflict Resolution* 25:329–48.

Morgenthau, Hans, and Kenneth W. Thompson. 1985. *Politics among Nations: The Struggle for Power and Peace.* 6th ed. New York: Knopf.

Murnighan, J. Keith. 1978. "Models of Coalition Behavior: Game-Theoretic, Social-Psychological, and Political Perspectives." *Psychological Bulletin* 85:1130–53.

Murnighan, J. Keith, and D. J. Brass. 1989. "Intraorganizational Coalitions." Presented at the fourth Conference on Research on Negotiation in Organization, Northwestern University, Evanston, Illinois.

Neale, Margaret A., and G. B. Northcroft. N.d. "Experience, Expertise, and Decision Bias in Negotiation." *Research on Negotiating in Organizations,* ed. B. Sheppard, M. Bazerman, and R. Lewicki. Greenwich, Conn.: JAI Press. Forthcoming.

Neustadt, Richard E. 1970. *Alliance Politics.* New York: Columbia University Press.

Olson, Mancur, and Richard Zeckhauser. 1968. "An Economic Theory of Alliances." In *Economic Theories of International Politics,* ed. Bruce Russett. Chicago: Markham.

Oye, Kenneth A. 1979. "The Domain of Choice: International Constraints and Carter Administration Foreign Policy." In *Eagle Entangled: U.S. Foreign Policy in a Complex World,* ed. Kenneth A. Oye, Donald Rothchild, and Robert J. Lieber. New York: Longman.

Porter, Roger. 1980. *Presidential Decision Making*. Cambridge: Cambridge University Press.

Pruitt, Dean G. 1982. "Integrative Agreements: Nature and Antecedents." Presented at the Conference on Bargaining Inside Organizations, Boston University.

Putnam, Robert D. 1988. "Diplomacy and Domestic Politics: The Logic of Two-Level Games." *International Organization* 42:427–60.

Putnam, Robert D., and N. Bayne. 1987. *Hanging Together*. Cambridge, Mass.: Harvard University Press.

Raiffa, Howard. 1982. *The Art and Science of Negotiation*. Cambridge, Mass.: Harvard University Press.

Rapoport, Anatol. 1970. *N-Person Game Theory: Concepts and Applications*. Ann Arbor: University of Michigan Press.

Riker, William. 1962. *The Theory of Political Coalitions*. New Haven: Yale University Press.

Rosenthal, H. 1970. "Size of Coalition and Electoral Outcomes in the Fourth French Republic." In *The Study of Coalition Behavior*, ed. S. Groennings and E. W. Kelley. New York: Holt, Rinehart and Winston.

Rothstein, Robert L. 1968. *Alliances and Small Powers*. New York: Columbia University Press.

Rothstein, Robert L. 1979. *Global Bargaining: UNCTAD and the Quest for a New International Economic Order*. Princeton, N.J.: Princeton University Press.

Rubin, Jeffrey, and Bert Brown. 1975. *The Social Psychology of Bargaining and Negotiation*. New York: Academic Press.

Schelling, Thomas C. 1960. *The Strategy of Conflict*. Cambridge, Mass.: Harvard University Press.

Schelling, Thomas C. 1966. *Arms and Influence*. New Haven: Yale University Press.

Sebenius, James K. 1983. "Negotiation Arithmetic: Adding and Subtracting Issues and Parties." *International Organization* 37:281–316.

Sebenius, James K. 1984. *Negotiating the Law of the Sea*. Cambridge, Mass.: Harvard University Press.

Smith, D., and L. Wells. 1975. *Negotiating Third-World Mineral Agreements*. Cambridge: Ballinger.

Snyder, Glenn H., and Paul Diesing. 1977. *Conflict among Nations: Bargaining, Decision Making, and System Structure in International Crises*. Princeton, N.J.: Princeton University Press.

Straffin, Philip. 1977. "The Bandwagon Curve." *American Journal of Political Science* 21:695–709.

Straffin, Philip, and Bernard Grofman. 1984. "Parliamentary Coalitions: A Tour of Models." *Mathematics Magazine* 57:259–74.

Talbott, Strobe. 1984. *Deadly Gambits*. New York: Vintage Books.

Talbott, Strobe. 1988. *The Master of the Game*. New York: Knopf.

Tollison, Robert D., and T. A. Willett. 1979. "An Economic Theory of Mutually Advantageous Issue Linkage in International Negotiations." *International Organization* 33:425–49.

von Neumann, J., and O. Morgenstern. 1944. *Theory of Games and Economic Behavior*. Princeton, N.J.: Princeton University Press.

Walt, Stephen M. 1987. *The Origins of Alliances*. Ithaca, N.Y.: Cornell University Press.

Walt, Stephen M. 1988. "Testing Theories of Alliance Formation: The Case of Southwest Asia." *International Organization* 42:275–316.

Walton, Richard E., and Robert B. McKensie. 1965. *A Behavioral Theory of Labor Negotiations*. New York: McGraw-Hill.

Wilson, James Q. 1975. *Political Organization*. New York: Basic Books.

Winham, Gilbert R. 1977. "Negotiation as a Management Process." *World Politics* 30:87–114.

Winham, Gilbert R. 1979. "Practitioners' Views of International Negotiation." *World Politics* 32:111–35.

Winham, Gilbert R. 1986. *International Trade and the Tokyo Round Negotiation*. Princeton, N.J.: Princeton University Press.

Winham, Gilbert R. 1989. "The Prenegotiation Phase of the Uraguay Round." *International Journal* 44:280–303.

Wriggens, W. 1976. "Up for Auction: Malta Bargains with Great Britain, 1971." In *The 50% Solution,* ed. I. W. Zartman. New York: Anchor-Doubleday.

Zartman, I. W. 1975. "Negotiations: Theory and Reality." *Journal of International Affairs* 29:69–77.

Zartman, I. W., and Maureen Berman. 1982. *The Practical Negotiator*. New Haven: Yale University Press.

Contributors

Max H. Bazerman, Department of Organization Behavior, J. L. Kellogg Graduate School of Management, Northwestern University

Steven J. Brams, Department of Politics, New York University

Ralph L. Keeney, Department of Systems Management, University of Southern California

D. Marc Kilgour, Department of Mathematics, Wilfried Laurier University

David A. Lax, Environmental Capital Management, New York, New York

Samuel Merrill III, Department of Mathematics and Computer Science, Wilkes College

Roger B. Myerson, Department of Managerial Economics and Decision Sciences, J. L. Kellogg Graduate School of Management, Northwestern University

Margaret A. Neale, Department of Organization Behavior, J. L. Kellogg Graduate School of Management, Northwestern University

Barry O'Neill, Department of Political Science, York University

Howard Raiffa, Graduate School of Business Administration, Harvard University

James K. Sebenius, J. F. Kennedy School of Government, Harvard University

H. Peyton Young, School of Public Affairs, University of Maryland

Index